AF489082

TOMBSTONE HISTORIES

TALES OF JEWISH LIFE IN HARBIN

DAN BEN-CANAAN

Tombstone Histories

By Dan Ben-Canaan

ISBN-13: 978-988-8769-73-5

© 2023 Dan Ben-Canaan

HISTORY / Asia / China

EB175

All rights reserved. No part of this book may be reproduced in material form, by any means, whether graphic, electronic, mechanical or other, including photocopying or information storage, in whole or in part. May not be used to prepare other publications without written permission from the publisher except in the case of brief quotations embodied in critical articles or reviews. For information contact info@earnshawbooks.com

Published by Earnshaw Books Ltd. (Hong Kong)

Contents

TOMBSTONE HISTORIES

*In memory of Zahava Abramowitz Mozes,
my mother, who kept her past concealed,
and of a father I never knew.*

Jewish community. This archive, today under the auspices of the Harbin Jewish Culture Association, a semi-governmental enterprise presided by my wife, is one of the largest depositories of primary and secondary sources in the Far East. It includes thousands of documents, relics, letters, personal materials, memoirs, diaries, historical and family photographs, films, interviews, and recordings. These are the foundations upon which this book has been formed and written.

To understand the Jewish experience in Harbin, one must grasp the meaning of the community's daily existence — policy choices made by leadership, individual aspirations, dreams and needs, and actions taken by the individuals and by the collective.

We also must take into account the forces and attributes that contributed to the journeys people made in relocating to Manchuria and Harbin. This process is widely addressed as migration, and more accurately as an international one because the movement of persons or groups from one country to another constitutes transnational relocation.

Migration, in our case an international activity of movement from one geography to another, has always been understood as a crossing-border process whereby a migrant moves between countries to seek opportunities elsewhere. What sets international migrants apart from internal ones is that they have to engage with rules and regulations imposed by the migration regime of a receiving nation. Overtime rules and regulations have become increasingly fine-tuned. This suggests that a growing number of migrants could be observed to maintain multiple ties and connections between either their former home, other societies which have groups of the same antiquity traditions and culture, and the host country. What they bring to their new location can be described as a "glocal" experience, that is the global has been mixed with the local.

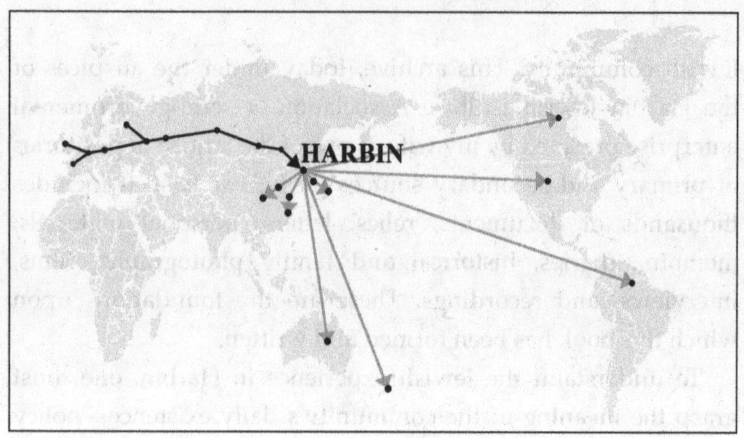

Migration into Harbin and out

Jews did not travel to Harbin because they chose by free will to live there. Most were forced to take the journey which with the global circumstances of the time brought about a resettlement process that they did not dream about.

When examining the stories, what I coined as their "histories", we find the reasons and motivations that people had to undertake the long and dangerous journeys.

Everyday life refers to the ways in which an individual, group, or society typically acts, thinks, and feels on a daily basis. The idea involves the definition of the self, and how people conceptualize relationships with the world and others, among them their sentiments to the collective. It involves the way people generate, establish, and interpret the meaning to their life.

Telling the stories can be done correctly by avoiding accounts based on selective memory, romantic notions, or nostalgia. The window through which historical reality can be presented should be given by the authors in a way that offered their remembrance, and then, the historian who examines and interprets these.

The past is a place of uncertainty. And the memory of it can be misleading and dangerous.

There is a fine line that separates nostalgia from amnesia. Both compete over control of memory. The danger of course is in that nostalgia, in many cases, overrides reality — historical reality.

Nostalgia has been defined in several ways. It is a longing for a home that no longer exists or has never existed. It is a sentiment of loss and displacement.[1] Nostalgia involves beliefs, discourses, and practices. Nostalgia refers to "a set of feelings and our interpretations of or beliefs about those feelings… nostalgia is "an emotional stance toward the past determined by a set of beliefs about its significance, desirability, and meaning"[2] For others, nostalgia is "a set of publicly displayed discourses, practices, and emotions where the ancient is somehow glorified."[3] Some see nostalgia as an incitement for political purpose as "acts of social renewal and change,"[4] and is experienced as a private and social emotion that helps shape both personal and collective identity.[5] Nostalgia also plays an important role in creating feelings of belonging to a community by linking a collective past to contemporary experiences.[6]

The nostalgic past, "is hardly the past as truly experienced. It is an imagined past, something that is idealized through memory and desire and is not factual."[7]

Starting at the end of the 19th century and for almost 60 years, thousands of Jewish people made Harbin their new home. Part of their legacy is visible on several sites around the city today. It is visible, however, only to those who are familiar with it, not to others, because what has been written about the Harbin Jewish community is based, in parts, on the inaccurate or nostalgic account. There are only a few texts that narrate the Harbin Jewish daily reality in full.

The most visible nostalgic accounts published in recent years have been several photo albums, "memoirs", academic papers, and autobiographies. Some were published in China in order to paint a picture that helps to reach political and economic aims. Others either drew materials from incomplete reports or were based on nostalgic and selective recollections. There are but relatively few accounts that should be considered real and factual.

A 2006-2007 investigation by the Chinese influential Southern Metropolis Magazine of the Heilongjiang Academy of Social Sciences[8] reveals for the first time an official policy that guides activities on "Jewish research". In order to achieve their aims, they have reproduced an imaginary history and painted it with romantic colors as "heaven" and "paradise" in their two publications of The Jews in Harbin albums[9], and a Collection of Research Papers published in 2004. Another such publication is The Jews in China,[10] a photo album described by the publisher as "An extensive, mainly photographic record, of the various Jewish communities in China from the mid-19th century through to the 1950s." There are several other publications that follow a similar direction.[11] Jews in Harbin: A Historical Perspective, by Xu Xin of Nanjing University; The influence and historical effect of Jews on Harbin in the first half of 20th century by Lishiliang Yangyanjun who writes in her conclusion "This is also the historical witness of friendly intercourse between Sino-Israeli relations, and directly affects economic and cultural friendly relations and cooperation of people of these two nations." Was it? Is it?

Among publications printed elsewhere are The Homesick Feeling of the Harbin Jews by Teddy Kaufman, a native "Harbinski" and for many years before his death, the president of the Association of Former Residents of China in Israel; and Charitable Activities of Harbin Jewish Association by Prof. B.B. Romanova, of the Department of Political History, Khabarovsk State Normal University, among others.

I argue that as years go by nostalgic accounts tend to take over what I call "historical reality", and that these should not be looked upon as complete reports of personal life and experiences because they lack full and intimate historical and factual encounters, and because many are based on the official policy of a present and personal selective memorabilia. They omit anti-Semitic and fascist conflicts under Russian rule in Harbin; they do not mention the 1911 memorandum sent by the Chinese Chamber of Commerce to the Minister of Trade in Beijing warning him of the bad consequences that will occur if Jews had anything to say in the formulation of a new treaty with Russia; they neglect the Japanese occupation, the state of terror — the horrors of kidnappings and murders, and they give no reasons for the dramatic dwindling of the Jewish community during the late 1920s, 1930s, 1940s, and 1950s.

In an album titled "The Pictorial History of Harbin" published by the Harbin City Planning Bureau, there is no mention of the Jewish active experience in the city. Within the album's more than 200 pages, there is just one small photo of a building described as "a Jewish Hall". Those few who are familiar with the photo know it is the New Synagogue of Harbin. But, to those who have no knowledge of the city's Jewish past, there is neither explanation nor any textual account of the Jewish community's existence collectively or as individuals.

There are several examples of insufficient language, misrepresentations, and lack of tangible information.

In his words of congratulation in the preface of the pictorial album 'Jews in Harbin', Ehud Olmert, Prime Minister of Israel at that time, writes: "The Jewish community of Harbin was lively and sparkling, reaching its peak of activity between the two World Wars and then thinning out to nonexistence."[12] Nonexistence? An absence of any existence and the negation of being is this what the former prime minister meant? The very fact, however, that he visited Harbin where his parents were born, and chanted together with his elder brother the mourners' Kaddish prayer while standing by the tombstone of their grandfather means exactly the opposite. Something does exist.

Olmert's writing is followed by Teddy Kaufman's letter in his preface to the same album: "We, who were either born in Harbin or came to live there for some time… still bear in our hearts the memories of our Harbin, because each of us has a Harbin of his own."[13]

Kaufman's decades of collecting and preserving materials at the Israel Association of Former Residents in China have presented historians with a key to a wider window. The key is in the periodical "Bulletin", and in the collection of Jewish newspapers published in Harbin and transferred intact to Israel. Here, through a journalistic narrative, one can find a less nostalgic picture of Harbin's Jewish people and their community. However, his book "The Jews of Harbin Live on in My Heart"[14] is a limited nostalgic account with a particular motive that cannot lead to an understanding of the community's functions, or his own. It is, more than less, a monument to himself.

In a letter to the author, dated May 27, 2006, Theodore Orosz of Valley Stream New York wrote:

"Our visit to Harbin was really the highlight of our trip to Asia. I had heard so much about the place for so long, but could never really get a 'fix' things because it was so remote, physically, and conceptually. Now it is all real for me."[15]

One should be interested in what Mr. Orosz has heard, why he "could never really get a 'fix' things", and how it has become "all real…" for him. His answers to these questions, arrived a short time after his first letter, but they are still vague. Nevertheless, in his later letter he reaffirms the thesis that only those who have had a direct or straight excess to a particular past can find themselves there:

"I had heard about Harbin, read about it, seen pictures and we had quite a bit of Chinese stuff in our house (rugs, ivory, dishes etc). But I really needed to see it (the space) to understand it fully."[16]

But what about those who are without a direct connection or excess? Can they depend, while reading historical accounts, on nostalgic and romantic notions? Should those who engage in research minimize their efforts to uncover historical facts by summing a past as the state of nonentity, unreality, or nonexistence? And what can one learn from others' "secrets of the heart..."?

Mordechai-Modka Olmert[17] opened a small window into the daily existence of a person, a family, and their relevant communal associations. However, the selective and nostalgic writings of his Harbin experiences gave rise years after his death, to manipulation by his elder son Amram, to suit a motive, a certain point of view, direction, orientation, or a particular favored agenda. In his memoir, Mordechai Olmert wrote that when the poor family relocated to Qiqihaer after Soskin offered them an opportunity for survival, they got, like every other Jewish family there, "a small house, several hens for eggs, and a cow for milk". But the elder son, in a book in Hebrew titled "My China", claims that his family was the first in China to own a dairy farm. His motive which he did not elaborate on, was to connect the advanced dairy farm near Beijing that Israel donated to China to his creation of a historical fallacy that made him an heir to the one cow first dairy farm in China. An analysis of the character and the motive is reserved only to psychiatrists.

In an e-mail letter, Wayne Mellon of the USA asks for help in deciphering his relatives' past in Harbin. I am looking for "resources regarding the Jewish community of Harbin. My mother, grandmother, and great-grandmother were all born in or near Harbin... I believe that my great-grandmother was interred in a Japanese concentration camp. If you know of anyone in China that could help me in my research, I would appreciate it."[18]

Wayne Mellon's wish to know about the faith of his mother, grandmother and great-grandmother under the Japanese occupation of Harbin has met a high wall of silence. Most, if not all, memoirs that were written by Jewish Harbinsty neglect to mention the years of cruel Japanese rule of the city. Studies have shown that most people try to conceal traumas and hardship.

Millions of people worldwide experience severe trauma in their lifetime. Trauma has immediate and long-term effects on emotional wellbeing. Moreover, the experiences of one generation may influence subsequent generations via social and biological pathways. Poor mental health and emotion dysregulation associated with trauma may affect parenting behaviors, which may have long-lasting effects on children's development.[19]

Trauma, including one-time, multiple, or long-lasting repetitive events, affects everyone differently. Some individuals may clearly display criteria associated with posttraumatic stress disorder, but many more individuals will exhibit resilient responses or brief subclinical symptoms or consequences that fall outside of diagnostic criteria. The impact of trauma can be subtle, insidious, or outright destructive. How an event affects an individual depends on many factors, including characteristics of the individual, the type and characteristics of the event(s), developmental processes, the meaning of the trauma, and sociocultural factors.

Historical facts come to illuminate aspects of the human experience — including scholarship, pioneering and innovative pedagogy, and a commitment to serve society or societies-- if we are to create a better understanding of a past.

History and archeology are not the same.

History, the discipline that studies the chronological record of events affecting a nation or people, cultures, countries, and regions, military affairs, economics, law, literature, sciences, art, philosophy, religion, and other fields of human endeavor, among them historical movements and events, is based on a critical examination of source materials and usually presents an explanation of their causes.

History relies on eyewitness accounts, biographies, memoirs, oral tales, and reports. History can only be told when these are present and without a place for speculation.

But archeology is the scientific study of human history and prehistory through the excavation of sites and the analysis of artifacts and other physical remains of past human life and activities.

While historians depend on the words, oral or written, archeologists look for physical evidence.

What makes these two sciences similar is the approach one takes in the analysis of the findings.

In such a case, Harbin appears both in words and in artifacts and other physical remains, among them buildings, and tombstones.

The concern I have is in and about the way in which nostalgia may override the scientific approach and avoid truthful facts in the examination of historical reality. History is for all people. But if it lacks reality, it may give rise to historical mistakes, imagined times, controversies, and intentional or unintentional misguides.

Historical reality can be achieved, in part, by examination of the daily life of families and individuals. These give meaning to the space and the time of those lives.

"Materials that have to do with history, culture, society, and many other subjects that humanists and social scientists teach... are bound to generate controversies because no two audiences are alike…"[20] And, as Theodor Kaufman wrote, "each of us has a Harbin of his own".

One perceives history according to his own experience, understanding, and accumulated "knowledge". The problem with "no two audiences are alike" is in that many chose to edit or reconstruct history, not to present it as was.

It is true that each person forms his or her notion of a place, an event, a life, from where he or she sees things. It depends on the focus, the angle, and things that were told and formed a perception. But there must be a common link and a certain bond between the writing. There was just one Harbin, but there may have been different perceptions.

Nostalgia describes a feeling of longing for the past, often idealized and unrealistic. It is an act of looking sentimentality to bygone things while generalizing or omitting many aspects of existence.

"Nostalgia, in fact, may depend precisely on the irrecoverable nature of the past for its emotional impact and appeal. It is the very pastness of the past, its inaccessibility that likely accounts for a large part of nostalgia's power… This is rarely the past as actually experienced, of course; it is the past as imagined, as idealized through memory and desire. In this sense, however, nostalgia is less about the past than about the present…"[21]

"The past is a foreign country; they do things differently there." said L.P. Hartley, in 'The Go-Between'.[22]

"History is a written narrative of events of the past. It is the aggregate of past events, and the continuum of events occurring in succession leading from the past to the present and even into the future."[23] Thus, written history is a record, a narrative, an account, a chronicle, of past events. But what happens when these records are based on a distortion of the past or an agenda that calls for its revision?

A thought in mind is the examination of recorded annals of villages, towns, and cities in China, in particular in the northeast of the country. In the 1980s, when China transitioned to the post-Mao era, a state-sponsored oral history scheme led to the publication of local, regional, and national histories. They took the form of written and transcribes individuals' testimonies of events that preceded the disorder of both the Cultural Revolution and, in many cases, the Communist victory in 1949. These publications, known as wensi ziliao, represent an forceful process of historical memory production... "Hitherto unexamined archival materials and oral histories reveal unresolved tensions in post-Cultural Revolution reconstruction and mobilization, informing negotiations between local elites and the state, and between Party and non-Party organizations."[24] The analysis took the northeast Russia-Manchuria borderlands as a case-study that created a post-Mao identities, political mobilization, and knowledge production in China. "The production of history and historical memory, a vital legitimizing task of the nation-state, took a particular significance during China's post-Mao transition, in the wake of the Cultural Revolution's destruction of not only the institutional infrastructure but also the historical identity of the Party. For these reasons, the post-Mao regime mobilized its subjects to produce historical artifacts in the form of written and orally transcribed memories; compiled, edited, and framed these narratives in a way that could be incorporated into new Party-approved local, regional and national histories..."[25]

Realism is commonly defined as a concern for fact or reality and rejection of the impractical and imaginary. "Historical reality", as I have coined the process of factual diggings, refers to the facts of events of the past as they occurred historically, whether they were external or internal to the subject confronted by them.

Historical reality deals with the actuality of existence. It is not fiction. There is no concern with the prettification of what was not with its ugliness. It is a presentation of the past as naked as is, as it was. In general, historical reality stands opposed to wishful fantasies and to everything within the mind that may be said to answer to the pleasure non-pleasure principle and its principal mechanism: hallucinatory wish-fulfillment.

Historical reality helps the reader to enter the experiences and feelings of those who lived in the past. It helps develop critical thinking through comparison of past and present and gives perspective on both dimensions. It brings a feeling of the continuity of time; see the present in the context of the past and future. It helps understand that there are not only political, social, and economic changes over time, but that there are universal needs and desires of individuals that are the same throughout different time periods. Moreover, it helps us see the interdependence of all people.[26]

The general frame of reference makes a distinction between two levels of scientific information, that is, descriptive/ explanatory information—knowledge/insight into historical reality, and procedural information—the skills to attain knowledge/insight and to evaluate its validity.[27] Both these procedures should be complementary so that a full account of the past becomes relevant.

The presentation of nostalgia as a means of recording the past may bring an "end of history".[28] History remains an irreducible component of human societies, and one cannot understand their total development without a reference to their reality of existence and values.

The great value of factual historical presentations is in their non-edited narrative. This way, it promotes, utilizes, and depends on historical realism with all its fortunate or unfortunate twists.

This is why I elected to keep the memoirs in this book in their own language, form and style.

There are at least two major approaches to the appearance of human beings. One approach is the spiritual-religious that follows the doctrine that God created all matters — earth, heaven, vegetation, animals of all sorts, and the human species.

This approach is concerned with sacred matters, religion, or the propaganda of the church, which eliminates any scientific discussion on the existence of earth and people. It is such a forceful narrative, that it pulls into it several scholars who, so it may seem to be, need the spiritual background for their own soul.

On the other hand, there is the "Darwinian" approach that brings forth the notion of evolution, a theory of the origin of species of plants and animals. The sequence of events involved in the evolutionary development of a species or taxonomic group of organisms can be described as a science.

While one approach relies on something which is imagined, the other takes the scientific path for revealing a factual past.

Most publications about Harbin attempt to paint the city as a haven for its Jewish community. This can be seen in all Chinese publications. But, was Harbin a true "Jewish Far-East Paradise — where the inhabitants of Harbin, endowed with hospitality and kindness unique to them, warmly accepted into their midst the Jews, perpetual travelers in foreign lands. In return, Jews who came to this city fell deeply in love with the land and people of Harbin. Harbin became a paradise for Jews who found a home in the Far East."?[29] This claim is false and has a political agenda that twists actual historical reality.

For most descendants of immigrants, their ancestors' past remains unclear and often a mystery. Only a few agree in their later years to tell their stories. It is a phenomenon that makes the unveiling of past accounts difficult and in many cases inaccurate. But some first-hand accounts do exist.

"Between 1921 and 1931 life was not as comfortable in Soviet-dominated Manchuria as it had been before 1921. Unemployment remained higher than it had been. The levels of prosperity reached between 1907 and 1920 did not return, and there was considerable tension between Soviet and non-Soviet Russians who lived as neighbors. During those years the city's population declined considerably from its post-civil war peak."[30]

But economic hardships were not the only concern. Harbin became, in a sense, a mirror of the Russian society as a whole—an arena for political, religious, economic, and social conflicts, as well as a fertile soil for the Russian extreme right and antisemitism.

"The aforementioned semi-fascist Russian extreme right has usually been called the "Black Hundred". The name refers to the paramilitary groups that belonged to the Union of Russian People (Soiuz Russkogo Naroda), the most important rightist party that had emerged before the first Duma elections in 1906. The new message of the Black Hundred was that the fundamental confrontation of the contemporary world was "Russia versus Jewry." The idea of a Jewish conspiracy against Russia was gaining ground among Russian nationalists mainly as a result of the appearance of the notorious Protocols of the Elders of Zion (Protokoly Sionskikh Mudretsov), an infamous forgery attributed to the tsarist secret service."[31] This did not only appeal to the orthodox Russian mind but found its way into the Chinese perception of the Jews. In a 1911 letter by the Harbin Chinese Chamber of Commerce, the writers warn the Minister of Trade in Beijing that the exclusion of Jews from the formation of a new treaty with the Russian will serve the Chinese government well because it will avoid manipulation by the Jews.

The anti-Jewish dimension of the Russian 'civil' idea had become a key issue in Russian domestic politics already by the 1880s and mirrored itself in Russian communities across Manchuria. Although this phenomenon differed from the traditional confessional anti-Semitism that had been cultivated for many generations by the Russian Orthodox Church, the new kind of anti-Jewish sentiment was based on what was to be called "political anti-Semitism".[32]

In her collection of poems Skin for Comfort, Nora Krouk paints a grim view of her personal history as an émigré in Harbin. Her poem "Yesterday" addresses the subject of Stalin's atrocities from the invaluable perspective of a voice with an intimate connection to the victims:

> … Efim and I dream collective dreams; He saves his Father Stops them in time; They're still in China He wakes with a smile; E. not all is lost; But I descend to the permafrost of the frozen bones; back to 1937 USSR and the mincer grinds; Krouk Lipa Yankelev; from Harbin; Spy for a foreign Power; On the same day; they collected Guita; seventeen-year-old enemy of the state; Wife Liza; taken in '38; Young Lilya; left to fend for herself; step back to the edge back to the walls'; congealed horror back to the cell; with the blood-sticky floor; back to improbably weird confessions; Signed.[33]

Jews came to Harbin for various reasons, among them economic opportunities as well as what they thought will offer a "pogrom-free" safe, and peaceful environment.

Mara Moustafine has put a new light on life in Harbin in what has been described as "heaven" or referred to as "Harbin became a paradise for Jews who found a home in the Far East:

"For Jews of the Tsarist empire, Russian Manchuria was the land of opportunity. The discriminatory laws and restrictions which prevailed in the empire proper—like those confining the Jews to live in the Pale of Settlement, excluding them from certain professions, and setting quotas for their numbers in schools and other educational institutions—did not apply there. Most importantly, there were no pogroms and little overt anti-Semitism, at least until the late 1920s... During the turbulent civil war years, while its political status was in limbo, the CER zone was a staging ground for the anti-Bolshevik White Guard and Cossack armies. With this came a rise in anti-Semitism, as the Cossacks regarded all Jews as Bolsheviks who deserved to be punished as perpetrators of the revolution... In 1919, my great-grandfather Girsh Onikul was captured by one of Baron Ungern-Sternberg's men, though miraculously he escaped alive... In 1924, after protracted negotiations, China recognising the Soviet Government and agreed to joint Soviet-Chinese administration of the CER... the division into White émigrés and Soviets would have far-reaching consequences for those who remained in Manchuria during the 13 years of Japanese occupation under the guise of the Manchukuo puppet regime. Life for Jews in Manchuria deteriorated seriously after the Japanese occupation. The Japanese... associated closely with militant anti-Soviet Whites, such as the Russian Fascist Party (RFP), whose ideology of anti-Bolshevism and nationalism was laced with virulent anti-Semitism... In the early 1930s, Russian thugs linked to the RFP engaged in a campaign of kidnappings, extortion and murder against wealthy businessmen, mainly Jews, masterminded by the Japanese military police, the Kempeitai. Faced with a declining economy, the rise in banditry, anti-Semitism, the takeover of their businesses by the Japanese and political intimidation (particularly of those who had Soviet citizenship), many Jews left

Manchuria… For many of those who stayed on in Harbin during the 13 years of Manchukuo, life was a harrowing experience…"[34]

Mara's mother Inna was excluded from school and had to study at home with a tutor. Later, when contact between 'émigrés' and 'Soviets' was forbidden she could no longer study music or participate in concerts at Madame Gershgorina's music school. She could not also, participate in either of Harbin's two Jewish youth organizations…

The émigré status of her grandfather's brother, Ruvim, did not save him. In 1940, the Japanese arrested him and took over his retail business at the Harbin market.[35]

To better understand Harbin and the worries Jews have had under the Japanese occupation as well as the conditions in the USSR, one should look at a letter that was sent from the Soviet Union to Harbin warning of the dangers there. The letter was written in a code trying to avert any possibility of harm to the writers.

> "Yakov is seriously ill and cannot write to you. And his illness is of the kind that used to be treated in Harbin by Dr. Mozgovoi."

Thus, the family of Berkeley's own Simon Karlinsky was secretly warned in a letter from an aunt that returning to the Soviet Union from Russian Harbin in 1935 could be dangerous: Dr. Mozgovoi had been the prison director in Harbin, so the letter meant that Uncle Yakov had been arrested.

Increasingly alarmed by fascism and the brutality of the Japanese occupation of Manchuria, many Jewish-Russian residents of Harbin fled in the 1930s to the Soviet Union, Israel, and, of course, California. In this way the multinational tapestry of Harbin society unraveled; the Chinese city of three million that stood in its place in 1999, has only its fanciful architecture as a reminder of its origins.[36]

The concern was not with Russian Harbin's dramatic denouement, but with its debut on the world stage at the climax of colonial ambition in late Imperial Russia."[37]

Reports, written by scholars, shade some light on Harbin and its turbulence, and sometimes confused past. But by in large, most accounts, official and private, tend to be edited to suit the writers' emotions, agenda, motives, and political goals.

A discussion about Harbin's past communities, the interaction between them, the daily tensions created by different elements within them, and their reasons, are unfortunately buried in memories that tend to smooth and beautify those years.

Serge Cipko claims that the Ukrainian participation in the colonization of Russian-occupied territories in the Far East was far greater than what has been written by Russian nationals. The Ukrainian settlement of Manchuria, which by the second decade of this century is said to have embraced over 22,000 families, has been documented even less. This, he writes, can be attributed partly to their Russo centric orientation. In reality, the Russian minority in Manchuria was not as numerous as previously stated. The Ukrainians formed a substantial proportion of those hitherto considered as "Russians" but owing to the dominant position of the local ethnic Russian group and the low national consciousness of many of the Ukrainian settlers, coupled wit unfavorable conditions for Ukrainian community leaders to redress this malady, they did not evolve as an influential minority tantamount to their numbers. But notwithstanding the fact that the Ukrainian influence in Manchuria was less pronounced than the Russian, the group was significant in the region.[38]

Serge Cipko is correct. The most vocal occupies center stage not because of its factual merit, but because the oppressed is more or less soundless.

Another example is in the noise that has been generated about the Jewish refugees in Shanghai by a small but vocal group of related offspring. What has been created is an unchecked glorification of a piece of history that was edited in order to suit aims, not historical facts. Harbin did not sound her voice for various reasons, thus was pushed off stage. So were Tianjin, Qiqihaer, Hailar, Manzouli and other towns where Jews formed small communities.

Furthermore, many of the "new" reports that pop out here and there are based on ignorance and denials.

Accounts of Harbin's political, social, religious, and imperial conquests are hidden within the memories of many of those who lived in the city and moved to other places. For most, however, nostalgia and other sentiments override the past as it was.

The reasons for nostalgic presentations of the past are many. They may belong to a "psycho-historical" analysis, which is another area of study.

A "creation" of history is another problem that should be addressed, and Harbin, like many other cities in China, has several good examples. For despotic regimes, history is a fluid process that can be, and sometimes should be manipulated by the authorities in order to achieve certain political, economic, and social aims. In such cases, as demonstrated by the manipulation of recorded history in China's northeat, the creation of history comes to put forward new agendas, reinforce nostalgia as a suitable medication for the masses, and tie all to a past that in many instances was different or did not exist. In turn, this new creation, if it survives the test of time, may become a historical reality years later.

A good case study is the newly constructed fake Memorial Cemetery for the Fallen Russian Soldiers in Harbin. Created

Fig. 1: Maurice Nigel (4-L) with workers at his horsehair factory in Harbin

Fig. 2: Resnikov Family Dinner party. Harbin 1925

in 2007, it seats next to the Russian Orthodox Cemetery in the Huangshan Public Cemetery on the outskirts of the city.

The Russian Orthodox Cemetery at Huangshan is decaying. It has seen very few visitors since its 1958 relocation to this site. The new cemetery, with its 60 tombstones, is a reminder of a past of Russia's dominance in the construction and development of Harbin that the Chinese do not acknowledge. For them, Harbin was always a Chinese city with a Chinese presence. The mark of Harbin's centennial was celebrated very quietly in 2006 — not in 1998, because Harbin, according to the official line has a long history that goes back at least 25.000 years.[39]

The "fake cemetery" with its plastic banners and Russian symbols, is a creation of history that never existed but that was necessary to make in order to warm up relations with contemporary Russia.

For the sake of the past, there is a necessity for historical presentations that are fully accounted for. The American journalist Edgar Snow gave a reviling and vivid account of Mao Zedong and China's struggle for independence[40]. His reports-books are serving historians until this very day.

All the stories in this book were chosen because they present factual realities, not a yearning for a past that never was.

If historical events are manipulated, for whatever ends, they become a simple tool of propaganda and misinformation in order to promote a particular goal, cause or need. It is then a concerted set of messages aimed at influencing the opinions or behavior of large numbers of people. Instead of impartially providing information, propaganda in its most basic sense presents information in order to influence its targets. Propaganda presents facts selectively to encourage a particular synthesis or gives loaded messages in order to produce an emotional (hence nostalgic) rather than rational response to the information presented. The desired result is a change in the cognitive narrative of the subject in the target audience. Nostalgia serves it very well.

It is natural that if the past is to matter at all if it is to enrich our lives on any level, we must be aware of its nature, its shifting meanings, and its vulnerability to present adjustments, causes, needs, and alterations.

We are not the guardians of the soul and life of neither Harbin, the Harbin Jewish community, and other communities, nor the Chinese experience in its totality. But in the journey to historical relevancy, the soul of Harbin and her communities should be unveiled fully. People provide this soul.

The role of the historian as a verifier and authenticator, through accuracy, independence, and integrity, is unique. It is in the ability to be real, useful, to make people understand without self-imposed commentary, know and think, that will help the past endure. While we figure out the reality of the past, we also guard the future. People's daily lives are archeological relics and artifacts of history. They tell the simple story of life within the larger frame of the events that shaped their own existence and those of the collective. They compose the tale of space and time.

Tombstones, a monument that marks a grave site, an inscribed memorial stone set at a place of interment. It is a marker that is placed over a grave. In most cases a tombstone has the deceased's name, date of birth, and date of death inscribed on them, along with but not always, a personal message, or prayer. Many tombstones erected by affluent families contain pieces of funerary art, especially details in stone relief. In several cases, inserting a photograph of the deceased in a frame is common.

The realization that the Harbin Jewish cemetery at Huangshan has no graves, just tombstones, expedited my conviction in the necessity to give the stones much more meaning. To carve a relevant history on each.

The old Jewish cemetery in Harbin is such a case. It was demolished by the authorities between 1958 and 1962. As the Chinese describe the destruction: it was "deep buried". The site is now the home of the Harbin Ice Palace and the city's fairgrounds. No tombstones, no graves, no cemetery synagogue, no purification facility. A void of an image of history, just a phantom of the mind.

I always wondered why people put much effort in placing a cornerstone on the site of the construction of a building. After all, these cornerstones are covered by cement and soil and then by a building. No one will be able to see the stone or what is contained there again.

But a tombstone stays erected in the open. It belongs to an individual, to a family, and to the public, thus, it presents a legacy, a heritage, a tradition, a history.

In early 2014 a Chinese television director named Lu Xiao-shu took interest in people who brought music to old Harbin. She learned that the most notable musicians in the city were Jewish, and decided to follow their trail and produce a television documentary about their life. In fact, she wrote, she was interested in the fate of those people. In a letter dated November 27, 2015, she asked questions such as why they came to Harbin, why they left, what happened to them after they left the city, and what kind of life they led after they left Harbin. Lu Xiao-shu thought it was not just the subject of music itself, but the fate of groups of talented musicians who lived and functioned in Harbin.

She decided to take the Harbin Symphony Orchestra which was founded over 100 years earlier, and most of its musicians were Jews, as a starting point for her film.

Their performances, she said, "were famous in the world".

She learned that the orchestra was founded as the Symphony Orchestra of the Harbin Railway Club and that the club was situated at the Harbin CER Railway Headquarters.

The building has an old locked underground basement, which was where all the orchestra's large wooden trunks containing equipment and instruments were placed.

In November 2015 Lu Xiao-shu was permitted to enter the basement. Searching in the cobwebs-infested dust-ridden space, her pocket spotlight illuminated parts of the walls and the trunks. These structures, made of bricks and wood, were full of signatures, short writings, and illustrated figures, carved or penciled by members of the orchestra.

The writings were all in Russian. Some were simple and others more intricate. One of the signatures was that of Kalman M. Shlifer. Born in Harbin in 1927, he spent his professional years as a member of the orchestra playing the violin. He left the city for Israel in 1951, where he joined the army and played in its orchestra. Many years later, when asked about the pencil signature he left on the wooden wall of the basement, he was very emotional and spoke about the group's wish to leave a mark on where they spent their time. We were friends, he told his niece. We spent most of our time rehearsing and performing. These were our lives, a daily struggle to be the best. Gary Brovinsky who was 4 years younger than me was one of my friends, he said. He too joined the Israeli army orchestra and here we spent a year and a half playing together again.[41]

Kalman M. Shlifer who never got married spent his last years at a home for the aged in a town named Zichron Ya'akov in Israel. He died just before Lu Xiao-shu was able to film an interview with him.

Jewish friends were among the top-level musicians. Among the names that Shlifer remembered were conductor Mettler, violinist V.D. Trachtinberg, pianist Gershgorina, who also was a very popular music teacher, pianist Dillon, violinist Goldstein who founded the Glazunov School of Music, Singer Su Shenlin, and violinist Helmut Stern.

Personal histories, families' past, individual recollections, and collective remembrance are too often presented in a way that makes it very difficult to decipher what really happened to a person or his family. These are written in a form of road markers with large black holes between them. It is also a practice of too many historians who tend to report on the macro rather than the micro.

Microhistory is a historical method that takes as its object of study the interactions of individuals and small groups with the goal of isolating ideas, beliefs, practices, and actions that would otherwise remain unknown by means of more conventional historical strategies. By examining the history of everyday life, microhistory is providing historians with a paradigmatic dimension to traditional research. Microhistory reinfuses the past with its own vibrant energy because finely crafted microhistories capture the drama of everyday life. They let readers understand people as agents of change for the worlds they live in, often in the face of overwhelming difficulties.[42]

What happens with an absence of the micro is a historical desert with just a few very dry vegetation. I named these "graveyard histories" and "tombstone histories" because the stories are told in a form of a tombstone — short writings of names, a place, two dates, and often a short statement.

There are, however, few memoirs and stories that expand the history they report on, and take painstaking efforts to describe the life of the person or the family in detail. By doing so they allow the reader to not only share and understand their experiences but shade light on their daily life and the environment in which they functioned.

Large and small Jewish enterprises provided working places for the Jewish and non-Jewish population. Enterprises on Kitaiskaya Street functioned with Jewish-owned shops, among them the men's fashion shop of Eskin, the pharmacy of Arkus, Hotel "Pekin" of Berkovich, "Shvedko" kitchen furniture and equipment shop of Genkin, famous coffee house "Mars" of Zuckerman-Drezin, Hotel "Moderne" of Joseph Kaspe, manufacture goods of Rabinovich, and "Optica" of Faingold. Out of 32 Hotels registered in Harbin in 1932, 28 belonged to Jews.

Jews in Harbin were furriers, bankers, bakers, shopkeepers, restaurateurs, accountants, lawyers, teachers, musicians, and people of letters and the arts. They owned coal mines, lumber mills, breweries, and candy factories. Among them were owners of small businesses such as grocery stores, dairy shops, shoemakers and watchmakers, tailors, and the like. The Jewish-owned Hotel Moderne boasted a restaurant, a cinema, an exclusive jewelry store, a large meeting hall, a concert and opera performance stage, a ballroom, a billiard room, a bar, and a barbershop.

History holds many mysteries and untold stories. Like the large trunks in the forgotten basement of the railway headquarters, no one knows what they contain. Time is just like the wind in the desert. It can cover everything and hide the stories. It can make a memory vague and obscure, or as real as life itself. Life is short and its shortness gives rise to the neglect of most tales of daily activities. History, then, becomes a collection of tombstones that are scattered throughout the long-distanced graveyard of time. What we want to know are the little details, the daily impressions of life that were and then gone.

The existence of Russian Jewish communities in China covers a relatively short period of time, only about sixty years or so (1898 -1962).

These years saw the Chinese revolution of 1911 that abolished the Imperial rule. And the communities that mainly concentrated in Harbin, Tientsin, and Shanghai, went through two world wars (1914-1918 and 1939-1945).

There was a major local war (Sino-Japanese, 1937-1945), a major local conflict in the northeastern part of China (Japanese occupation 1931-1945). And the Chinese civil war that led to a communist revolution in 1949.

During this period the Harbin community went through another war (Russo-Japanese. 1904-1905), another major Sino-Soviet conflict in 1929, and an external revolution and civil war in Russia, 1917-1920. Harbin lived under five different political authorities: Tsarist Russia 1898-1917, local warlord Zhang Tzo-Lin between 1917 and 1931, Japanese Manchukuo puppet state between 1932 and 1945, Soviet Red Army occupation between l945 and 1947, and the People's Republic of China (PRC) since 1949. These turbulent political events and diverse local administrations shaped the rise, growth, and fall of the Russian Jewish communities in Harbin and in other parts of China.

From a historical perspective, the internal political conflicts within the community are equally significant. The struggle between secular groups and orthodoxy, between Zionists and Bundists socialists, the struggle to maintain a Jewish community far away from its members' original geographies in Europe, and the Jewish confrontation with anti-Semitic Russian extremist elements, are all part of the history of Harbin.[43]

In 1917, after the February Revolution in Russia, the Kerensky Government abolished all restrictions based on nationality or religion. In Harbin, this was reflected in a total reorganization of the community institutions. An Interim Committee, elected at a general community meeting held on April 30, 1917, was charged with the task of the community's reconstruction. The Committee consisted of 31 members, 13 Zionists, 4 Orthodox, 2 Marxist Bundists, and 12 others representing the non-partisan Jewish voters. Most of the early Jewish pioneers, seeking their fortunes, found it either in industry or trade. The Jewish community contributed its share to the city's growth. Jews occupied positions of responsibility and trust on the Stock Exchange, and the city's Chamber of Commerce, and played important roles in trade and professional associations. With material success came community and cultural institutions — synagogues, a cemetery, a hospital, a home for the aged, a residence for invalids, support for the sick and for the poor, schools, youth organizations, clubs, various publications, musical performances, dramatic productions, and lectures.

Traditional observance of Purim, for example, included a costume ball in the Commercial Club. The men wore dinner jackets, and the ladies wore evening gowns, many of which were created for the occasion by the local fashion house Mme. Antoinette — Mrs. Meller, a creative fashion designer. The artistic program at the ball, produced and directed by a local Russian choreographer, was performed by the Jewish society ladies.[44]

The life of the Jewish community in Harbin which started in 1903, came to a halt in 1962. This is just one side of a paradigm. The other, and mostly untold, is the daily life of individuals and families that were part of the community. Through their memoirs, letters, and photographs we can decipher the kind of life they had, their needs and necessities, their interactions with friends and foes, their dreams, cheerful moments, difficulties, and triumphs. It is a complicated story, but one that can give history a personal touch — a meaning. Yet, even in these, we may find insufficient evidence because most tend to bring just important dates and names and not much in between.

I named this "Tombstone History" because grave marks carry names, dates, and maybe a one-line that comes to honor the dead.

However, these tombstones are grand. And being so, they can hold more than just dates. These tombstones carry the stories of their owner.

Harbin's short historical time, yet large space, tells a story of a convergence of human experience that established a pattern of daily life that was brought by the newcomers from their old geographies while trying to cope with the new.

Northeast China known as Manchuria at the time, was a wild region with small Manchu settlements, 40 or so ethnic minorities living in their ancient compounds, fishing and agricultural villages, inns, a fortress, several distilleries, widely stretched opium fields planted and harvested regularly, and small administrative towns like Changchun, the capital of the Manchu Qing Dynasty.

It was here, in the center of this region, that Harbin grew from desolate beginnings into an important commercial, financial, and industrial center... The site that was chosen for the new town was nearly indistinguishable from the virgin wilderness. "A few Chinese houses and a small customs outpost along the riverbank and a distillery a short distance inland were the only permanent structures."[45]

It was in 1896 that a treaty with China gave Tsarist Russia the right to construct a railway that will run through the wilderness of Manchuria, connecting Moscow with the strategic warm-water port of Vladivostok. The control of the railway gave the Russians a strong colonial hold over Manchuria with Russian law, police, courts, and the presence of its army. The works on the China

Eastern Railway (CER) started in 1898 and were completed in 1903, opening the region for imperial exploitation.

The center or hub for the proposed railroad and one of its principal administrative locations was to be in a location on the Sungary River that was given the name "Harbin". Until 1898 the place was a cluster of small fishing villages on the Songhua River and a modest trade center for lumber, fur traders, and opium. The construction of the new railroad turned Harbin into a magnate for new industrial activities, an opportunity for a myriad of new commercial services, and a boom climate for all types of commercial and domestic construction.

The beginning of the 20th century marked the arrival in China of thousands of Jews, some with commercial interests, many as émigrés, and the rest as refugees escaping Russian pogroms, persecutions, and the after mass of the 1917 Russian Revolution, and the Nazi Holocaust. They hoped to find sanctuary in China, especially in Harbin, where they could build a new life for themselves, and a successful community and left its cultural marks after they left.

The first Jewish family arrived in the new town of Harbin in 1899. The head of the household S.I. Bertsel was a railway engineer who worked for the CER.

Thousands more arrived as refugees from the Russian Revolution of 1917. A wave of Jews was to arrive in the 1930s and 1940s, seeking refuge from the Holocaust in Europe.

The Harbin Jewish population built strong roots in the city and many considered it to be their home. That explains why the community of Harbin had both domestic and international influence. It was conceived to be permanent home.

Harbin was the center of the largest Jewish community in China and the Far East. The Jewish active presence in the city lasted until the last family immigrated to Israel on December 31, 1963.

By 1900, the town had 45 Jews, and by the end of 1903, Harbin had 500 Jews and more than 15 Jewish-owned shops. It was then that the first Harbin "minyan"[46] took place.

In 1903 the Harbin Jewish Religious Community Association (HEDO) was established in order to attend to the religious and cultural needs of its members. Under the Russian provisions, the Jewish community was to be recognized only for its religious purposes.

The committee consisted of Israel Meerovich (Gabay), Eugen Dobisov (Treasurer), Khatskel Furvich, and Mordechai Samsonovich (Committee Member). The formation of the HEDO was accompanied by setting up the first synagogue in Harbin in a rented house[47], a Burial Society, and commencing a Jewish cemetery.

The Jewish community employed a Rabbi, a Mohel (circumciser), and a Shochet (slaughterer) who was responsible for the slaughter of animals according to the religious ritual. The Mohel and the Shochet traveled to other places in the region and performed circumcision and ritual slaughter for the Jewish communities there. The Burial Society buried the community's deceased in accordance with Jewish rituals. The society maintained the Jewish Cemetery and owned a hearse.

Rabbi Lev Levin was the first full-time Rabbi in 1903. Under his supervision, all religious functions were put in place and a school in the synagogue's yard was established. In the course of just a few years, the Jewish community established all the institutions that are traditionally an inseparable part of the life of the community — a Mikveh (religious body purifying bathhouse) for men and women, and a bread bakery that supplied Chala bread for the Shabbats, and Pesach matzoth to all the other Jewish communities in the North-East of China, in Hailar, Qiqihar, Manzhouli, Hangdaohezi, Zhengyang, as well as more distant cities like Qingdao, Hankou, and also the communities in Japan: Kobe, Tokyo, and Yokohama. Since the very first days of its existence, the Jewish community made sure that Jewish traditional values were preserved, communal help was promoted and Jewish costumes kept.

During the War between Russia and Japan in 1904-5, the community took care of Jewish soldiers fighting in Manchuria. After the Russian defeat, many demobilized soldiers settled in Harbin and were joined later by their families. At the same time, an increasing number of Jewish refugees came fleeing from pogroms in Russia. The number of community members increased to 5,000.

In 1906 the Women's Welfare Organization was founded. The organization helped establish workshops, supplied clothes, and supported education. In 1907 the Jewish Free Soup Kitchen was opened to all needy persons in Harbin. A "Committee for Social Security" (1916) was founded and provisional organizations such as the "Committee for Support of the Jewish Victims of the War" (1914-1920) were formed.

The Harbin Jewish population reportedly topped 23,000 at its peak in the 1920s. There were two major synagogues, the Main or "Old" Synagogue and the New Synagogue. The Jewish community also established a library, a Talmud Torah[48] school, an elementary and a secondary school, a cemetery, a women's charitable organization, a soup kitchen, a home for the aged, and a Jewish hospital, which treated both Jews and non-Jews.

Jews were the first to begin the soybean and fur industries in Manchuria. They built factories, had holdings of the region's timber, and operated coal mines throughout the region. They founded the Jewish Commerce Association, the Jewish Far Eastern Bank, and the Jewish People Bank.

Harbin's cultural life was often compared with Paris and

other European cities. Operas, operettas, musical concerts, and plays were frequently performed. They were held mainly at the Hotel "Moderne" or at the "Commercial Club", both located in the heart of Pristan district, the main Jewish area of Harbin.

Jews established a theatre and the Jewish cultural club "YILMADAG", which presented lecture series in Russian and Yiddish, dramatic performances, and musical evenings. Some special training schools such as the Music and Art School "Lotus", where mime, art history, sculpture, and drama were taught, all were set up by Jews. In 1912, a Jewish Library was founded with about 13 thousand books.

Between 1918 and 1930, about 20 Jewish newspapers and periodicals were published in Harbin. All but one — the Yiddish Der Vayter Mizrekh (The Far East) — were in the Russian language. Russian was the lingua franca for Jews and gentiles alike, as well as for their Chinese employees and business associates.

World War I and the Russian Revolution brought scores of anti-Bolshevik White Russians to Harbin, along with a virulent strain of anti-Semitism, and bullying of Jews by Russian hooligans became common.

Under the cruel rule of the Japanese army, starting in 1932, Jews began fleeing Harbin for Tientsin, Shanghai, and destinations abroad. By the end of World War II, only about 2,000 Harbin Jews were left in Harbin to greet the Soviet Red Army that had taken over the city from the Japanese. Between 1945 and 1947, the Soviets arbitrarily arrested the leadership of the Jewish community and "repatriated" them to Russian gulags. They arrested many others and shot them dead at the border.

Following the victory of the Chinese People's Liberation Army in 1949, about 1,000 Jews left Harbin for Israel. By 1955, only 319 Jews were left to maintain the dwindling Harbin community institutions.

In 1958 the city government ordered the demolishing of all cemeteries within the city. The government allowed the relocation of the Jewish and Russian Orthodox cemeteries to Huangshan, a new burial place outside of the city. Between 1958 and 1962, 816 tombstones out of about 3,400 graves were chosen for relocation to the new cemetery. Only 512 tombstones were actually moved. The rest of the spots are marked with metal plaques.

The Jewish community stopped its functions in 1962. A year later, in December 1963, Podolsky, the last family, left for Israel. The last Harbin Jew, Hana Agree died solitary in 1985. Miss Agree found refuge quarters in a room at the Old Synagogue. In her room, the last of the Jewish leadership left the community records, those that were not destroyed earlier. After her death, the authorities confiscated the records and put them in the Harbin Archives. A few months later the central government issued a decree shutting down the Jewish archive and prohibiting any entry, research or other activity.

Jewish entrepreneurs arrived in Manchuria at the turn of the century and played an important role in developing the natural resources of the region. They were followed by white-collar professionals among them doctors, lawyers, architects, teachers, accountants, and pharmacists, as well as tradesmen, merchants, jewelers, tailors, shoemakers, watchmakers, and the like. The community had all it needed in order to function in relative comfort.

The turbulent events of the 20th century made Harbin a temporary refuge to all of them. Those who could secure funds and necessary affidavits moved to destinations across the seas. Others moved along the east coast of China to other cities from which they thought it would be easier to depart to other places. And some with stateless status and no passports were stuck until someone found a way out.

The pasts that are presented here are of individuals and families that found temporary refuge in Harbin. Each past has its own unique story of triumphs or defeats, struggles and celebrations, worries and dreams, birth and death, a restless movement from one geography to another, and the formation of identity or a need to assimilate and hide.

Each past has its own life and daily events, but when all are put together, they unveil another history, a larger one, a greater record, and a narrative that describes all the pasts as almost one. These, when put one after the other, give a deeper meaning to the daily life of the Jewish inhabitants of Harbin that was just another railway stop in the long journey to a final destination.

What is in the name

A cemetery is made of graves where the bodies of the deceased are placed deep underground. Above the grave are the tombstones. These marble stone structures come to memorize the dead. The problem is in that they hold only names and dates. The details are buried under.

To many, history is like a tombstone, a marker with highlights only. The grave — the history in many cases, is bound to fade as the body decomposes and only the dry bones are left.

Historians love dates. But dates hold nothing except if they can tell a story, a detailed one, that can answer many questions and paint life with full colors transforming the tombstone into a book of life.

This book aims on focusing on small matters such as those that make daily life in order to answer big questions. And, if you ask unexpected questions in small detail, very soon that will lead to larger questions that the secondary sources do not touch on. It leads to all kinds of questions because the answers depend on them and never end.

Sometimes, however, there are only tombstones and no graves. The Harbin Huangshan Jewish cemetery is such a case. The dwindling Jewish community in the late 1950s, which numbered only a few dozen families, could not and did not supervise the relocation process of what was to be about 800 graves and instead left it to the Chinese workers to move only slightly more than 500 tombstones to the new location on the eastern hills of Harbin.

Thus, when one stands in front of a tombstone, he or she can just imagine the one who was to occupy the underground space. And if there is no story attached to the empty plot what is left are only names, dates, and a symbol.

It is, therefore, a virtual grave and so is its history if no one bothered to preserve it.

Imagining history is a fascinating subject. It deals with what would have been rather with what actually was.

While archeology examines physical evidence, history deals with the words, written, spoken, or recorded.

Many have asked why people, rich, well-to-do, or poor, exchanged their old geography with a new one, which is situated in a region that was far away from their civilization. There are many answers as the reader will find in the histories presented here. But, the main one, so I believe, is that ever since the destruction of life in ancient Israel, the diasporic experience of the Jewish people has been of dispersion or spreading from the space that was originally localized in their homeland and that it has continued over the centuries because this group of people has been, tragically, at the center of hate and genocide that forced them to move from one geography to another while looking with a certain degree of hope to find a resting place until another event will force them out to a new space.

This unfortunate condition created at times the necessity of finding refuge in a faraway place.

World War II was a catalyst for attempts to settle tens of thousands of Jews in unimaginable regions, hostile to their background, tradition, and culture. Although all suggestions did not materialize, they do point to the question whether Jews are capable to adapt to conditions well beyond their cultural, and traditional traits. The answer is in the affirmative. When there is a need a will can be found.

Nevertheless, it is about an imaginary concept of 'what if'. What would have happened to these people if these were to materialize? Imagine the delicate Austro-German Jewish ladies, for example, walking barefooted in the jungles of south China by the borders with Burma and Vietnam. Or the city dwellers of Vienna working the sun-scorned fields of the Kimberly wastelands in Australia trying to raise grain or vegetables.

When people embarked on their long journey to the far away Far East, they had no idea what they would find there. Harbin was, for them, an imaginary space alien to everything they knew.

They were lucky to find another Russian city with elements that could remind them of their former spaces. And it was in this place called Harbin that they built their lives, adapting to new circumstances until they moved again.

There are, however, other dimensions to the experience of individuals or the collective. I call it "historical réalité" which means a history that may have happened but did not, and that in such a case we should look at the question of what could have happened to individuals or groups that were lifted from one geography and were placed in another, sometimes extremely hostile. What would have been their daily life experience and did it, or did not, affect their identity?

These are difficult questions to answer because the attempts to resettle Jewish refugees in various parts of the world, including Manchuria, the south of China, and Australia, did not materialize.

The Japanese attempt to get "Jewish money" is a good case study.

In the first years of the 1930s, Japan was expanding its political, economic, and military resources on its China-Manchukuo strategy to the limits. In 1933 the Japanese looked for ways "to centralize their influence and control over the Jews with BREM [the Bureau of Russian Emigrant Affairs] under their auspices serving as a role model... In 1937 the Japanese approached Dr. Abraham Kaufman, president of the Hebrew Association of Harbin, asking him to organize an umbrella organization of Hebrew associations in China and Japan. Dr. Kaufman complied with this 'offer that he could not refuse', both in order to win Japanese support for diminishing the rampant Anti-Semitism inspired by White Russians in Harbin. Even more important, Kaufman hoped to persuade the Japanese to offer protected areas for settlement by Jews fleeing Nazi Europe. Thus, at the "Jewish National Council of the Far East" at the close of the final conference in December 1939, Chairman Kaufman signed a petition to the Japanese minister, Abe Nobuyuki, expressing his gratitude for the "protection without prejudice" that the Japanese authorities had given to Jews in East Asia. The settlement plan failed, both because of active aggressive Japanese activity against China and the Soviet Union, and because the Jews of America, led by the president of the American Jewish Congress, Rabbi Stephen S. Wise, refused to give any support, financial or political, to enemies of America.

But Dr. Kaufman, who "visited" Japan twice and had audiences with high officials as well as the emperor himself, saw the necessity of counteracting the danger stemming from the newly signed Agreement on Cultural Cooperation between

Japan and Germany. Certainly, it would have endangered all Jews of the Far East if an anti-Japanese policy had been adopted by the Jewish organizations of the Far East.

Following the occupation of Manchuria in 1931 after the Mukden Incident, Japan initiates several steps to tighten political and economic control of the region. Their policy had two principal objectives: First, to force the Soviet influence out of Manchuria and to take control of the CER, and second, to take over or at least to receive a substantial share of the businesses owned by non-Japanese, including Chinese, Russians, Jews, Poles, Tatars, and other Western foreigners. This brought the destruction of many businesses in the city, including those of Jews. The 20th anniversary of the founding of the Weekly "Jewish Life" was marked in 1941, but buckling under the pressure of the German Embassy in Tokyo, the Japanese authorities decided to close the Zionist publication "Hadegel". In 1943, again under the pressure of the German Embassy in Tokyo, the Japanese authorities in Harbin closed the "Jewish Life".

Why did the Japanese threaten the Jews in such a fashion? Most Japanese have never met a Jew in their lives and generally were not affected by Christian anti- Semitic beliefs.

The Japanese, who throughout the first thirty formative years maintained a relatively small community in Harbin and were not immune from anti Jewish sentiments, engaged in a secret 'sticks and carrots' game of which they believed would bring them economic, political, and civil benefits.

Chizuko Takao[49] states that "the Japanese understanding of the Jews between the two wars can be roughly divided into the "useful Jews" theory which was aimed at taking advantage of the political and financial influence of the Jews in international scenes, and the "Jews as conspirators" theory which advocated the threat of a Jewish revolutionary plot in Japan, based on a view that the Jews and Bolsheviks are the same.[50] Japanese understanding of the Jews was very theoretical, regardless of pro-Jewish or anti-Semitic sentiment. It was not formed by real contact with Jews."[51]

According to Chizuko Takao "In 1921, the Japanese government formed an intelligence office in the Ministry of Foreign Affairs (MOFA) as it felt during World War I, particularly at the Paris Peace Conference, that Japan's intelligence and propaganda activities were lagging behind other countries. The report titled "Research on the Jews" was written in 1921 by Kenkichi Mori, who belonged to the third department in charge of propaganda of the intelligence office. In this report, Mori pointed out that Japan has little understanding about the political influence of the Jews. Mori advised the Minister of Foreign Affairs, saying, "from now on, our authorities will have to associate and get in touch with influential Jewish people in a timely manner through Japan's embassies and consulates in the UK, France, and the USA".[52]

Examination of files on the 'Jewish question' at the Diplomatic Record Office of the Japanese Ministry of Foreign Affairs in Tokyo shows that Foreign Minister Yasunari Uchida sent Mori's report titled "Research on Jews" on April 20, 1921, to Japan's embassies and consulates.[53]

After their invasion of Manchuria in 1931 and the start of their occupation of Harbin in February 1932, the Japanese divorced themselves, publicly, from anti-Jewish beliefs or practices, while on the other hand engaged firsthand, or used and enjoyed the services of the Russian extreme-right and other criminal elements in the city, to pressure the leadership or individuals within the Jewish community to deliver economic benefits or goods they were in need of. Among these tactical hushed games was the 'Fugu Plan'[8], a secret Japanese plot designed to recruit "world Jewish money" and use it to enhance Japan's war-torn economy.

It seems however that through the 1930s and by the 1940's, anti-Semitism had become an integral part of ultranationalist thought actively disseminated and promoted by Japan's major newspapers with the approval of the Japanese government. It reached every corner of the country.

By now many Japanese believed that Japan and Germany were engaged in a single struggle against a common Jewish enemy and that Japan must expel Jewish influence from Asia. The Japanese government was exploiting anti-Semitism at home to enforce ideological conformity. However, the Japanese official policy of wartime anti-Semitism was not used to openly persecute the Jews. 18.000 German, Austrian and Lithuanian Jews were allowed to find temporary refuge in Shanghai and Kobe between 1938 and 1941.

On December 6th, 1938 the Five Ministers Conference (Gosho Kaigi), consisting of the Prime Minister, Foreign Minister, and the ministers of the Army, Navy, and Treasury, adopted the following three principles towards the Jews:

1) Jews living in Japan, Manchuria and China are to be treated fairly and in the same manner as other foreign nationals. No special effort to expel them is to be made.
2) Jews entering Japan, Manchuria and China are to be dealt with based on existing immigration policies pertaining to other foreigners.
3) No special effort to attract Jews to Japan, Manchuria or China is to be made. However, exceptions may be made for businessmen and technicians for utility value for Japan.

The Japanese rulers of Manchuria realized that Japan would need huge investments to develop this vast region for their benefit. At first, they tried to attract European and American investors...

The founder of Nissan industries, Ayukawa Gisuke, wrote an article entitled 'A Plan to Invite Fifty Thousand Jews to Manchukuo'. He hoped that America would invest one hundred million dollars in the resettlement of German Jews in Manchuria. While his article was received with interest, Ayukawa Gisuke's plan could not succeed if the Jews kept leaving Manchuria and taking their capital with them. In order to persuade them to stay on, Colonel Yasue Norihiro was appointed as the chief liaison officer of the Japanese military forces in Manchuria. Colonel Yasue had been interested in the Jewish question for years and had written many articles and books on the 'Jewish problem'.

The three "articles" however, were just a cover for wider Japanese considerations. They hoped to soften the Jewish leadership's refusal to provide them with needed money in order to help Japan's crumbling economy.

The Fugu Plan did not succeed in Manchukuo. Records of Dr. Kaufman's deals with the Japanese are hidden and not to be found, except, maybe, in the locked and well guarded "Jewish Community Archives" in Harbin, which according to government officials hold extremely sensitive political documents that can make the Israeli government uneasy. One may get only a very narrow sense of the atmosphere of the time from the Jewish or other official newspapers published then in Harbin.

Harbin was not a paradise or heaven. Plagues, devastating floods, criminal and fascist gangs ruling the streets and terrifying everyone. Kidnappings, and murders, were all part of the daily agenda of the citizens' life. Those were just part of the scene. There were also celebrations and parties, and the Jewish holidays were observed by most members of the community. These 'happy times' have been recorded by almost all. But accounts of the years of worries and traumas are hard to find.

During the Japanese occupation, lives were controlled by military orders. Many private establishments—residential and commercial—were confiscated, most social activities were stopped and special permits were issued only for an extraordinary reason.

In 1997, Irene Clurman interviewed Charlie, her father who was born in Harbin and was sent by his father, Izko Chaim Gershowitz Clurman, for new and secure life in the United States.[54]

> "Grandfather (Izko Chaim Gershowitz Clurman—in Russian, Isak Grigori) built this building in 1936 as a Japanese hotel during the occupation of Manchuria. The last building grandfather built before his death, it occupied almost one square block... Because of the long Harbin winters, the building was under construction for about two years. It was built largely from recycled materials salvaged by my grandfather. Essentially, we were wreckers and dismantled everything, even a huge circus building constructed from wood, freight railway cars, and a couple of riverboats. This made for excellent well-seasoned building materials...
>
> The Japanese Hotel on Yamskaya Street was built as much for public relations as for income and profit. It was never sold. After the war, the Chinese expropriated it. It was well built over about one square block and heated by steam heat with a boiler fired by hard coal. The father of Efim Krouk was a plumber and he installed it. After the war, Efim moved to Hong Kong, then Australia with his wife Nora..."

In a letter to his daughter dated June 16, 1997, Charlie offered the following comments on the difficulties of life in Manchuria at that time in history:

"...Japanese troops marched into Harbin and gradually occupied the entire country in 1931 when I was 13 years old and Johnny was 3. I stood on the street corner and watched Japanese mechanized Army units roll into the city. There was no organized opposition as the main body of Chinese Nationalist troops under Chiang Kai-Shek was engaged in a civil war against the Chinese Communists and thought it was more important to defeat the Communists than to fight the Japanese. The Chinese government in Nanking had no interest in Manchuria. To them, it was just an uncivilized faraway border state. The central government also was very weak and riddled with graft.

Not unlike the German Nazis, the Japanese did not reveal their final plans and worked gradually to take over the entire country. Manchuria was destined to become an economic base to support Japanese military adventures to the south. We were totally defenseless and had no one to turn to for help and protection. The final stroke came when Red Russians sold their half of the Chinese Eastern Railway and pulled back to Russia. Gradually, like the Nazis, the Japanese tightened their hold on Manchuria and then the atrocities really reared their ugly heads. Japanese were not anti-Semites like Germans. They just wanted to eliminate the ruling class and Jews and Chinese merchants were it...

This is the period and the conditions that prevailed under which we were living and trying to survive.

Father for one did not survive. I am sure you have heard all this before. I consider this period as the beginning of World War II.

The White Russian remnants of the defeated Imperial Russian Army went to work for the Japanese and made sport of denouncing Jewish people to the Japanese Kempetai [secret police]. Father had good connections with the Japanese since we traded with them before the occupation. He used to help our people when they were taken by the Kempetai headquarters for interrogation. Unfortunately, when he was taken, there was no one to help him. I was already in the United States for six months when he was taken. Father actually sent me out of Manchuria to save me so he would have someone abroad to help the family..."

In an audiotape made on October 28, 1982, in Reno Nevada, Ethel Rachel (Roza) Clurman,[55] Isak Grigori's wife, tells the story of the family:

"This guy was kidnaped and killed, Mark Abramovich. He was a very good athlete... Isak Grigori carried a pistol when walking the streets of Harbin. He was also known to use his fists on people who got in his way — and sometimes men crossed the street to avoid running into him. Once while walking to the synagogue, Isak Grigori saw some young Russians harassing an old bearded Rabbi. Even though he was wearing his Sabbath finery, Isak Grigori pulled the young men aside and beat them up. The family never made it to the synagogue that day... I never saw a Jewish beggar or a Jewish prostitute, criminal or dope addict. I never

saw a Jewish man drunk on the street. Saturday was
an alms day."

In May 1938, Isak Grigori disappeared while on his way to work
in the lumberyard a few blocks from the family's apartment
building. No one ever saw him again. The family and the Harbin
Jewish community believed that the Kempetai, the Japanese
secret police, had taken him into custody tortured him, and
either sent him to the medical experiments camp (Unit 731) or
possibly buried him in a mass grave."

. Such accounts of Harbin's political, social, religious, and
imperial conquests are hidden within the memories of many of
those who lived in the city and moved to other places. For most,
nostalgia and other sentiments override the past as it was.

The reasons for nostalgic presentations of the past are many.
They may belong to a "psycho-historical" analysis, which is
another area of study.

The Baal Shem said:

> *"What does it mean, when people say that Truth goes over
> all the world? It means that Truth is driven out of one place
> after another, and must wander on and on and on..."*[56]

This venture into the personal histories of individuals touches on
the collective as well. It is also an attempt to apply perspectives to
the study of identity and its relation to space and time, especially
to ways identity, geography, and memory may intersect and
change. It presents some cases of recollections, oral and written
memories, diaries and publications based on motives, nostalgic
remembrance, selective memory, psychological blocks and
forgetting, or political manipulations. I call these "imagined
history".

Many attempts to tell the stories of individuals have

transformed the pasts of Harbin into mental geography, sometimes imagined. These pasts have been packed into suitcases that moved from one space and time to another, changing, creating new stories, or hiding portions, while neglecting to note what was actually happening.

A study of teller's motives suggests a need for a new approach comprising not just historians, but other disciplines, among them psychology, law, anthropology, sociology, and literature.

More than 40 foreign nationalities gathered in Harbin to make the city an international cosmos. Among them, and speaking 45 different languages, were Russians of several colors, Jews from different geographical locations, Japanese settlers and later invaders, Koreans, Poles, Ukrainians, Danes, Germans, Portuguese, Latvians, Armenians, Georgians, Tartars, Italians, Greeks, Belgians, French, Swedish, Swiss, Americans, British, Indians, and others.

They brought their former spaces with them, created a new local existence, maintained global connections, and influenced global events, hence forming glocalized[57] communities. And, "by dwelling in the diasporic past, the global village create[d] its spiritual and intellectual theme park."[58] In this case, although Harbin was referred to as 'global village' I prefer to label it a 'glocalized space' with special spatial dimension. The suitcases that new comers took with them on their journeys were full of memories of other spaces, some real and others imagined.

Upon leaving Harbin years later, they added another past to the suitcase, and this they brought to a new place. Over time, these pasts lost their boundaries and became almost one. This was the case, for example, with Rosa Clurman whose mother bought a small porcelain Buddha in a Harbin street bazaar in the 1920s and took it with her to San Francisco after she left China in the 1940s. She put the porcelain Buddha in her living–room and created a new glocalized space.

It is natural that if the past is to matter at all, one must be aware of its nature, its shifting meanings, and its vulnerability to adjustments, causes, needs, and alterations.

"Place defined not simply in terms of location and topography, but of the memories enshrined in myth and rite which render it unique, the center of the world for those whose place it is", or those who made it their new home. "In being lost—often long lost—these places have also lost their particularity; the nostalgia is no longer for places, but for place imbued with an Edenic innocence."[59]

The 1930s produced several proposals to the Jewish problem, which I have marked as the "final geographical solutions". These were extraordinary ideas to resettle very large numbers of Jewish refugees in faraway geographies, especially in East Asia. These ideas never materialized, but they do raise questions about why these were not realized, what were the politics behind the rejections, what if these would have happened and what kind of adaptation or changes would have occurred to the relocated individuals or groups? Would these helped change their identities?

The German-Austrian Jewish doctors, for example, that found jobs in Harbin tried their best to maintain their Germanic cultural attributes while trying to compete for their survival in the city. Those who kept clinging to their former habits lost their ways and were rejected.

The study of identity and its relation to geography and time, especially to ways identity, space and memory may intersect and change, can be subject to a lengthy discussion on the "wandering Jew" and the many garments he had to change along his journey. The proposed settlements of Jews in the Far East bring about the question 'what would have happened to people if all of these suggestions have materialized'? It should be followed by the understanding that the rejection of the resettlement ideas came out of traditional anti-Semitism and stereotypical notions.

The Jewish People encountered migration more than any other national group. In trying to find a peaceful space to settle into, they as a group and as individuals became human cargo for suggestions that met political maneuverings, consideration based on economics and social transformation, moral briberies, colonial purification, and mostly bigotry. It seems, even in the most sincere designs, that these were influenced by the then very popular notions set by the fake "The Protocols of the Elders of Zion". History is a fluid subject that changes time and again by governments and politics according to time, needs and wants.

Burning Europe and the plight of the Jews in it brought about several suggestions for alleviating the "problem". What is so interesting is that all the ideas were to be materialized at the end of the 1930's as if there was a global conspiracy behind the suggestions.

Although there is no reference to it, I suspect that the ideas of resettling Jewish refugees in various parts of East Asia came out of three models, two of which were of Jewish design.

At the Sixth Zionist Congress in Basel, Theodor Herzl suggested establishing the Jewish national home in Uganda, Africa, of all places.

When Herzl began his pursuit to establish a homeland for the Jewish people, he looked for the support of the great powers to help achieve his goal. In 1903, Herzl met with Joseph Chamberlain, the British colonial secretary and other high-ranking officials who agreed in principle to Jewish settlement in East Africa.[60]

On August 26, 1903, Herzl went on and proposed the British Uganda Program as a temporary refuge for Jews in

Russia in immediate danger. The congress decided to send an "investigatory commission" to examine the territory proposed. Three days later the British government released an official document allocating a "Jewish territory" in East Africa. The Uganda Program was finally rejected by the Zionist movement at the Seventh Zionist Congress in 1905 because it was conceived as anti-Zionist, although there were attempts to continue the scheme. What kept the idea alive for nearly two years was a combination of the seriousness of anti-Semitism and at the same time the failure of the political dimension of Zionist activity.

After the rejection of the Uganda scheme on the grounds of impracticability by the British, new ideas followed about settlement in Canada and Australia. But opposition from local residents led to the abandonment of the scheme. Expeditions were sent to Iraq, Libya and Angola, but nothing came of these excursions.

The Galveston scheme, which considered the settlement of Jews in the American Southwest, in particular in Texas, had some concrete success. The project received the assistance of Jacob Schiff, the American Jewish banker, and some 9,300 Jews arrived in that area between 1907-1914.[61]

Jacob Schiff will play a role again 20 years later in another scheme to resettle Jews, this time in Manchuria, China.

The suggestions of Jewish resettlement took hold by now. This was followed by the resettlement of Jews in southern Siberia in the Far Eastern part of the Soviet Union. This relocation was the only one to be carried out in very large numbers.

The plan that was implemented was that of Joseph Stalin who established the Jewish Autonomous Oblast in Birobidzhan, in Siberia, at the border with China in 1928. the plan was carried out later and thousands of Eastern European Jews whom he described as "rootless cosmopolitans" found their way there.

In 1924, the unemployment rate among Jews in the USSR exceeded 30%, partially as a result of pogroms but also as a result of the policies of the USSR, which prohibited people from being independent craftsmen and small businessmen. The government established the committee for the agricultural settlement of Jews, and thought of resettling all Jews in a designated territory as an alternative to Zionism, which called for the establishment of Palestine as a Jewish homeland.

The location that was initially considered in the early 1920s was Crimea, which already had a significant Jewish population. However, an alternative scheme, perceived as more advantageous for the USSR, was put into practice.

Eventually, Birobidzhan, in what is now the Jewish Autonomous Oblast, was chosen by the Soviet leadership as the site for the Jewish region. It was an area that had been chosen for military and economic reasons, as it was often infiltrated by China, while Japan also had an appetite for the provinces of the Soviet Far East. According to General Pavel Sudoplatov, "The establishment of the Jewish Autonomous Oblast in Birobidzhan in 1928 was ordered by Stalin only as an effort to strengthen the Far Eastern border region with an outpost, not as a favor to the Jews. The area was constantly penetrated by Chinese and White Russian terrorist groups, and the idea was to shield the territory by establishing a settlement whose inhabitants would be hostile to White Russian émigrés, especially the Cossacks. The status of this region was defined shrewdly as an autonomous district, not an autonomous republic, which meant that no local legislature, high court, or government post of ministerial rank was permitted. It was an autonomous area, but a bare frontier, not a political center."[62]

By the 1930s, a massive campaign developed to induce more Jewish settlers to move there. The campaign partly incorporated the standard Soviet promotional tools of the era and included posters and Yiddish-language novels describing a socialist utopia there.[63]

A third model was that of the Japanese, which followed the Soviet scheme and elevated it further. There is a correlation between the Soviet actions in regard to the settlement of Jews in a designated area and the formation of the same idea by the Japanese authorities in the 1930s. After all, Japanese army officers that studied in Moscow, brought upon their return home the beliefs put forward by the Russian anti-Semitic invention of the fraud Protocols of the Elders of Zion, which they acquired in the Soviet Union.

Imperial Japan proposed to settle Jewish refugees escaping Nazi-occupied Europe in Manchukuo where Harbin is located, the Japanese-controlled puppet-state in northeast China's Manchuria, as well as in Shanghai. The proposal, called The Fugu Plan, was prepared in June and July of 1939, and sought to gain the benefit of the supposed economic prowess of the Jews and convince the United States, and specifically American Jewry, to grant political favor and economic investment into Japan.

The plan included how the settlement would be organized and how Jewish support, both in terms of investment and actual settlers, would be achieved. It addressed the size of settlements, allowing for the populations to range in size from 18,000, up to 600,000 persons.

The Japanese officials insisted that while the settlements could appear autonomous, controls needed to be placed to keep the Jews under surveillance. It was feared that the Jews might somehow penetrate the mainstream Japanese government and economy, influencing or taking command of it in the same way that they, according to the false and libelous Protocols of the Elders of Zion, had done in many other countries. The Jewish world community was to supply the settlers and fund the settlements. The plan was not implemented because of the refusal of the American Jewish leadership, including Jacob Schiff, a Jewish-American banker, to go along with it and invest 50 million US Dollars in Japan.

Harbin and Shanghai were not the first choices for Jewish refugees. A 1939 American Jewish proposal was to create a large settlement of Jews in one of the southern islands of the Philippines in a neighborhood with the radical Muslim community and ancient tribal groups. It was thought that this would have allowed them easier access to the USA. Although the settlement of thousands of Jews in that part of the Philippines was perceived by the authorities as a creation of a buffer zone between the mostly Catholic nation and the hostile Muslims, it did not materialize because of fears of introducing a new element that would be in conflict with the state religion, and also, by a refusal of the local Jewish community to allow such migration that may jeopardize its status quo conditions.

A similar solution was suggested in regards to Indonesia. A Muslim dominated nation with a small Jewish community. Both rejected the idea.

In China, on 17 February, 1939, Mr. Sun Ke, the elder son of Dr. Sun Yat-sen[64], and Chairman of the Chinese legislative body, made a proposal to set up a settlement in Southwest China for Austro-German Jews who were fleeing from their countries.

The proposal[65], which never materialized, saw the settlement of Jews in the border region of Yunnan province. The plan was to settle 50,000 Jews on the border with Burma, and 50,000 on the border with Vietnam[66]. There were economic considerations in Mr. Sun Ke's proposal, which were borrowed from ideas put forward by the Japanese and the notion that one can benefit from "Jewish money".

The plan, Sun Ke said, would relieve the pressure of arrivals that Shanghai was finding hard to bear, and it would also help strengthen China's relations with the U.S. and the U.K. These were the countries with the world's strongest Jewish communities and which China needed most in her life-and-death struggle with Japan.

"We can see similarities between Sun's proposal and the Fugu Plan of the Japanese. Both saw the global Jewish community as wealthy, powerful and talented—and a group to have on your side in the world war. Yunnan was, like Manchuria, a remote region rich in natural resources but sparse in population; neither China nor Japan had the capital to develop them — both looked to the overseas Jewish community to provide funds—just as Britain and France had introduced Indians, Chinese, Lebanese and other foreigners into their colonies in Africa, Fiji, and the Caribbean."[67]

General Long Yun, chairman of the Yunnan province government, sent a telegram of support to the central government in Chongqing, saying that he welcomed the Jews to help cultivate the land: "Yunnan is a large area with a sparse population and fertile soil. The Jews have rich knowledge and abundant financial resources. If they could settle in Yunnan and cultivate the empty land, it would bring benefit to everyone."[68]

The plan never materialized. The only 'migrants' were 10 Jews who arrived in Yunnan in 1939 to work as drivers and in the provincial salt management bureau.[69]

Around that same time, in Australia, the Kimberley Plan, was a failed scheme by the Freeland League for Jewish Territorial Colonization to resettle 75,000 Jewish refugees from Europe in northwestern Australia before and during the Holocaust.

The Freeland League was formed in the United States in July 1935 to search for a potential Jewish homeland and haven. The League was a non-Zionist organization led by Isaac Nachman Steinberg. In late 1938 or early 1939, the firm of Michael Durack in Australia offered the League a sale of about 16,500 square kilometers (6,400 sq mi) in the Kimberley region in Australia, stretching from the north of Western Australia into the Northern Territory. The League sent a Yiddish poet and essayist Melech Ravitch to the Northern Territory in the 1930s to investigate the region and to collect data on topography and climate. Ravitch, in his report to the League, suggested that the area could accommodate a million Jewish refugees.

A 1944 opinion poll found that 47% of Australians opposed the scheme. Opposition was primarily based on concerns that the settlers would inevitably drift away from Kimberley and begin migrating to the cities in large numbers. In July 1944 the scheme was vetoed by the Australian government and Labor Prime Minister John Curtin informed the League that the Australian government would not "depart from the long-established policy in regard to alien settlement in Australia" and could not "entertain the proposal for a group settlement of the exclusive type contemplated by the Freeland League".

It is not surprising that along with Herzl's reasoning, all plans, including the Chinese, came out of stereotypical beliefs, or the usage of both, that anywhere else will be labeled as anti-Semitism. And it is not odd that four of these proposals were formulated around 1939.

In his book, Der Judenstaat, Herzl writes:

"The Jewish question persists wherever Jews live in appreciable numbers. Wherever it does not exist, it is brought in together with Jewish immigrants. We are naturally drawn into those places where we are not persecuted, and our appearance there gives rise to persecution. This is the case, and will inevitably be so, everywhere, even in highly civilized countries..."

Harbin was such a case.

This discussion offers an opportunity to imagine what would have happened to the identity of these Jews if the plans had materialized. Could one imagine the nature and identity of Austro-German Jews who found themselves in the tropical jungles of south China? What kind of people would they have turned out to be in the wilderness of Manchuria under the Japanese? And what kind of a Jewish community would have been formed in the northern wilderness of Australia?

Harbin could not handle such large groups of refugees. There was a need for larger spaces that not only accommodate the refugees but that some of the benefactors will gain a nice profit out of these.

A careful study of the personal histories in this volume may suggest that in spite of all difficulties people encountered in their daily life, the umbrella of Jewish tradition and culture, including life under hostile rules, contributed to the formation of a strong community with relevant diasporic attributes, that catered to those who were not as fortunate as others.

This undertaking thus establishes a detailed account of the daily life of the tellers and in some cases the handling methods that they employed to dodge their experiences.

It does so while trying to preserve the original language of the storyteller in order to safeguard its authenticity.

Most members of the Harbin Jewish community lived a life either full of goods or overwhelmed by shortages, misfortunes, and difficulties.

It would be safe to note that many members were passive in face of the various policies implemented by the various regimes, yet active in face of the hardships. This demonstrates how motives of self-protection and survival beneath the acts of superficial compliance directed the people's everyday life.

The individual histories presented here focus on the detailed examination of the everyday life of people of various economic conditions, exploring more specifically the aspects of education, economy, housing, and healthcare, as recorded in their stories.

By looking at these core elements that constituted the everyday life of ordinary people, we find that they managed to adapt to several ways of survival.

Sol Kerson had survived the Pogrom of 1905 at age 11 in his native Belarus by hiding under a stone bridge as the Czar's soldiers burned the houses of his extended family, friends, and neighbors with the people inside, asleep and burning to death. There were some survivors, he and his mother among them.

The same soldiers prevented Sol from traveling west, so in 1913, at age 19, he escaped to the east, hitchhiking on trains and wagons across Europe and Asia, until he reached Harbin, in Manchuria part of northeast China.[70]

Sol was born on March 3, 1894. But in order to get out of Belarus, then part of imperial Russia, Sol had to list his birthday as 1899, five years later than it actually was. He needed to do this to get out of the Russian military draft. Thus, he could travel with Russian papers that listed him as 14 rather than 19.[71]

Sol spent several months in Harbin trying to get by with temporary shelter and food he could obtain by asking. Harbin was not his final destination because he wanted to get to New York in America. He spent his days in the new town contemplating how to continue his way to the 'new world' where he would build his permanent life. Yet, as he told Paul Kerson, his nephew in a 1973 interview, Harbin was his start. His old country was as if never existed and Harbin in China's Manchuria was his new birthplace.

Sol found out that Harbin was a part of a Russian enclave within China.

The Russians leased this area from China in order to build the Chinese Eastern Railway that broke away from the Trans-Siberian Railroad from Moscow and ran south and then east to Vladivostok, the Russian Far Eastern Pacific warm water port city.

Once the railway was built, Russians, among them many Russian Jews took it to Harbin in search of opportunity. What Sol Kerson found was a Jewish community complete with synagogues, schools, hospitals, medical offices, many stores and bazaars, a cemetery, a beer factory, bakeries, hotels, and numerous other commercial establishments. Harbin, so he was able to gather, was a place where the rich got richer and the poor tried to survive.

It was a new city, complete with all the necessary services that enabled it to function and grow. For Sol, Harbin looked like a Russian city. On the streets, he heard the Russian language, and the storefronts were covered with names and announcements written in the Russian language. Yet, there was something else there. For the first time in his young life, he was seeing, hearing, and bumping into Chinese people. As a matter of fact, half of the city was Chinese and they lived, so he discovered, on the other side of the railway tracks. The Chinese were curious and very welcoming people. It was here that he found the Chinese guide with his rowboat who would venture on a dangerous journey.

Sol was looking for partners for the voyage east. Several victimized Russian Jews that held a strong will to continue their journey somewhere else, to another geography, and from there to a new destination of their choice. Sol did not have any money to venture on an ocean voyage on a large ship. So were the 4 other "passengers" he was able to recruit. The plan he created in

Harbin was as simple yet courageous as anyone could imagine. With no money to buy his way, he was able to convince a fellow Chinese who owned a tiny river rowboat, to sail the Sea of Japan and cross the water from the shores of China all the way to Japan. For this, he did not need much, just clothes to cover his flesh and a few items such as Russian black bread that was called kleb, a salami or kalbassa in Russian, a spicy sausage that looked like a tube of meat with spices that is usually eaten cold in slices, something that the Chinese call xiāngcháng, meaning Italian sausage. And, of course, one bottle of vodka either to warm his body from the cold ocean winds or to deep his worries in the Russian alcohol.

Thus, Sol fled across the Sea of Japan in a rowboat with four other persecuted Russian Jews, a Chinese guide, and just a few eatable items to keep him simply alive.

It seemed then as it is always the case that people's need and desire for a better life are stronger than perhaps life itself.

Sol reached Japan, walked across it, and in Kobe boarded a freighter bound for Seattle, Washington in America. In 1916, the only requirement for entry into the United States was five dollars. If one didn't have certain health conditions, was not Chinese, wasn't an anarchist, communist, or any other restricted participation. The U.S. did exclude certain categories of people even then.

Sol did not have this then-large sum of money, so he borrowed it from a fellow immigrant getting off the boat. When he arrived, the U.S. Immigration Officer standing on the dock stuck out his hand and said "Welcome to America". The U.S. Immigration Officer changed Sol's Russian-sounding last name to the Americanized version of Kerson and carry forward into the future.

Sol picked apples in Washington State to earn the

transcontinental railroad fare to New York where his two uncles, Louis Kalmanoff and Louis Kaplowitz, preceded him. This trip around the Earth seeking freedom, dignity, and life itself took three long years.[72]

Sol Kerson's story is just one of many. It demonstrates as others do, a strong will to live, to survive, to look forward to some kind of permanency and safety, to a space that can offer peace of mind, a resting place where worries are in the drawer only. His dream was not Manchuria but New York in America. Harbin, where he assembled a simple daily life and few necessities, was his jumping board to that destination.

For others, Harbin was a new home where they could build a new life, sometimes a new identity, and erect a sense of permanency in what they conceived as the farthest place on earth.

Here, in this booming Russian enclave, they started building a form of life that was, so they thought, free of the evils that they knew in the past.

Some were very rich, industrialists who came from Odessa, St. Petersburg, Moscow, and Vladivostok, and who looked for new opportunities. Others belonged to the "white collar" middle class, among them, journalists and writers, doctors, teachers, musicians, actors, accountants, lawyers, real-estate middlemen, and the like. Many others were refugees, stateless people, who escaped misfortunes, revolutions, and pogroms, and reached Harbin penniless.

A closer study of Harbin, from its inception in 1896, its establishment in 1898, through the Russo-Japanese war of 1904-5, the end of Czarist rule and the Bolshevik revolution, the two devastating plagues of 1911 and 1919, the Japanese invasion of the region in 1931 and occupation of the city in 1932, the Soviet invasion in 1945 through 1947, and the formation of the People's

Republic of China in 1949, reveal a different picture. Each with its own understanding.

"My late Grandfather's brother, Sol Kerson, resided in Harbin in 1915..." writes Paul Kerson. "He had lived through and survived the Pogrom of 1905 at the age of 11. He was determined to escape to freedom, and at the age of 18 in 1913 he commenced walking east. He could not go west because of the Czar's bureaucrats and army, determined to prevent anyone from leaving their jurisdiction. Sol walked and hitchhiked to Cathrinaslav, Ukraine, where he managed to board the newly built Trans-Siberian Railroad. He got off in Irkutsk and found his way to Harbin, which he described as an international city. It took him the better part of two years to get this far. In 1916, with four other Russian Jews led by one Chinese with one salami and one bottle of vodka, he escaped the Eurasian landmass in a rowboat and crossed the Sea of Japan. He walked across Japan. This took six months. He then boarded a freighter in Kobe and arrived in Seattle in 1916, penniless... Sixteen productive American citizens now exist because the Harbin Jewish Community and the Chinese City of Harbin took Sol under its wing in 1915, and somehow helped him into that rowboat. I learned this story in detail on June 2, 1973, when I was 22. I interviewed Sol extensively in his retirement high-rise apartment in North Miami Beach, Florida. Sol was then 78, but he remembered his odyssey clear as a bell... When I interviewed Sol in 1973, Ida his wife did not want to tell her immigration story, or perhaps could not. American Jewish immigrants of their generation were often reluctant to recount their heroic odysseys. They very much wanted to blend into the American life, and not be called 'greenhorns'..."[73]

A bird that you set free may be caught again, but a word that escapes your lips will not return. What you do not see with your eyes, do not invent with your mouth.

– Jewish proverb

Histories

Well-to-do Jewish households employed amahs — nannies, women that were hired to suckle a child of someone else, cooks, servants, and house workers. Many of them lived with the family in a special part of the house. Others lived in the Chinese quarters of Harbin and arrived each morning at their post. Other families found ways to take care of their households by having workers come each day or once or twice a week. Chinese labor was cheap and many could afford the luxury of having outside help.

The community was a mirror of the life of the Jews anywhere at the beginning of the 20th century and onward. Its composition was made of differences in social rank and status. These were industrialists with old money and high status. There was a middle-class made of white-collar occupations among them lawyers, doctors, accountants, civil servants, artists, and journalists. And there was a large presence of the poor, who needed the help of the community in order to survive.

This was the reality of the past. Nevertheless, many years later, after Harbin had no Jews to count for, what the Chinese inhabitants of the city can see are the luxurious Jewish constructed and owned buildings on Zhongyang Dajie that was once called Kitayskaya Ulitsa, the Hotel Moderne in the center of the mile-long street, the architectural wonder of the two synagogues, the old European style of the Jewish Gymnasium, the villas of Skidelsky, Soskin and Krol, the exhibition of the history of the Harbin Jewish community on the second and third floors of the

Moorish styled New Synagogue, and the silent tombstones that face in all directions at the Huangshan Jewish cemetery.

All of these present only a slice of the community. Most of the tombstones at the cemetery were constructed by rich Jewish families. Nearly all of them are very large, made of granite and with intricate decorations. Thus, the cemetery gives a false impression of the composition of the community.

The exhibition of the history of the Harbin Jewish community that was set up in the New Synagogue by the Heilongjiang Academy of Social Sciences and was curated in a way that it presents the Jewish industrialists and the well-to-do only. It follows the official line of "all Jews have much money" and thus can bring investments and prosperity to Heilongjiang's capital city.

As said, this is what the citizens of Harbin or any visitor to the city can see. This in turn formulates an imaginary history far from being real and true.

The stories presented here are of people, some rich, some poor, and many in between. They are told in their authors' language and color so that the reader can recognize a character with his or hers way of expression and grammatical mistakes, hear the tone, can feel the emotions, attach colors, and can be part of the tale.

Cecelia Hurwich

Cecelia Hurwich, the daughter of Jack Steinberg, who was born on December 21, 1919, recalls her childhood years in Harbin. Her first memories as a child were of eating in their warm Harbin kitchen with her amah and numerous Chinese servants coming in and out. When servants entered the kitchen, they hurried to the stove for warmth, rubbing their hands against the chill. Harbin's temperatures were bitterly cold in the wintertime. She felt they were hungry and offered them part of what she might have been eating. The servants were very thin, but they usually shook their heads "no" because they felt it inappropriate to accept food from the child of their master.

In her father's Jewish Russian society[74], food played an important role, with social occasions revolving around tables laden with sumptuous food. She asked her father where their servants lived and ate, he waved "out there." Once playing in the garden, she noticed that there was a pile of bedding in a wooden storeroom and surmised that this was "out there."

Cecelia liked watching all the activity on the street below through the huge picture windows of their mansion. Rickshaws, peasants pulling carts with fresh produce, and items for sale passed before me she recalled.

"One exceptionally cold day when I was three and looking out our windows, a large horse-drawn wagon loaded with cabbages drove by. Two peasants pulling small carts ran in front of the wagon. In order to avoid hitting them, the driver turned the wagon sharply to the left. The wagon overturned, throwing hundreds of cabbages onto the street. Within seconds, a mob of men, women, and children, descended on the street, ravenously eating raw cabbages. The driver frantically tried to stop the mob from devouring his cabbages, to no avail. Minutes later, all the cabbage disappeared, eaten or tucked away in carts, aprons, and dresses. In that instance, hunger, starvation, and poverty became real.[75]

Father and his brother were taught to work in the family business. In Harbin, my father officially took his place in the Steinberg family business.

My parents first set up their own flat with a cook and amah. From my amah, I learned my first words of Mandarin and by the time I was 2, I could speak Mandarin and Russian fluently.

Jack Steinberg was a charismatic, lovable, wheeler-dealer businessman and gambler, who collected mistresses.

Cecelia's grandfather Gregory had a wonderful personality, loving and gay. She described him as being "a witty person and loving company. He was a terrible flirt, and he was always flirting. Everyone would come up to him and borrow money, even though he couldn't afford to give it to them. Jack Steinberg was that way too. Neither of them could say no. Grandfather wrote a book that was published in Shanghai. Grandfather Gregory's short stories are witty with Russian humor.[76]

Gregory had a Torah in the house in Harbin, and when the Jewish holidays came, the synagogue would be held in our living room. Later they built a Russian club, and they would bring the Torah to the Russian club, and then the Jewish holidays were held there. Both my grandfather and his sons could read from the Torah.

"Garibaldi lived in Harbin. He was the grandson of the famous Giuseppe Garibaldi[77]. Of course, we Jews used to have a peculiar feeling about him.

Garibaldi was strongly anti-clerical and anti-papacy. However, in some writings, he supported Christianity. "I am a Christian, and I speak to Christians—I am a true Christian, and I speak to true Christians. I love and venerate the religion of Christ, because Christ came into the world to deliver humanity from slavery…" he wrote.

My father who was a big fan of horse races told me that Garibaldi's wife would dress very elegantly at the races. Garibaldi was very antisemitic so I guess we took it for granted that his grandson would be so also. Jack never alluded to the plight of Jews in Russia. All he and his father and brothers talked about was business.[78]

"One of the popular customs in Harbin was that in the fall there would be a sheet of paper in the newspapers, and the woman would give their homes addresses. In the afternoon you'd get on a rickshaw with a paper in front of you, and you'd go to tea in these homes. That was the kind of life we women led in Harbin during the social season. If you didn't play cards or mahjong, you were left out of another social clique. Everyone dressed to the hilt and we danced. There were dances on Wednesday and Saturday nights. It was quite a social thing, anybody that was anything turned up at these.

The Harbin Jewish Community was well-organized, with private clubs, social gatherings, dinners, a synagogue, and programs for the new immigrants who escaped Russian antisemitism. These poor immigrants came with nothing on their backs, except their suitcases. The Jewish community took care of the immigrants, and no one lacked food or a place to live. My grandfather Gregory Steinberg and other business people found jobs for the newcomers and taught them the ropes of doing business in China."[79]

Cecelia Hurwich's parents lived a privileged life in Harbin. They attended many parties and dances, picnics on weekends, and dinner parties in friends' homes. Cecelia remembered her father and mother dressed up in a tuxedo and ball gown, stopping to give her a hug and kiss and say goodnight before they left for the evening.

Her mother ran the household with the help of cooks and servants and entertained guests at large dinners while learning Mandarin. Jack Steinberg, her father, spoke six languages.

For Cecelia, life in Harbin was full of luxuries and few worries. Yet her mother's parents who worked hard running a grocery store did not share such experiences. Their Harbin world was quite different.

Ethel (Roza) Keilis Clurman

Ethel (Roza) Keilis Clurman was born on February 20, 1900, in Odessa, Russia, and died on April 4, 1994, in Reno, Nevada in the United States. She was the daughter of Naum and Yelena Keilis and the oldest of their eight children. Ethel was the wife of Isak Grigori Clurman, who was abducted and killed in 1938 during the Japanese occupation of Manchuria and Harbin. She was the mother of Charles (Ruvim) Clurman, Sylvia (Tziva) Clurman, and Israel (Izra, Izrik, Johnny) Clurman, all now deceased. At the time of her death, she was the grandmother of five, and great-grandmother of nine.[80]

Ethel Clurman was a lively and energetic woman. After she left Harbin in the early 1950s and established residence in San Francisco, her home became a gathering place for many former Harbinsty, where they would meet every week for a long game of mahjong and reminisce about the life that they left in their "old country", Harbin, China.

Ethel brought several artifacts from Harbin. But the most important relic she cherished was a porcelain Buddha which she placed in the center of her living room. She bought the traditional Chinese figure on one of her visits to the second-hand market in the Daowai district of Harbin. The Buddha was made by a person in the south of China and she named it the "Jewish Buddha".

Ethel's father Naum Keilis left Odessa in 1903, and went to Harbin. In 1904, her father visited them in Odessa, and then he left returning back to Harbin. In 1905, a pogrom broke out in Odessa. Ethel's mother Yelena Keilis was pregnant already.

Ethel Clurman was trying to put her thoughts in order. Reno, Nevada, was not a natural place for her. It was just a temporary space. Later she will return to her home in San Francisco, and there among her Chinese relics and her Jewish Buddha, she will find comfort.

My mother's younger sister's wedding was that day, Ethel remembered. And usually, in Russia, the wedding was in the yard, under the sky under that canopy. And for the wedding reception, usually, you rent a hall. So my mother went to set the tables, everything, when my aunt's fiancé came he said that they are killing Jewish people. My grandmother stayed with us—that's my mother's mother. When she heard that, she was in tears.

Finally, my mother came. She was stopped on the way. They asked her, "Ti xhidovka?" (Are you Jewish?) And she said "Nyet." She had on a headscarf, and she looked Russian, blond, blue-eyed. And that saved her. She came back home.

There was no wedding and there was no reception, and we went to the attic. You know, in Russia, on top of the house, there's an attic, not inside but outside. And we went there, no food, nothing. But we had a Russian maid. It happened that she gave birth to an illegitimate child, and in Russia, at that time, with a child, nobody wanted you. So my mother hired her. And she brought us food upstairs to the attic. Yes. Well, it lasted a few days, the pogrom. We were dirty in the attic, not washed, nothing.

A man came and called up "Yelena Keilis!" She was afraid to answer. Then, he called again. My grandmother said, "Answer!"

She said, "I'm Yelena Keilis."

He said, "I'm from Harbin, just a few days ago, I came back from Harbin. Your husband was very good to me."

This man was a barber. He went to Harbin, he couldn't get a job, nothing, and no money to go back, so my father gave him money to go back, and helped him out.

He said, "Come to my house."

So we went down, they gave us water to wash ourselves, food, and we stayed there until the pogrom was over.

The hooligans approached. The houses in Russia are built around a courtyard. So there was an iron gate, closed. They approached it. In front, there was a Greek café. The Greek people came out with an icon and they swore on the icon and said, "There are no Jewish people here." And the hooligans left. That's how we were saved.

After that, we came to Harbin and we lived there, settled there. There was no place to live. We were at that time three children. My brother was three months old. My mother, my father, we all lived in one room. My sister Nina too. She is in Russia now, I don't know whether she is alive or not. And my brother Sioma. He died in 1979 in Israel.

That book that Pearl Buck wrote "My Two Worlds," I think.[81] A child of missionaries living in China, Pearl Buck was treated as a foreigner while living in a place that has long been her home. American by blood but Chinese by culture, Peal was misunderstood and mistreated because of the rising fear and political strife within the country. Throughout her life, Peal moves back and forth between China and the United States. Both places were her home and both people were her people, so she believed. Following the wise words of her mother, Pearl pursues her dream of bringing her two worlds together.

When I read it, Ethel said, I saw China the way it was when I came there in 1905.

Ethel said that when her father came to Harbin, there was nothing Jewish there. Absolutely nothing Jewish. There was no shul[82], nothing, absolutely nothing. That's why… my parents were not kosher. That's the reason. Later on, they, the community, built a synagogue, and there was a Jewish school. There was a rabbi, a shochet. But when we came, there was nothing.

After that, as I say, people were coming from Russia to Harbin and houses started to be built, so we could get an apartment. But the apartment had ice on the walls!

Our winters, you can't imagine how cold was our winter. Harbin is on the border of Siberia and Mongolia. The winter lasted until April, then the river which was frozen, the ice broke. It's windy and from the steppe of Mongolia comes the dust. You have never seen such dust. It's like little stones. You come home, your face and everything is black, your mouth is full of that.

We had a very short summer, it used to start in July. On the 15th of August in the evening, you had to put on a coat. You couldn't go out without a coat. September in the daytime it was nice, warm, but in the evening it was cold.

My mother came from a kosher family too, a strict kosher family. On Friday my mother put on candles, but my father did not. He was not a religious man. And when we had so many children, to go and buy kosher meat ... we were eight, and with mother and father is ten, and man that worked in the family butchery is eleven, and this fellow and a boy that helped out is thirteen, and a Russian woman that took care of the small children, that's fourteen people to feed. Besides, there was not a day that one or two more wouldn't come. So how much meat we had!

That's one thing, my mother, when we had filet mignon, everybody ate filet mignon. Then my father used to send — it's a French word, we use it in Russian — "entrecote." It's the prime rib. So everybody ate entrecote. My father hated ground meat. We ate only good meat. But to go and buy it kosher was impossible. So I didn't grow up on kosher meat.

It was enough that my father could support us. Can you imagine eight children? We were all well dressed, and well-fed. We lived very good. Not like some people who say they get up in the morning and not to find food. I didn't know that.

My mother, her bread was delivered. Loaves of round bread.

And bagels, I don't know how many bagels were delivered.

My sister Nina, she went to school, she graduated from the Russian school and there was a hospital where you could study to become a registered nurse. And when she graduated as a registered nurse, she wanted to become a doctor, and there was nowhere to go and study to be a doctor. At that time the Revolution broke out already in Russia, so she went to Russia. She went to university there in Tomsk, in Siberia.

I went to elementary school at Gymnasia Oksakovskaya. Mainly Russian people. In Harbin, the Russians wanted to discriminate, but we had a very fine governor, a Russian with German roots. And he said to them, "You can't do that. That's not the Russian territory. It's the Chinese territory. You cannot apply the same law." Horvat,[83] was a very fine governor.

There was no discrimination in the school, nowhere. You could go to school together with others. In Russia, you could not do that. In Russia, only a percentage of Jews were allowed into school, just like in university. But in Harbin, there was no discrimination, so I went to school.

And then when I was about 10 or 11 years old, I went to Shanghai, was in a convent, in a Catholic convent, St. Joseph's Institution. It was actually in the French concession, and it was called Institut de St. Joseph. That's the beginning of my English. My parents were liberals. They didn't worry about sending me to a Catholic School. They just wanted me to have an education. I was there for about four years.

Then I came back to Harbin. The reason they didn't send me back to school was that my father was in the butchery business and he had trouble with cashiers, so he tried me and I stayed there. I was a bookkeeper and a cashier. Retail butchery business, beef mostly.

Ethel poses. She moves in her chair trying to make herself

comfortable. It is hard for her to talk about a past that made her what she has become. To talk in a strange place and in other than her native language about another faraway life.

Then I met my husband Isak Grigori Clurman. I got married. I was 17, close to 18 years old. I tell you how we met. He courted my cousin. I was a teenager when he courted her.

He was in the States during World War I. Then he came back and in order not to be a soldier, not to go to fight for Czar Nikolai, he underwent an operation, and the big toe on one foot was removed. And that's what helped him stay away from being drafted. There was a doctor, he was a Turk. I remember him very well. I can see him as I talk to you. He was the one that operated on and removed that toe. He started to help out the Jewish boys not get drafted and somebody put the finger on him. He could make that one leg would be shorter, one leg would be longer. So somebody put a finger, and he had to leave Harbin.

After the war, Isak Grigori came back. He was about two and a half, three years in the States. He didn't like it because he had to do physical work and he was a businessman. Natan, Isak's brother, was a window washer in New York and so was Isak.

So right after the war, Isak came to Harbin and I was working as a cashier in the butchery. And he brought from the States tire rubber, not for cars — we didn't have cars — but for carriages. So when he sold it, he would come and weigh them on the butcher's scales. They were sold by weight. And that's how we started. But I knew him. He first courted my cousin. And then we courted and he proposed to me and we got married.

It was the Russian Christmas. The butcheries in China, they used to work six and a half days a week, only half a day on Sunday they closed. But Christmas was closed all day long. So they decided the only day to get married was on Christmas Day. Russian Christmas is on the 7th of January. It's a 13-day difference.

So I got settled, and our son Charles (Ruvim) was born in 1918. And a few years later in 1921, Sylvia was born, and ten years later in 1928, Israel was born.

Isak Grigori came from a very small place, Orinin, Kaminisk-Podolsk in Ukraine. The men, used to get married and the wife used to work and the men used to sit and pray. My husband didn't like his father. Even Natan didn't like him. Because when they were children, their mother had to work. She would bake bread and sell it, and that's how they made a living, while her husband didn't do anything except study Torah. Their mother died young and their father married again, to his third wife.

My husband was 15 years old when he came to Harbin with his brother. You know what he had? He told me, "I had one ruble and 50 kopeks." And he went to work with the Chinese. He worked just like the Chinese. Finally, he built up himself and the Chinese worked for him later. Yes. And without education. Very poor education. His writing was terrible but he used to read every day the paper, Every day. His mind was a brilliant mind.

When I lost him, came a Russian man, an engineer. He was an engineer who build bridges. And he came to see me and he said, "If this man had had an education, he would have been a genius."

I'll never forget men that came from Russia and they were selling old wagons. My husband had a partner, Berihovich was his name. Yosia was his first name. He said, "Yosia, I'm going to go buy these wagons. Do you want to go in with me?" And Berihovich said, "No, I don't want to. Buy them yourself."

So my husband went and bought those wagons, and he made a fortune, a fortune. Chinese took the wheels apart and there were handles made of brass. Everything apart. And Isak told me, he said, "I'm earning $200 a day."

The wheels were broken, and the Chinese would come and buy them by the pound and make shovels because they were cast iron. The handles the Chinese used to buy also were brass and they could make things from brass. And from the wood, Isak took it to his yard, and he built houses. From the scraps, they built houses. Very little new material went into houses and they're still there, staying there.

Isak Grigori was a good working man. He was not an alcoholic, not a gambler, not a skirt chaser, that's why I married him. Right away when he came from the States, he went into business. He rented a big yard and we had everything in that yard. We had wood, all kinds of wood there. And he built a small house for himself. He didn't plan to get married. Then he built flats and we moved to another place.

Ethel starts laughing. These pieces of memories make her feel good. It has been a very long time since she lost her husband, but whatever she remembers makes her feel good.

He was a good provider so I didn't have to do anything. I'll never forget, he once came and said to me, "I married you not because I needed a cook. I can hire a cook. I want you be a wife, a mother, and know what's going on in the kitchen." He didn't like me in the kitchen. I liked it. I didn't cook … but I loved to bake. So I baked all kinds of cookies and cakes and things like that.

Isak was a hard-working family man. When he used to come home, the first words were "Gdye dyeti?" "Gdye dyeti?" — Where are the children? That was it.

The only thing was that he was short-tempered. But … we say in Russian, "Krasatoo i manyeri, na tarelka ne polozhish." — You can't put good looks and fine manners on a plate. I would keep quiet, he would get over it, and I would do what I wanted.

We never came home after going out to a show without bringing the children chocolate. He used to put it under their pillows. In the morning they would know already that there's something under the pillow. And he tried to give them an education. Not educated himself but Charlie went to gymnasia, we had to pay for the gymnasia. Charlie didn't study, he didn't do his lessons at home, so he had a tutor. He was behind in English, so we had to have an English tutor. Then he wanted to draw—he draws very good. We had a teacher who came specially to teach him to draw. Then we had a Hebrew teacher. That's what it is.

And Sylvia, the same thing, she had the same tutor. She didn't have an English tutor and she didn't have a drawing tutor. But she had music, piano lessons. Twice a week with the teacher and every day for one hour a girl the teacher recommended used to come for one hour, she played piano with her.

I had a maid and a governess for them too because they didn't go out by themselves. We were afraid to let them go out. Up to five years for Charlie, I had a nurse. From five years, I had a governess. And once a month, I had a woman to help out with the cleaning and then we had a Chinese that took care of the yard because we owned the apartment house.

So the new month would come, can you imagine the expenses? And Mrs. Clurman, I, would go and order a hat for $20-25! Clothes we had to order. You want good clothes. We used to go and buy materials. And I had a seamstress and she had all the fashion magazines, she had McCall's and she had Vogue and everything. And I would pick out what I wanted and she would sew. Then I had to go and she would try it on me. We were all well dressed. So as I say, it was a good life, especially for the Jewish people.

The Jewish community had only 10,000 people, including men and women and children, and there were two synagogues, beautiful, they were all maintained with private donations. Can you imagine? We had a hospital, it was all built on private donations. We had a Jewish bank, it was built on private donations. We had an old age home, it was on private donations. And there was a cafeteria[84] for people who could not afford to pay. They used to come and if they couldn't afford to pay in full, they could pay a quarter and get a full meal for a quarter. And the second floor was for the old age people, and people didn't have to pay. And then they built another place for chronically ill people. All from private donations.

I liked always to read. I belonged to the library. I liked good pictures, and movies. We used to go. And I liked legitimate theater. There were so many operettas. I love operettas. For the Jewish people really it was a good, good life. But it all changed, all was changed.

We had to watch the children because of the kidnapping. We had Chinese bandits. We called them "hoohoozi." It wasn't so bad at the beginning, but later on, it was very dangerous. Isak Grigori used to go to his slaughterhouse at five o'clock in the morning in winter to start the day, and he used to carry a big revolver.

The kidnappers took men for ransom and sometimes the victims didn't return. Abramovich was kidnapped. He was 19 years old. He didn't come back. And there was Galimpolski kidnapped. They paid $25,000 to get Galimpolski back. Was Raii's cousin, her first cousin. Raii was the wife of Isak's brother Nathan Clurman. Galimpolski came back, but he died soon.

When I came to the States, a former Harbinite told me that Abramovich was taken by mistake. They wanted to take Charlie. We lived on Yamskaya Street, it was the sixth street, and they lived on the fifth street, not far from us. But Charlie was already away in school in California. That's why we sent Charlie away, as I say. It was very dangerous.

They didn't take women, but they took children. They took

men. Boys, men. It was hoohoozi, bandits. Mostly Chinese. There were probably rings. But when the Japanese took over, there were already Russian kidnappers. They kidnapped Kaspe. There were still Russians there and the police were involved in it. They kidnapped Kaspe.

They killed a butcher. He was driving—they had like those horse race carriages called an "Amerikanka." He was riding to the slaughterhouse and they attacked him. They probably wanted to kidnap him, but they shot him and he died. So life was not easy. It was dangerous for people who were well off.

What happened in 1938 was terrible. Only Izra (Johnny) was home. Charlie was away. Izra was ten years old. Isak Grigori promised to go with me shopping. I loved to go shopping with him. Not groceries but goods! I could buy what I wanted. Well, it was twelve o'clock, he didn't show up. One o'clock, two o'clock. It made me really angry. Then came night. Izra went to bed. He had his own room. I went to bed. But I was so angry.

Izra was very attached to his father. Wherever he went, he took Izra with him, because he was the only one left at home from the family. The first thing when I went into his room in the morning, Izra said to me, "A Papa prischol?" Did Papa come? Then he said, "Mama, what happened to Papa? It never happened before that he didn't come home to sleep."

And that's true. He would come late at night, twelve o'clock, eleven, but always he came home. That's when I came to my senses. And I was waiting maybe for a letter of ransom, something like that. I was afraid to say. There were only the manager and grandfather and me and Izra.

A Japanese, he was with the police, came. He said, "Clurman-san."

I said "Clurman-san is not home."

A few hours later, he came again.

I said "Clurman-san is not home."

Finally, he said to me, "You know that you can be arrested?"

I said, "Why can I be arrested?"

He said, "Because you should report to the police that somebody is missing for 24 hours."

So I went to report to the police.

No information came from the authorities. Isak Grigori was never seen again and his body was never found. The family assumed he was killed and his body dumped in a mass grave, or he was kidnapped and put in the Japanese medical experiments camp.

When my husband left the house, the whole building changed. They, the Japanese tenants stopped paying rent. They used to come drunk. They beat the Chinese. They smashed the windows. Izra and I would stay in fear. I'd rather not think. And the manager started to take advantage of me because I was afraid to open my mouth.

If I went out and didn't come home on time, Izra would run, look for me. And one day I came, he was crying on the street. I said, "Why are crying?"

He said, "I'm afraid from the Russian. Where were you?"

I said, "Why are you crying? You are a grown person."

"Papa was also a grown person," he said.

After I lost my husband, I would say to my daughter "Sylvia, what do you want to do tomorrow? She'd say, "Nothing. I'm going to the Café Mars."

Then she would come back to dinner, and I'd say "Where are you going now?" She'd say, "I'm going to play mahjong."

But finally, once she was in the Café Mars, and there was a German young man working that day. And he gave her a check, and on the back of the check, was "Don't come back here. This is not a place for you."

Because there were spies there in Café Mars. Everywhere you had to be very careful. You couldn't even trust your own friends. They would be working for the Japanese. And that stopped her from going.

The good thing was that we had no pogrom. In Russia, before a holiday, Easter or Christmas, Jewish people were afraid. Because usually before the holiday, the hooligani used to get drunk. So who's the scapegoat? It was the Jew. In Harbin we didn't have that. We weren't persecuted. And business was very good. Antisemitism started after the Revolution when the White Russian officers came. That's when it started. We had fascists then.

Some Jewish people were religious, some not. But as I say, they kept up the shul. Beautiful, two synagogues, built on private donations, and on private donations, they were kept up. Two synagogues. At first was built one, but when more Jews came it was too crowded, so they built another one. We used to call it Staraya Sinagoga, Novaya Sinagoga — Old Synagogue and New Synagogue. And they built a Talmud Torah school. That's a Jewish school. They taught in Russian but they also taught Hebrew. Charlie didn't go there. But the boys that went, when they went to Israel, it was easy on them. Because they knew Hebrew already. They couldn't speak but they could read and write. You could get a job.

Then there was a Jewish organization, Brit Trumpeldor. Charlie belonged to it and Sylvia belonged to it also. When the holidays came, they used to make a stage play. It was beautiful. With an Israeli flag and all marching in. But then as I say, after the war, some young people went to Israel because there was nothing for them to do in Harbin.

We didn't think of going to Israel. We lived in Harbin and that was our country. My father, my family, during the last war, they were in Harbin. When the first war broke out, we didn't feel there was a war. But the second war, we felt because the Japanese occupied Harbin.

In 1942, Ethel, Sylvia and Johnny left Harbin for Shanghai. Charlie was already in the U.S.

Many people from Harbin were in Shanghai. Harbin was a Russian town and Shanghai was a foreign town, so everything was different. They had modern houses and hotels, 15-16 floors. We didn't have that in Harbin. Three floors were the highest. And there was a Japanese store that had four floors. But in Shanghai there were elevators. It was different. And we had furnaces in Harbin, we had to use coal. In Shanghai it was gas.

In Harbin there were only 800,000 people. In Shanghai there were millions. And Shanghai was very poor in natural resources. Everything had to be imported. While Harbin was very rich in natural resources. That's why Japan moved into Harbin. It's near Japan and it's very rich in everything. They started to send the resources to Japan so we couldn't get nothing. From Mongolia we had beef. Cattle. Wild partridge, pheasants. You could buy a pair of pheasants, a female and a male, for 50 cents. It was delicious. So tasty. All kinds. We had wild game. Sheep, anything. Milk. Everything. Iron, wood, coal. In Shanghai there was nothing. Absolutely nothing. Had to import.

Shanghai is a beautiful city, international city, but the climate is horrible. In Shanghai, you can be on the 15th floor and everything turns green and it smells. So there's nothing much I can tell. I was so glad when I got out of Shanghai. But Harbin was a dream.

In 1949, Ethel and Johnny left Shanghai for San Francisco, where Charlie was living. Sylvia left for Israel.

These are the best memories of Harbin, best memories. Now sometimes I hum to myself—a Russian song ... We used to

Fig. 3: Ethel (Roza) Keilis Clurman

sing with the Russian people, we used to dance. But then with the Revolution, there was trouble with the Russian antisemites.

Charlie was once in a fight. We were on a way to a show and we saw the Jewish boys running and Isak Grigori said, "We are going back home." Charlie was hiding and some more Jewish boys were hiding in the house. My husband had a big cane and Charlie had taken that cane and hit somebody on the head. So we told the Chinese to lock the gate and not to let anybody in. We were so happy when we got him out of Harbin because on the word "Jew," he would fight, and how.

And he broke that cane in half. It is not easy altogether when children grow up, especially in Harbin, was very hard, and that's after the Revolution. Chinese never threw a stone at you. Chinese never molested a child, no. So I have the best memories of the Chinese people. But after the Russian Revolution, yes. It was terrible.

Charles (Ruvim) Isaac Clurman

Charles (Ruvim) Isaac Clurman was born on October 31, 1918, in Harbin to Ethel Keilis Clurman and Isak Grigori Clurman. He married Miriam Grant (nee Grodsky) in 1946 in San Francisco, California. He died on July 8, 2001, in Reno, Nevada. It was far away from the space that shaped his perception of life.

Charles Clurman spoke directly to the microphone on the

table in front of him. He spoke English with a Russian accent. His English was not as good as that of the American natives but he managed to tell his Chinese experiences in full clarity.[85]

...So here would be our city. He pointed to the map. This is the river Sungari (now Songhua). Then there would be an embarcadero along the river. Then here would be the bridge across the river. The only way that you could cross from here to here would be the bridge. This was almost a mile wide river, very fast, fantastic current.

The Amur River[86] was north of us. And this is the railway bridge. When the ice would flow on the river in the fall, you could not cross on a boat because the ice would crush it. So you could walk across but you couldn't drive across. During that time, no carts could go across.

We were on the main side in Pristan (now Daoli District). Pristan means like a pier. And here was Chingche, a suburb. Here was Nahalovka, another suburb. Nahalovka means "squatters," taking advantage of the place without rights.

And here was the drive-over, and this was Fifth Street and here was our lumberyard. And here was Kitayskaya Ulitsa[87], which means Chinese Street, and it was the main street of Harbin. Here on Komerchaskaya Ulitsa (Commercial Street) was the city jail. And here was the main police station and here was the Russian church and here was a stadium, a big stadium. And here "Za Sungariu" (today Sun Island) — on the other side of the Sungari — were all the summer resorts and all kinds of ... flimsy things for summer only. Couldn't live there in the wintertime. It was too cold.

Right here was the main railway station. And the railway went to Russia. Here was the old city. And here was the racetrack, horse race track. And all these people with horses lived here. And here on this side was the Chinese city. That's where all the

Chinese lived. There were no Russians living there at all.

In the olden days, by the river was a swamp. So the old city started here. Then the suburb Madyugo. Then Novii Gorod. Then Pristan. It was called Pristan because it was right on the pier of the river. And on this river, Charles points to the Amur, were big river boats. They used to go to Russia and all that. This Amur is the boundary between Manchuria and the Soviet Union. And forever they were fighting here, because when the Japanese took Manchuria, they put troops on the Amur. And they were big skirmishes between the Russians and the Japanese. Practically a war going on. Many, many Japanese were killed there, on the Amur, and so were Russians.

Harbin was a village... Manchuria was very sparsely populated... with big chunks of land totally unpopulated. So, Harbin was nothing. It was just a sleepy small village and swamps and everything until they put through the railway from Russia and to Dairen.

The Russians when they were building the railway, they developed the entire country there. They started to cut timber, ship lumber, and there were a lot of natural resources. Lumber went south also to the rest of China. Lumber went to Japan. Then meat and hides and casings and bristles. Manchurian bristles. Because it's so cold, the prime export was hog bristles, because bristles they grow 6-7 inches long and the best paintbrushes and all kinds of brushes used to be made from Manchurian bristles, because pigs in north Manchuria grow these bristles 7-8 inches long. And these bristles were processed and packed and graded and shipped out. And also pelts, all kind of pelts.

So when we talk about Harbin, when my father came there, about 1904, it was absolutely nothing. There was nothing there. Then when the railway came, the railway developed the country. As they developed the country, they also developed the freight that they would ship. So they put in ... a university in Novii Gorod, a polytechnic, the Railway Polytechnic, for engineering sciences. Then they brought opera. Then they brought high schools. Then they brought the veterinary sciences. They brought in agricultural seeds. They brought in breeding animals. They brought in everything, everything from Russia to develop Manchuria — agriculture, industries, and everything, from Russia. The whole country was revitalized. The railway connected the wilderness to the civilized world.

Harbin was the biggest of all the railway cities because it was the center, a railway hub, through which all the network of railways went south and north and west and east. That's why it grew up so big. The railway was owned 50 percent by the Russians and 50 percent by the Chinese. Used to be called the Chinese Eastern Railway. The Russians in the olden days considered this country as their property. But all this, I'm talking loosely, because in those days there were no such controls. It was a wild open country, just like in the Wild West. One sheriff for the whole state of Texas.

The Russians had a small garrison of troops in Harbin and they maintained law and order and collected some taxes ... but basically, they were guarding the railway. During Czarist time, there was a general in charge, his name was Khorvat. He was the head of the railway, the Russian representation in Manchuria.

Along the railway, the Russians were able to maintain peace because the Chinese were not armed properly. They were armed with spears and swords and bows and arrows and things like that... But in 1917, when the Revolution came to Russia, these Imperial troops were cut off from Russia because it became Soviet, and the Chinese took advantage of that and disarmed the Russian garrison and took over Manchuria.

At that time rose a common bandit to power but he was a

very astute person, Chang Tso-lin, who was referred to as The Old Marshal. He was very successful. He was very wily. And he was able to rule Manchuria. There was a Manchurian cavalry and things like that and my father used to sell the horses for the generals and the officers.

All these Jews came there because it was such a booming city. Fortunes were made overnight. It was like a boomtown, exploding in all directions. My father went to the US from Harbin during WWI and brought back indoor plumbing and things they didn't have in Manchuria. There was no indoor plumbing. He brought in central heating — radiators and boilers — and he made for himself a fortune... He was very smart of course. Even how he designed buildings. He learned many things in the States. He picked up a lot of things from the States and brought them to Manchuria because it was an innovation.

We wrecked probably a hundred railway cars for scrap iron. And we used to sell scrap iron to the Chinese foundries that used to smelter them... We used to winch up the thing on the tripod like this, big tripod, then loosen it, drop it and break it to sell for scrap. The whole city shook, and all the buildings collapsed. We had to move three times!

Charles Clurman laughs when he thinks of that.

When we had a chance in '38 to leave during the Japanese occupation of Manchuria, my father wouldn't leave, because he said, "I built this whole country and I'm not going nowhere. Japanese come, Japanese go, and the Japanese can never control China."

Al Maisin's father who was a baker never left either. And he was baking bread for the Communists all the time until he died in 1952. And they didn't bother him. They just let him bake the bread.

We never had cars. There was only one car that belonged to

the cousin of Tyotya Ria the wife of Nathan Clurman, my uncle. Chinese had some cars and police had special trucks, and then the fire department had fire engines and buses, there were buses. Oh, and Alex Turk of course had a car, don't worry about that. His father had the Ford agency in Harbin. But really privately owned cars, there was only one guy that I know of.

All other cars were taxis, and there were jeepneys — cars that would take 5-6 passengers. And there were buses and there were trucks. But there were no private cars. Gas was so expensive. And there was no place to go because the roads were bumpy, paved not with asphalt but cobblestones. We had beautiful horses. We could outrun a car on cobblestone streets! We had very good horses.

Maisin's bakery always delivered on horses. Wagons driven by horses. There were whole big stables. That's why Al Maisin likes to ride horses, because he used to ride those horses that used to deliver bread in the morning.

And the man would come in with a big round bread like that, and say "How much bread do you need today?"

You'd say, "Give me one or two pounds."

So he'd cut from this steaming big bread...

Most of our teachers in our school, the First Harbin Public Commercial High School, were old Russian staff officers, Imperial Russian Army officers that migrated out of Russia. We had a Russian education. We had a very good school.

All of us were very law-abiding and all of us succeeded in every field we chose... So we just learned to survive and we learned to live by our wits and pursue our goals and succeed in what we're doing. You can say there are some better people, some worse people...

We all had fun. We would go to the river. We would row. I used to row. Sail. Swim. Play volleyball, basketball. We had our dances. We had our parties.

Then there were the Trumpeldor scouts. We had athletics. We had a skating team. Boys and girls. We were preparing to go to Israel to fight for the independence of Israel. China was not our country. We considered ourselves Jewish. We did not even consider ourselves Russian. We were paramilitary. This was in 1933, maybe 1934. All these guys are in Israel now.

Although young people had many cheerful times, kidnapping was an ongoing fear for foreign families.

The bandits in China, they kidnapped people for ransom. Then they cut off an ear and they send the ear... I think kidnapping originated in China, particularly in Manchuria. They were brutal, I mean, they cut off fingers, ears, noses, and send it to the family with the ransom note to prove that they're holding them.

Everybody used to laugh at me, because I'd go to a party, then my father would come to pick me up. He wouldn't let me go alone. It was dangerous.

White Russians fleeing the Bolsheviks brought antisemitism to Harbin, and Russian hooligans began attacking Jews.

I never got beat up. I could beat anybody in fighting. The one time I got beat up was in a boxing match. But in the street, I never got beaten up.

My father carried a gun. My father never went without a gun. I always carried this kind of stick like my father carried. I carried it right here, in my sleeve. When I walk on the street, they never know, but I have this billy club here from ironwood, a piece of black ironwood. Something happens, I'm just ready to go and I pick it up and I have it in one second. I always carried it in my sleeve. And my books, I never carried them in my hands. My books were always in my belt, so both arms were free.

Because my job was to see that we did not get in the short

end of a stick. So anybody would pick up on the Jewish boys in school, I had to go and fight with them. But then we would have challenges. This guy challenges this guy. So I had to go and fight. But I never fought with a Jewish boy. I never hit a Jewish boy.

One time both of us got beaten up, my best friend and me. And he wouldn't tell his mother what happened. So the mothers got together, and his mother said, "They must have fought each other."

And my mother said, "No. He wouldn't fight your son, because we don't do that. So they must have been together in some kind of fight."

We had a lot of these fights because a guy called me, "Dirty Jew." And I said, "Bang!" and hit him. They used to bait me like that. One time, a guy called me "Dirty Jew" and I didn't see anything, and right in front of the teacher...(bang!).

We had a special kitchen for poor people. We had special barracks where all the refugees lived and were supported by donations. And we fed them and took care of them and then they got visas and continued on. Some stayed but many continued on. They went to Shanghai, Tientsin, to other countries. Harbin was like a clearing point.

All the Jews who were old-time settlers helped because the Jewish community in China was very philanthropic. They helped all Jews. We collected money for Israel. We collected money for German refugees. We collected money for everything. And we were forever collecting money and sending all kinds of donations all over the world to support destitute Jews everyplace. For tree planting in Israel we donated, for buying land we donated. We were forever donating money. And all these people were always taken care of in Harbin by the old-time settlers who were well off. We were very charitable.

Then in 1931, the Japanese rigged up a provocation in Mukden and the Japanese moved in to "make peace and order and to save the populace." And it wasn't true. It was all provocation.

We knew the Japanese were in the south of Harbin. The newspapers and everything were announcing that they were going to march into Harbin. And the Chinese troops were retreating through Harbin. So we knew, all these movements of troops and everything. Even in our school. The Chinese cavalry occupied the school. We couldn't go to school because they requisitioned the whole school where we were and the cavalry would put horses in the garden and everything else.

The Japanese Army marched into Harbin in 1932. I stood on the street and I was watching the Japanese Army march into Harbin. They were riding Ford trucks, Harley-Davidson motorcycles, and practically all their equipment was American-made. Because United States was in Depression and was selling all kinds of things to Japan. The U.S. sold them all kinds of stuff—airplanes, everything.

They landed airplanes on the racecourse, the horse track. Because we had no airfield at all in Harbin. So we used to bicycle there to look at the planes. We'd never seen an airplane.

There was absolutely no resistance. Because the Chinese didn't have arms. Nothing. So they went all the way through Harbin and occupied Harbin, and then they went alongside the railway. It took them some time to occupy the whole of Manchuria. But they never conquered the whole of Manchuria because until World War II there was an insurrection in the Manchurian countryside.

Trains were wrecked. Japanese were attacked. And came so bad that they would not even allow sorghum to grow near the railway. Because sorghum grows in Manchuria about ten feet tall, eight, nine feet tall. And the sorghum would be planted right near to the railway, miles and miles of it. So the Chinese guerrillas—well, Japanese referred to them as bandits, but nonetheless, they were guerrillas, remnants of the army—they would come close to the railway and blow up the railway and wreck the troop trains of the Japanese.

When the Japanese came, they blocked the Sungari River. They didn't understand it and flooded the whole city. During the flood, we were supplying the people that were stranded with food.

And then, when the water receded, outbreak of cholera. Thousands of people died. And you'd see corpses lying in the street in the Chinese section of Harbin, and the flies. And even on the garbage pile, they'd throw these cadavers there and wild dogs would go there and eat.

When I was going to the States, the Japanese guy would pick out all my old books that referred to Manchuria.

He said, "Why is it Manchuria?"

I said, "This is a very old book."

"No, no. You shouldn't take this to United States. It is Manchukuo now."

So he confiscated all my books with reference to Manchuria! Took 'em out. But I knew how to handle these guys. I said, "Sure, take them."

"And do you have any relatives in the States…?"

I said, "No, no."

"None of them are writers, newspaper people, journalists?"

I said, "Of course not."

Because they were afraid of bad publicity all the time. Even the mail was censored. They would pick through your mail and everything. So there was tremendous oppression and before you could speak to anybody, you had to know to whom you were speaking, because they would denounce you…

Charles Clurman left China in 1937 to study in California.

A year later his father was abducted and killed by the Japanese Kempetai. They wanted to expropriate his cattle operation.

Shimon Leib Fix and Evgenia Samuilovna Fix

Jean Ispa's[88] grandparents Shimon Leib Fix and Evgenia Samuilovna Fix (nee Beskin) arrived in Harbin around 1906 with their 2 sons: Alexander whom they called Sasha, and Mulia. Alexander was sent to the U.S. at the age of 16 to attend college. Jean's mother Mariam, nicknamed Mira, was born in Harbin in 1917. She left for New York in 1939.

Their street address was 7 Luteinaya Street, a block or so from the New Synagogue on the south side of Kitayskaya Ulitsa.

For a decade or more, starting around 1906, Shimon Fix, was the manager of a storage & trucking facility that received and sent goods from the railway. It was called the Russian Transport Company—Rossiskaya Transportnaia Obshestvo. Evgenia Samuilovna Fix took art lessons in Harbin and became a rather accomplished artist.

Fig. 4: Shimon and Evgenia Fix. (courtesy of Prof. Jean Ispa)

Later the family income was from renting out rooms in their house and the backyard shed.

Shimon Fix was an excellent writer. His and Evgenia's letters to their son Alexander (nicknamed either Sasha or Sashura) can stand witness to his talent. He wrote his letters with much Jewish humor and with detailed wits and emotions, describing the daily life of the family, the events of the time, and the people that were entangled in their life.

Shimon Fix wrote his letter in an orderly way, while his wife Evgenia had her way in being "a matter of fact" writer.

The letters that were sent from Harbin to the United States are scattered throughout these texts because they are so detailed that they add reality to the pasts that are presented here.

February 19, 1922

Dear Sashura![89]

As always, the week raced by. Papa and I write on Saturday evenings or on Sundays. What happened during this time? Nothing special. We quarreled with Tasia and told her to find a position. We had our stove fixed and it turned out that the handyman didn't charge a lot. We bleached and painted the stove and the surrounding wall blue-green and now Nickolai and I enjoy admiring our pretty kitchen. Misha Shriro had an ear infection and Gelenor prophesied death — I visited him two times a day and came home broken from seeing him and his mother suffering so much. He's better now; the danger has passed. I am just worried about their situation. They won some sort of court settlement and received 400 yen but two days later the money disappeared, so what comes next? I want to think that God will not abandon such good people. They told me that they wrote you a letter.

A man told me that his nephew completed an engineering degree in 4 years, and when he finished his 3rd year, he got a job as a draftsman for 120 dollars. Another someone was saying that the climate in San Francisco had a healing effect on his acquaintance.

Maria Borisovna doesn't look good. Lev Yakovlevich's lips are swollen. Things are very, very bad for them and they can no longer stay strong. And Nikolai asks to send his greetings. Mama.

Then Shimon adds: Eldest! Mama filled her letter to you without any particular "substantive substance" — the material there is a sort of chronicle of the week. And I will add to the week's chronicle of our dull everyday life.

A few days ago, Patushinskii, a local old-timer, died. The funeral was very pompous. After the funeral procession, Zinovi Semenov Vaisenberg came over and at this time Y.M. Broine, a christened Jew, was sitting with us and starts sharing his impressions of the grandiose funeral and, by the way, says: "While the synagogue choir was singing, I found my friend and chess partner in the crowd — Fonfatik (a convert to Christianity) and that Fonfatik, under the influence of the singing of a poem and apparently deeply moved, began singing Heine's poem to himself but aloud:
"Nach meinen starbens Jage,
"Wird man Keine Masse singen
"Keinen Kadish sagen . . .
Having said this, Zinovi Semenov suddenly realized that in the house of the hung one must not speak of a rope, — and what Mr. Broide was going through was visible on his face. There is nothing else of note in our weekly chronicle. Papa
"Nach meinen starbens Jage,
"Wird man Keine Masse singen
"Keinen Kadish sagen . . .
"After my dying hunt,

"No masses will sing

"No kadish would be said . . .

My dear Sashura![90] Mulya and I calculated that in three or four days there should be a letter from you if yours was en route for 32 days, and if less, then we can expect it even sooner. And now when the mailman arrived our hearts beat joyously. Dear Sasha, write, did you already receive the money that we sent (a transfer) addressed to Senate Hotel? You probably are overdue for new shoes and a summer hat.

The Vaisorelds ask you to fulfill their daughter's request to buy some sort of books and he will pay us back whatever the cost. He in general asks that in every letter we send you his greetings. In general, he looks great and his health has improved (though he still drags his leg, poor thing), and his mood has changed somewhat, and even a lot, for the better.

Then Mama adds: Yesterday Papa suggested to me that we go to the theater and, can you imagine, we went to Palermo (before 12 o'clock) since they were putting on a Jewish piece. We haven't been to a Jewish theater production for several years and it was just interesting. The actors were good but the repertoire was poor. They were playing little scenes from American life, with a focus on "bluffing" — that is, deception. In general, I don't like operettas. I was amazed by the character of the theater Palermo — formally it's a pub but it is unique in that people sit quietly. Write about American theater.

Recently in the movie theater, I saw a film and it was a true pleasure. It was called "Two Paths." If it plays there you should definitely go and see it. In the film, there is a girl from high society who catches syphilis from her fiancé and when she finds out from her doctor what kind of illness she has, she refuses treatment. All she cares about is her burning desire for revenge. The doctor takes her to a hospital ward and shows her the consequences

Fig. 5: Alexander Fix (Sasha — Sashura).
(courtesy of Prof. Jean Ispa)

of neglecting to treat this illness. Here on the screen, we see the stages of untreated syphilis. One woman's spinal column is damaged — she drags her foot, another's nose has collapsed, sores and ulcers, insanity, etc., etc. And all of this is shown in stark detail. One syphilis patient has a sore on her lip — the result of a kiss with a scoundrel.

When I say that I had a sincere pleasure, of course, it is not from viewing this human suffering, but from awareness of the beneficial influence that such a film can have on youth, and actually on everyone.

My dear one, don't be insulted if I remind you to wash your hair more often, and your feet. I am asking you to do a good job washing the bathtub before you get in it. Write everything, everything about yourself — we will be so grateful.

A big kiss, Mama

March 15, 1922

Dear Sashura![91]

Today everyone has joyful faces, smiles to their ears — your presents arrived. I, Mulya, and Mira went to the New City to the Chinese post office to get the packages. On the way, we tried to guess what it could be and decided that it was probably from you. But suddenly we were seized by doubts, what if it's the typewriter from Dairen? On the way back, we already knew from whom the packages were and managed to open the corners of the little packages inside just a little to find out what was in there. First Mulya got a sense of what was there when he saw the stamps. You should have seen his joy! But his happiness reached a peak when he saw the film and then the camera. Still, it seems to me that most of all he was excited about the stamps. Papa was so happy about his present that he didn't want to take the note off the package. Mama's face warmed from her presents and from seeing everyone's happy faces. Mulya already photographed all of us and soon you will receive photos. And it turns out that yesterday was Purim and Mr. Merkin reminded us that these were Purim presents. Kisses, Mama

June 4, 1922

Dear Sashura![92]

We received your three photos with letter N. 37. Terribly happy to see you. Today I sent to you, with Henven's son, a violin, a white linen suit, and three sailor shirts. There is another suit I sewed for you, that is, not I, of course, but Ya's son, who still has your measurements. I'll send that one to you by mail. Before you try on the white suit, get it laundered because I bought it ready-made and since they don't finish them, I got it two sizes too large so that after laundering it will be just right. If, even after the first laundering, the pants are still too long, don't cut them, but instead, fold them over toward the inside since after the second cleaning the fabric will shrink some more. Take it to just regular cleaners. They say that in America there are cleaners that are much cheaper.

Try to speak English with your friends. Write about your progress in the English language. What classes are you going to? How much do shoes cost there? If they are more expensive than here, put each foot on a piece of paper and trace it with a pencil and send your measurements and I will send shoes from here. They say that it doesn't make sense to send chesuncha from here. Look in the San Francisco newspaper and see if you can find out what the market is for squirrel pelts. They say that in America fur costs very little, and that explains why Harbin furriers went broke. Find out anyway and write; maybe it will turn out that it would make sense to send some. Here squirrel costs 2 rubles plus they say that customs takes 50%. How much is it there?

Sending you a big, big kiss and I ask you not to be lazy. Mama

Young Henven borrowed 25 yen from Papa and promised to pay it back to you. That of course will be after he gets settled.

And Shimon adds: My son! Enclosed—a transfer from the Russian-Asian Bank (The Crocker National Bank, San Francisco, N. 18913) for $50. Your orphaned Papa

Harbin, June 25, 1922

My son—my friend![93]

Here already, it seems it's been a whole month since I—except for short notes added to Mama's and Mulvechick's letters,—wrote anything to you. The reason—a beaten down soul, depressed mood, a broken spirit. If you were to look from the outside, it would look as if everything were as it was, nothing changed. A person sits in his office, in a wide armchair. He has even been clean-shaven by the hand of Mulvechick, he is in a white sailor's shirt, laid out for him by the morning by the caring hand of Mama, but scratch this "person" a little deeper under the sailor's shirt—and a "little river of grief, a bottomless little river" gushes forth.

Sasha,—my papa is no more!

The eloquent lips are closed; no longer does the hand rise that over the course of 27 years, since the day of my departure from my parental home, wrote letters to me so intelligent, so substantive, so full of literary content, letters that truly sowed in me what is "rational, eternal, good." There are no set boundaries to human dignity, there are no boundaries to the humanity in people, but I would be completely happy if you, my son, grew up to be as good a person as my papa. You may strive to be better educated, more developed, smarter than your ancestors — but to be a good person — it would be sufficient to be like — of blessed memory — my papa.

We live not according to our own will and die not according to our wishes. Living and dying, we fulfill someone's directive from above — and we do not have the will, the strength, the power to defy it. And given that we live lives forced upon us, if I may express it this way, then we must fulfill its laws, one of which is — love and care of parents for their children.

Is the date of your arrival in America officially recorded, and how many years must elapse between the recorded date of arrival and the date when you may acquire American citizenship? This is very important given the present state of things. How things will be in the future — it is hard to foresee.

In one of your letters, you ask how things are for us. Since you are already our grown son, I will briefly lead you to knowledge of our circumstances or, more exactly, of my job situation. It is, in terms of my comprehension of my official status, immeasurably better than last year, when the former auditor, V.P.I., literally yanked on my nerves, harassing me with his nasty pickiness, which was rooted in antisemitism. In a material sense, of course the business doesn't give much: 150 yen for salary + the apartment with heat and light, and there are percentages based on the results of one's work — but in advance it is hard to know what to expect. Profits from the house, lately reduced a bit, taking into account expenses for insurance, cleaning, taxes, repairs, and so on and forth, clear about 200 yen per month. In general, judging by how many of our acquaintances have gone broke and have nothing, we are still fortunate, and I would be happy if things continued as is and we could continue our way of living, but unfortunately, there is no basis for counting on things staying comfortable given the current state of affairs. I am trying to stretch it out. I think that it can last another year. More than that — unlikely. But to run ahead and worry in advance isn't worth it.

I must finish writing because the time is near for the evening prayers. I will rush there where "the offended one has the feeling of a corner" — in God's temple — to chant Kadish for my, — of blessed memory, — my deceased (how frightening this word is) papa, may he rest in peace. Be healthy, son of mine — Papa. About three months ago I received an award of 1800 yen for my 25th work anniversary.

Harbin, 26 November 1922

Sashura![94]

I believe Mulya wrote to you to ask that you go to the publisher of the Yiddish magazine, Hatoren — The Mast, and request that they send me the first issue of the magazine, which I didn't receive. If you haven't done this yet, kindly fulfill this request. I would like to have the full set. A few months ago I sent $5 to this publisher, i.e., the cost of an annual subscription, but I don't know when they begin calculating the subscription year, whether according to the Jewish or the Christian calculus. Therefore I don't know when my paid subscription ends. Please find this out as well and write to me. In addition, besides the magazine for me, ask the publisher to send one more issue from this subscription year (best — from January 1, 1923, not January 1, 1924) to the following address: Jacov D. Frizer. Birsewayer Street, N 40. Harbin, China.

Find out how much will be due from me for both issues, and I will transfer it — and for now they should send the magazine for me and for Jakov Davidovich Frizer without delay. You should not pay from your money because I have some amount of credit there. In addition, there was a notice from the publisher that as a bonus for orders of two magazine issues they will send out a free copy of a book titled History of Jewish Philosophy — by D-ra Neimark. Since I am paying for two issues of the magazine, have them send me the book. Also ask them to send me, just in case, a catalog of their Hebrew books.

I would like to get into some sort of business deal with America. Get your uncle's advice as to what can be done in this connection. Would it not make sense to send you silk to sell. You of course won't be able to occupy yourself with this business but maybe your uncle will see this as a potentially profitable opportunity. I can't put a lot of money into this business, but if it turns out that it would be profitable, then after a period of two or three months maybe New York buyers would make a bank transfer for their purchases or they would arrange for a bill of credit at a bank. Get thorough advice and write to me in detail. If Uncle Hessel won't take this on, get the advice of Lishchiner's brother. It is necessary to create some sort of business because Rostran[95] — is at the sunset of its existence.

In the month of September, Rostran will stop renting the apartment and the storage shed on our site. Also the goods in the shed are themselves "finished" since they were sold at auction. From among all the storage facilities, only one remains, the one leased at Zotov's. So that I am not left without a renter, I decided to move everything from the shed at Zotov's to ours. But since the things stored there are valuable and can't be kept under an open awning, I had to arrive at a financial sacrifice — build a covered zinc shed. This cost came to $1\frac{1}{2}$ months of yuan. The shed turned out large and attractive but the issue is that when there are no longer any goods from Rostran, the shed will be of almost no value. For the apartment with the shed I get 300 yuan per month. So, here I am taking you a little into the circle of our financial life.

You know, in the Talmud it is said that a single bad deed

evokes many bad inclinations,—while a good deed prepares the soul to do what is good all one's life. I recalled this when I received your present and I thought to myself: one or two good deeds give one a good habit—good habits. If you stitch good character, good character will lead to human charm, and human charm will give you happiness in life. Let it be so. —Papa

Harbin, October 23, 1922

My dear Sashura![96]

Mulya isn't completely pleased with his classes in medicine. The subject matter is interesting, but the instructional staff is only so-so; there is only one professor among them. For now, it's impossible to get into Russian universities. Leonid Stanislavskich is moving from us to the New City since the consulate was moved there. He was reluctant to leave us. We became good friends. He recommended his room to his friend who now rents it. This fellow is as sweet as he is. In the evenings, Papa plays checkers with him. Three days ago little Sasha L. was here and played in such a way that you, too, would have been pleased. Also Polina Borisovna came with V.A. The wife of Gad, our former renter,

Fig. 6 Mulya Fix. (courtesy of Prof. Jean Ispa)

Simona, Sarah. The latter came to see Mulya and even more to see Leonid Stanislavovich, more than to see me. When the grown-ups left, the young people started singing, with Sara Kuchevat accompanying them. Mulya imitates you in all ways and attends to all of your young ladies. I don't have anything to write about and am just writing the first thing that pops into my head. Papa wants to change jobs. If he succeeds, we will write. We already got a letter from Leshcha Nerov from Moscow. It seems to me that they are sorry that they left Vladivostok. Mama.

Shimon: Over all this time I have written you only one postcard. There isn't even a twig's worth of reason for this: if sometimes we do something without the slightest reason, then all the more it is possible to do nothing for no reason. It's just that I couldn't gather my thoughts. And there is nothing here to write about. Everything stands on a foggy point, unchanged, as it was when you were here. Only nature has changed. "Surely the skies breathed of autumn," so looking out the window in the morning, the neighbor's roof is getting whiter and somehow one starts to feel less cozy. But, after all, everything is transient.

So far, Mulya hasn't been able to travel. No one here is getting visas. For now, he is studying medicine. Do you think that is a good idea? To me it's good if only in that he at least has something to do, and it also gives him knowledge and furthers his development. It seems to me that it would be a mistake to go to the trouble of applying for a student visa because it only gives the right to study in a university and absolutely forbids the student to work under penalty of exclusion from student status and expulsion from America. In such a case I would have to take upon myself the responsibility to send Mulya money for all of his expenses during his stay as a student, that is for 4 or 5 years, and this, according to my current financial situation is completely impossible. Understand that even support as little as 40 American dollars per month comes to around 100 yuan, today the exchange rate is 2 yuan, 62 sen to the American dollar, and this is very difficult for me right now. I am applying for a position in various agencies and would be glad to get one for 150 yuan—therefore it is necessary to direct all of our efforts toward getting Mulya a visa, but only as an immigrant. Let this require a delay in his departure, but—otherwise, it is impossible.

Mulya's application for a visa lies in line at the consulate here, but when it will come forward—that is unknown. If you can, there in America, do something in connection with this—do it, but it must be for immigrant status so that he will have the right to work. In general, Mulya has turned into a good fellow.

Now, about you. Try to go without deviation, straight to your intended goal. I want very much to hear from you that you have enrolled in your new technicum, and how you have settled in terms of your living arrangements.

In a word, I confirm our agreement that in the future, when you are permanently settled, and when we will know exactly everything about your life, all your aspirations, and hopes, then you may send us just short picture postcards. When will we see each other again? And meanwhile, Papa

Yaacov Liberman

For Yaacov Liberman, Harbin should have been a paradise, a place of hope, a home, even if a temporary one. With great eagerness, the Jewish emigrants to Harbin established businesses—factories, restaurants, import-export offices, and shops. Those with fewer means, as well as the younger generation, including new entrepreneurs, found employment among the affluent members of the community. The more destitute were assisted, first on an individual basis, and then gradually, by organized charitable institutions and societies. Unique bonding of individuals and community soon came about.[97]

Whether moderately well-off or penniless, the Russian Jews of Harbin were united in a common desire to create an acceptable environment in which to live, work and worship with as little outside interference as possible.

"My parents contributed significantly to this community's

solidarity. My father, Semyon Liberman, emigrated to Harbin out of economic necessity. Born in 1893 in Sevastopol, in the Crimea, he grew up in a home in which money was scarce. Immediately upon graduating from high school, he had to help support his three sisters and a brother. When in 1916 he was offered a job as an accountant in Harbin, he moved his siblings to this story-book city in the faraway Orient, where they began a new life."[98]

"My mother, Gisia Zuboreva, was born into wealth in the city of Nikolaevsk on the Amur River, a city of Russia's Far East. Her father was the respected head of an industrial fishing complex that operated its own fleet of barges and ran a canning factory. For many years, until the Communists took over, the small lake by my grandparents' estate, in Grandfather's honor was named Zuborevsky Protok [Zuborev Channel]. In 1918, as the Bolsheviks approached, Grandfather Zuborev escaped empty-handed with his family to Harbin. With him went his wife, his two sons, and two daughters. My mother was among the family members who fled. However, her older sister, Sarah, by then a married woman, remained behind."[99]

In Harbin, the Zuborevs found a small apartment on Birzhevaia Ulitsa [Stock Exchange Street], where they set up their housekeeping.

My parents were married in 1921. "Although Dad was not ideologically inclined, he joined the General Zionists of Harbin. However, communal activities were more to his liking, and his favorite would be the founding of the Jewish Hospital and Clinic (Mishmeres Holim), of which he was a long-term president."[100]

Education in Harbin was given by several educational facilities. Most of the Jewish youth attended to the Kommercheskoe Uchilishche (the Commercial School). It was a Russian-language high school with very high standards and the graduates could enter with ease the best European and American universities.

"The Talmud-Torah school occupied a very special place in the life of the Jewish community of Harbin and loving memories of the devoted leaders and teachers of the only Jewish institution in town remain in many hearts."[101]

The main synagogue was not only the religious center of the community. It was a social center as well. Jews attended the magnificent structure on holidays, to mark a Bar Mitzvah[102], "to observe memorials, and to attend communal meetings of protest and solidarity. The presence of the talented Cantor Zlatkin and an excellent boy's choir enhanced the services. Other functionaries in the ritual life of the community were its shochet, Reb Litvin, who for many years supervised the ritual slaughter, and our mohel, Reb Rolband, who was a master of the ritual of circumcision."[103]

"The early Jewish arrivals were not a homogenous group. Although schooling and a house of worship were of primary concern to the early settlers in Harbin, the newcomers came with wide-ranging and extremely diverse ideological affiliations. Social and philosophical quarrels were endemic to the Russian Jews. Debate was continuous among Russian Jewry in general. Political tolerance within the community would only come with its maturity."[104]

"That spirit of rapprochement and consolidation, however, eluded the Bundists, whose politics were a mixture of Judaism and Socialism. A continuous source of dissent and divisiveness during the formative years of the Harbin Jewish community, the Bundists in their opposition to Zionism were remote from world Jewry's goals of political rejuvenation and Jewish solidarity. Gradually, Zionism prevailed, the Harbin Bund disintegrated and the unity of the Jewish community was assured."[105]

Yaacov Liberman's first recollection of the city goes back to the year 1928 when his family anxiously awaited the arrival of his Aunt Sarah from the Soviet Union.

While many Jews living in Harbin had escaped from Russia immediately after the Bolshevik Revolution, only in the 1920s, and after hair-raising border crossings, did most refugees settle in this Manchurian city. Until Stalinism made attempted flight futile and suicidal, refugees continued to pour into Harbin. Among them was Liberman's aunt, a resident of Vladivostok.

"My parents were anxious to see Aunt Sarah and Uncle Mulia emigrate to Harbin much earlier. Uncle Mulia, the manager of the Russian branch of Lurie & Co, a large international trading firm, felt that he could not abandon the home office without salvaging whatever he could. Soon thereafter, Mulia was arrested by the state security organ, the GPU. After weeks of agony and despair, Sarah learned that her husband had been thrown into a local prison. Arriving one morning at the prison gates and bearing her usual dry food, socks, a warm sweater, and a change of underwear, she was informed that Mulia was not in his cell. Running from one official to another, she finally had a bundle of old clothing thrust into her arms. When Sarah asked what had become of her husband, the official replied: "He was eaten by dogs." Hours later, friends found my aunt lying unconscious in the snow by the prison yard fence. After her hazardous journey by foot, rowboat, and horse-driven cart, Sarah Feinberg finally managed to cross the Manchurian border. Like many others, she had been accompanied by provodniaki, special guides who made their strange livelihood guiding desperate refugees past barricades and across borders toward China. Aunt Sarah stayed with us for many years following her escape, but she never recovered completely from her deep misery and depression.

"Socialization between Jews and Gentiles was minimal and, consequently, they were perceived as two exclusive ethnic entities. Gentiles became categorized as White Russians, whereas the Jews preferred to be known as stateless Russian Jews or simply as Jews from Russia. Nevertheless, the two separate communities of Russian and Jewish immigrants made joint and commendable use of the various existing facilities in town and patronized Russian cultural institutions. Both groups enjoyed Russian theater, ballet, and occasional performances by local and visiting opera ensembles. They also mixed socially in various clubs, commercial societies, and sports organizations, and occasional friendships were forged in school. Of course, there was no lack of competition and a healthy rivalry that sometimes erupted into unpleasant confrontations and intense animosity.

"Both groups read Russian-language newspapers and journals, frequented libraries and public concerts, lectures, and discussions. All derived their news and information from the two leading dailies in town: Zaria (The Dawn) and Rupor (The Mouthpiece), as well as from the weekly Rubezh (The Frontier)."[106]

A gang of Russian anti-Semites, led by the infamous Konstantin Rodzaevsky used the daily newspaper, Nash Put (Our Way), for ethnic provocation and personal blackmail to color up its pages. The Jewish community had its own Russian-language biweekly, Evreskaia Zhizn (Jewish Life), published by the Zionist organization and edited by the head of the community, Dr. Kaufman. In the 1930s, a second Zionist biweekly came to life and became a popular mouthpiece of Betar and the Revisionist Party.

"It was not unusual for a middle-class family to hire a nanny. I was introduced to my first niania (amah) at the age of five. A heavyset, meticulously dressed woman in her late fifties, she always wore starched dresses that buttoned down the front, trimmed with white lace collars. Once, after a particularly heavy rainstorm, on our daily walk through town, niania attempted to take me by the hand so that I would not splatter myself in the filthy puddles along the pavement. That kind of coddling was not for me, and, pulling her toward a large pool of water, I jumped into it with both feet, splashing her from head to toe. The next day my mother was busy interviewing a succession of nianias for her mischievous son.

"As I approached my eighth year, it no longer became necessary for my parents to surround me with overseers. My father then decided it was time personally to take charge of my upbringing. Only once was I whipped by my father; but then I crawled under my bed and was spared a real beating."[107]

One day when Yaacov was grounded for doing something nutty, he wanted his freedom, and composed a short poem in Russian. It was an apology and a promise to change his ways. His father was pleased with his ability to lever rhymes that he agreed to pardon his son and offered to take mother and son to the movies. "As it happened, we went to the premiere of an early talkie, The Merry Widow, starring Jeannette MacDonald and Nelson Eddy."[108]

"As manager of an international trading company, owned by the well-known Kabalkin family, father held an important job. Thanks to his wit, charm, and talent for telling jokes and anecdotes, he was often the center of attention at the many parties in town.

Since most of us lived in Pristan, the lower part of town, we walked to work and everywhere else. During the 1920s, and even later, no one in Harbin owned a car. The most popular way to get around town was by izvoshchik — a cabby with a carriage. For rare trips to Novyi Gorod, the New City, and the elevated part of town, we used public buses. Some of my friends were the proud owners of bicycles, but these were costly."[109]

Chinese Street, Kitaiskaia Ulitsa in Russian, was the main

street of Harbin, its heart and its soul. Wherever one went, he was bound either to pass or cross this street that mirrors the life and the mood of the city and often reflects its major events. For a boy like Yaacov, no street could match the Chinese Street. It had a main thoroughfare, a shopping mall, a promenade, a restaurant row, and a parade ground.

"To the Jewish population, Chinese Street had its own significance. One could note that Chinese Street branched into dozens of smaller streets, one of which was the Kommercheskaya Ulitsa (Commerce Street). Occupying a large part of this street stood the Hall of Commerce, housing one of the largest Russian-language schools, a theatre, a library, a spacious playground, and a restaurant. Next to this complex lay a large open field with a wooden hut, serving as a space for track and field events during the summer months and as a skating rink in winter. Further down the street lived hundreds of foreigners, among them many members of the Jewish community.

"Among the non-Jewish shops on Chinese Street were many corner kiosks that sold booza, a Caucasian soft drink, and baklava, a Greek pastry, gastronomic delights that were ever so popular among our youth. Scores of other shops on Chinese Street belonged to Jewish merchants who traded in women's clothing, furs, jewels, shoes, and hats. The Victoria Cafe, owned by the Bresler family, and the Cafe Mars, owned by the Zukermans, were among the best in town. Further down the street one could catch the enticing aroma of a first-class delicatessen that sold red and black caviar straight from the barrel at a few pennies a pound. Another delicatessen around the corner on Artillery Street belonged to a friend of my father, Owsiej Lias, whose son became one of my closest and dearest friends. Lias sold milk products and pickled vegetables. Many of my younger contemporaries would stop by for a glass of kefir, fermented goat's milk, which is no doubt the mother of all yogurts.

Amidst all these shops and restaurants, and majestically towering above all of them, loomed Churin's department store, the largest in town, where one might shop to one's heart's content or rendezvous. Next to Churin stood the architectural pride of the city, the Hotel Moderne, which housed the largest auditorium, used for theater, movies and concerts, a ballroom, restaurants, and shops. The hotel was owned and managed by a prominent member of the Jewish community, Joseph Kaspe, whose personal tragedy had a deep and lasting effect on every Jew in town."[110]

In 1945 leaders of every community were invited by the Soviet authorities to the Hotel Moderne. They now controlled the town with cruelty and an iron fist. None of the gathered leaders, including Abram Kaufman and several other members of the executive committee of the Harbin Jewish Spiritual Association, returned home that night. The group included Moses Zimin, Israel Orloff, and Alexander Raskin, all of whom were transported secretly across the border and eventually incarcerated in the GULAG, with but a few survivors.

"Many others were arrested and transported to prison camps in the Soviet Union. Two of my Betar colleagues, Yosef Halperin, the talented poet, and Misha Kachanovsky head of the Betar Tel Hal Fund, were among them. Yosef died in a camp somewhere in the Soviet Union, while Misha was rescued, thanks to the efforts of his family and the State of Israel."[111]

A growing boy, Yaacov was unaware of the future implications of the political involvement by groups such as Betar. His activities now drew him to the young people's community center and recreational center. Here he met many youngsters his age and developed friendships. "By coincidence, the Betar summer facilities were located next door to the recreation area called the ploshchadka (literally, little market square.) The two properties were separated by a long fence with many cracks between the boards, which made it extremely easy to peer from one into the other. The ploshchadka space encompassed a large playground, a garden, a small shell-shaped outdoor stage, a room for crafts activities, and a roofed shelter, while the Betar area held a small building, two dressing rooms, another roofed covering used for boxing and physical exercises, a large glassed-in hall, which in winter was used as a dressing room for skaters, a large track and volleyball and basketball courts. On the Betar side of the fence, in large letters, a sign read: 'Vzdorouom tele, zdorovyi dukh' — 'A healthy spirit in a healthy body'."[112]

Freezing winters brought about seasonal pleasures: in the afternoon, the boys were active in ice-skating in rinks, sledding down snowy river banks and traversing the frozen Sungari River, by means of the tolkai-tolkai — push-push, in pidgin Russian. In the evenings they were fortifying their bodies with Siberian dumplings called pel'meny; and then after dark, nourishing their souls with an evening at the theater. The "Stop Signal" restaurant on the other side of the Sungari River, on what is now Sun Island, used to serve many of Harbin's special foods and recreations. To get there, in winter, one had to cross the river on a tolkai-tolkai, a local winter transportation, a contraption that looks like a chair, or sleigh. It was driven by a Chinese who pumps a spear-like stick between his legs that hits the ice below and created a motion that can generate a frightening velocity. A passenger would sit covered with blanket in the chair and enjoy his frozen dreams while of the boiling soup and pel'meny was waiting for him.

Although a freezing weather, Yaacov's house was warm, protected by cotton-insulated double windows. Each year, From October to March, wall stoves, heated with wood and coal, burned 24 hours continuesly. Winter brought the youngsters outdoors to the public skating rinks. It was there where bands would play in the evenings, and pairs and singles would perform figure and race skating to the delight of those who came to learn or simply to watch.

"As I grew older, I often wondered what the Chinese population was doing while we continued to enjoy life in this city. Hardly any Chinese youngsters shared our activities, and the grown-ups seemed to have moved out of sight in order to leave us, their guests, in total privacy. The Chinese outnumbered the foreigners more than a hundred to one. We lived among the Chinese masses in splendid isolation and our paths would cross only when our own needs depended on their assistance as shopkeepers, street peddlers, brokers, salesmen, cooks, drivers, or amahs."[113]

Jewish women were the first to learn some of the Chinese language and to use it loudly during their daily games of mahjong. They played the game with ivory-colored cubes, with various Chinese lettering drawn on the white side. Thy put the ivory pieces on a foot-long wooden container, and when a woman would throw in her matching cards, she would shout out in Chinese, "Pong, Kong or Chow!" Once the right combination was assembled on the container, the winning lady would display her winning set, and exclaim, "mahjong!" "Between the shuffling of the ivory pieces and the ladies' excited screams of different Chinese words, the noise level in the house would become deafening. In fact, it was rumored that on more than one occasion, robberies took place in homes or apartments during mahjong games, and not a single player noticed the rude intrusion."[114]

Most of Yaacov's friends, he said they came from many different backgrounds, attended summer camp at the ploshchadka. During the summer months, he first met some of the girls and boys with whom he was destined to share many years of friendship. Yaacov became active at the ploshchadka together with his two cousins, Bertha Oppenheim and Boris Zuboreff.

In the summer days, they were active in sports, arts and crafts, singing, and folk dancing. "We all, except for Ura Horosh, managed to rid ourselves of our governesses! To supervise his every step, Ura's mother, however, had insisted on keeping his old German governess, Frau Pauline. The whole town came to recognize Frau Pauline in search of her elusive charge as she would shout "Urikum, geh nach haus!" — "Urik, go home!" Among the many games we played, there was one that eventually helped me make the baseball team in high school. It was called lapta, from the Russian word lopata, or shovel, and it consisted of fielding and batting. The game required no bases, and those in the field ran a straight line at a distance of thirty to fifty meters from the batsman. Positioned next to the batsman, the pitcher would throw the ball gently into the air, about two meters high, the batsman would then smack it and run. The only way to get the batsman out was for the fielding team to catch the ball in mid-air or to pitch the retrieved ball at the runner and hit him before he returned to the baseline from which he ran. A cheap sport, it could be played with any ball the size of a baseball, and any bat, even a heavy tree branch. Nevertheless, it was considered a rough game and was usually played only by boys. During my lapta phase, I discovered that I could run faster than my peers, a capacity that I began to develop."[115]

In the same year of the great Harbin flood in the summer of 1932, was a turning point in Yaacov's life. One afternoon his father returned home with mail from the post office — because of the flood there were no home deliveries. Aunt Nuta and Uncle

Yasha Veinerman in Shanghai sent a letter, inviting him to stay with them during the coming school year.

It was difficult for a nine-year-old to leave a happy home and friends. For him this was Harbin, a vibrant living city with his own family and friends.

At the end of that summer Yaacov Liberman made said a sad farewell to everyone who had contributed meaning to his life, and was set to leave for the journey. After a long and boring sea voyage, his mother brought him to the Veinermans in Shanghai. Yaacov Liberman wrote that he arrived there miserable and brokenhearted. He was angry as one could be under the circumstances.

It was his farewell to Harbin that hosted his young life.

Roman M. Kabalkin

The Harbin Jewish Entrepreneur Roman M. Kabalkin, partnered with a British national and jointly established "The Sino-Anglo Orient Trading Co." in London in April 1914 with a branch in Harbin. The company was located at Horse Street in the Pristan District.[116] The Harbin branch began to export grain, soybeans, and soybean oil to Europe and the US.

Kabalkin who pioneered the export of soybeans from China used to walk in the grain market with his son at his side. He used to point out the sacks of the soybeans describing the grain as the "black gold of Manchuria".

Many of the Jewish residents of Harbin built their homes in the tradition of what they had before coming to the city and mixed it with the prevailing winds of the trends and fashions. The Skidelsky, Krol, Soskin, and Kabalkin families built grand villas on the upper side of the New City, on the hill climbing from the train station and in the vicinity of the administrative buildings. Other Jews built their business structures in the center of Pristan or Daoli district, many on Kitaiskaia Ulitsa, now Zhongyang Dajie or Central Pedestrian Street. The spaces next to these main avenues were streets where members of the Jewish community built their homes, apartment buildings, offices, banks, and stores. Joseph Kaspe's Hotel Moderne, on the corner of 7th Street and Central Pedestrian Avenue, the most lavish enterprise in China in those days, symbolizes the eclectic nature of Harbin's architecture.

In April 1936, a secret special investigation made by the Harbin Japanese Commerce & Industry Bureau stipulated that the Jews occupy a large proportion of commerce and industrial proprietors. The Japanese clandestine report showed that in 1936, the commercial and industrial proprietors holding Soviet nationality were 50, and 41 were Jews, among them, I.M. Lifschitz photo studio, and I.A. Bent Brothers Trading Company. 82% of the total stateless owners of commercial and industrial proprietors (Belarusians) were 442, of which 113 are Jews, among them the Maikin Bakery, and I. Katz Watch & Jewelry Shop. About 26% of the total Lithuanian commercial and industrial proprietors, altogether 96, 70 or about 73% of the total were Jews, among them M.M. Kotz's Geneva Watch & Jewelry Shop, and Eskin Brothers Chamber of Commerce. Several Jews in Harbin were of Polish nationality, among them the Executive Director of Northern Manchuria Sugar-Refining Company L.G. Zickman, and M.P. Pines, wool spinning products shop on Kitayskaya Street. There were also several Jews of English nationality, among them R.M. Kabalkin of the East Trading Company, and Steinberg of the fur importing and exporting business. Some were of American nationality, P.C. Belwin of Kulayev Father and Son Mortgage Company, and Ackerstein the owner of the American cinema. There were several of French nationality, among them E. Gilberstein of the Louis

Dolev Manchurian Special Products Exporting Company.

On December 20, 1935, Kabalkin's son, Simon Ruvimovich, died and was interned at the Jewish cemetery of Harbin.

In the summer of 1938, Under Japanese pressure to seize his properties, Roman M. Kabalkin was unable to keep the operation of the Sino-British Oil Mill, and he sold it at a very low price to a Japanese agent. The mill was renamed the "Manchurian Oil Co. Ltd."

Moses Grossman

Dr. Moses Grossman was born in Kiev and at the age of six moved with his parents to Harbin after an opportunity came to join the rest of the family who lived in the city. His uncle owned a business in Harbin. The city was a terminus of the Chinese Eastern Railroad, with all the businesses surrounding it, many cargo insurance businesses, and others.

Not long after the family arrived in Harbin the region became a puppet state of Japan, named Manchukuo.

No one in the family knew Chinese and none ever learned Chinese, except for a few words. Moses Grossman had home tutors until he was nine. Then he was enrolled in a Russian émigré school called Commercial School. It was a very good school in terms of education but he went there for only one year because it became clear that a Russian education and Russian credentials in those days would not lead him to any university or to any institution of higher education. Moses's mother had hoped that he would become a physician and his parents were quite anxious that he will attend a proper university that would be accredited. After one year in the Russian school, he and his cousin, transferred to a German school.

It was a very good school, with German teachers. But in the

second year, it became very clear that it was not for him. The Nazis had taken over Germany, and the principal had a swastika on his armband.

At that time the family decided that the only kind of education that made any sense for those days, roughly 1934, was an English education. He then transferred to a German school run by Russians. It was called the Harbin English Secondary School. The principal was an American. The other teachers were Russians. The instruction was in English. Some of the teachers spoke good English, some did not. The math teacher was excellent, he was a former artillery officer, but his English was very poor. But you don't need to know much English to teach math. Moses went there for two years. However, it became clear that getting a degree from that school, would not lead him to any university. It was decided then that he and his cousin should go to a proper English school. There was no American school nearby, but a British public school that was allied to Cambridge University. Here, if you passed the Cambridge University local examination successfully, then you could go to any university. It was in Tientsin, where they lived in a boarding house.

Moses Grossman had an uncle in Harbin his name was Zikman, who had arrived in Harbin in about 1913, being a representative of a large Russian insurance company.

He did very well for himself, was quite an entrepreneur, began dealing in sugar, and eventually bought a sugar factory. It was he who offered Moses's father employment so all the family could come to Harbin.

In 1936, when he was 50 years old, he came to the United States to celebrate his birthday. He was a multi-millionaire. He brought a lot of his money with him. He spent a lot of money and when he was finished with his United States celebration, he had just $25,000 left. Instead of taking it back to China with him, he bought United States Steel stock, rented a safe deposit box at National City Bank in New York, and put the stock in there. When the war was over, that's all he had left.

Moses Grossman left Harbin in 1941 and went to the USA where he studied medicine.[117]

Alexander Fix

Alexander, the elder son of Shimon Fix was popular among the girls in his school and community. Several of them kept sending him letters after he left Harbin for San Francisco. Their letters give sense to the time and space of Harbin of the period, to the difficulties in making a decision, and the misgivings they had about the opportunities Harbin had to offer to young people.

Harbin, January 7, 1925

Sweet Sasha![118]

A big, big thank you for your congratulations and for remembering me. I was very touched by your attentiveness. I also got your postcards and letter, but couldn't get myself to answer. In terms of promptness in correspondence, you and I deserve each other.

Sashenka, don't be so laconic in your letters, write details about your life, how you pass time, your work, your studies.

Are you thinking of coming to Harbin?

I am seriously preparing to leave for Moscow. I will see new places, try to get into a university. They say that admission to higher education will open up next year. Sitting around in Harbin—just doesn't make sense. I am going at my own risk, exchanging a peaceful life for an unknown one, but I want to try. Maybe I will take on Party work in Moscow. Harbin is a place of moral hibernation and the foxtrot. The latter interests me very little. Besides, staying in Harbin means putting an "x" on further education and, in general, making oneself into a philistine. I am thinking of starting my journey in August.

I won't be able to take the high school graduation exams this year because a week after you left, I fell ill and was sick for 1½ months. This, of course, had a very bad effect on my health. But in my opinion, whether I go a year later or a year earlier doesn't matter.

I am planning to have my photograph taken and in my next letter will send you a photo.

In 10 days, I will turn 18, childhood will end. It's time to step into independent life.

I am at your house every day, taking lessons with Alex your tenant. Your Mama misses you very much and waits very impatiently for your letters. I almost never see Sima and Sara. It seems they often spend time with Mulya. Good-bye until we meet again—not soon, I press your hand,

Lida

Mama wrote:

Dear Sasha![119]

Polina Borisovna is in an insane asylum. Klabanskaya got married to a 30-year-old who got married for the first time. How do you like "Energetic Chin?"

We've received the little package with the gramophone record of Chaliapin—thank you. Unfortunately, it arrived broken.

I wrote to you that Mulya had enrolled in a Russian university in Paris. This university, in quotation marks, was established by refugees from Russia. He wrote earlier that he was thinking of living in Montpellier and getting the lectures by mail—in a word—ridiculous.

I haven't seen Lida Vaisfeld. She's at a dacha with her mother on the other side of the Sungari River and we haven't seen her, that is, we haven't been there yet. You must remember that

Vaisfeld owes us 130 rubles and all this time hasn't mentioned it even once. He did some work for Papa. Papa thought that he would pay down the debt, but that hasn't happened. Esther Borisovna called Papa into another room and asked him not to hold them to a payment schedule on the debt because they are in need of money now — that was fine. But then a month ago they asked to borrow another 50 rubles. If there were any certainty that they would pay it back, we would gladly give it to them, but since there is no such certainty, Papa refused, and taking my advice, for a reason, reminded them of the old debt.

Lida is a good young lady, but now she looks completely lifeless, skinny, and boring. Simona also looks awful, she coughs, and her family conditions are not good. Her mother smears herself in make-up, flirts, people say she goes beyond flirting, plays cards all day long. They live in poverty. Their house has been mortgaged over and over but looks as chic as if they were rich. For a whole year they haven't paid Shpunt, the variety shop where we buy things, the 5 rubles they owe, and when they came to change a 5 ruble bill, he happened to be there and stopped them and made a big fuss. That's how a surface sparkle can trick us. And then they hired a foxtrot teacher for the mother, daughters, and son. Actually, they didn't want to teach the son, but since there was no beau, as Simona explained, they were forced to take the son along for the dancing lessons.

After lunch we were on the other side of the Sungari and met Lida. She sends you greetings. She changed her hairdo and seems prettier. She doesn't have any lessons with pupils. They are thinking of going to Russia in the fall.

Mira went today with Ekaterina Lvovna, our German governess, to the park. As you advised, Ekaterina Lvovna did not live with us this past winter. Instead, she came for lessons from the New City and got 10 rubles per hour. Since at home we knew that very, very often she was starving, at first, we just fed her breakfast every day and then very, very often, supper also. This meant that I was saved only 5 rubles since before she was getting only 15.

As summer began, we had to correct this mistake because Mira was disappearing like the wind from my field of vision, making friends with all the children on the Seventh Line and since the children, one meets her are, as one might say, street children, this was becoming very unpleasant. Now she, that is Ekaterina Lvovna, comes in the morning, leaves in the evening, and gets full board according to the rules. . . and the same 10 rubles. She goes with us to the other side of the Sungari River and since Mira speaks with her in German all day long, lately she has begun to speak fluently in this language.

The second half of my letter wears the character of gossip, but I want to gradually introduce you to Harbin's character and the particulars of our life.

I am writing to you "in flight" standing with one leg in the room and the other on the threshold prepared to leave for the office. Of course, nothing useful can be written in this "situation." Therefore I am limiting myself to just a greeting and my wishes for you: — be healthy, my son, and may your memory always be strong so that you remember and don't forget to write often to your mama and Papa.

Zeev Rubinsohn

In January 1939, 7-year-old Zeev Rubinsohn and his parents set off from Berlin to the faraway Harbin. They arrived in Harbin in April 1939, as German-Jewish refugees and rented an apartment at 54 Commerce Street. Their place was on the first floor. There were 7 apartments in the house, all belonging to Jewish owners who moved to the town of Natanaia in Israel.

Their beginning in Harbin was full of difficulties. The job that was promised in Berlin by the Jewish Relief Society in 1935, did not exist. Therefore, little Zeev's father, Dr. Hans Rubinsohn, had to open his own doctor's office, where he gained a good reputation over time. The daily number of patients who visited him ranged from 20 to 30 people. Among his patients were many Chinese. As thanks to his services, some Chinese patients gave him calligraphies and Chinese paintings. To help him at his work, Dr. Rubinsohn hired a Russian-speaking Chinese man named Vasja. In addition to his work as a translator, he also was a cook for the family. He was a very good cook who prepared both Jewish, Chinese, and Russian food, and was paid a monthly salary.[120]

Dr. Rubinsohn's wife, Fanya, worked for a short time in the countryside with Dr. Muhan Ravel, and later also in his own ambulance. Both practices brought a good income and the family living conditions had improved over time.

Faniya's health had deteriorated and because the work in the doctor's office was stressful, Dr. Rubinsohn hired a domestic worker to help his wife with the housework.

When the Rubinsohn family arrived in Harbin, the little son Zeev had just reached school age. Because of the Jewish community's strong support of the family, his parents sent him to the Skidelski Talmud Torah school, a Jewish primary school, with only 5 students in his class. Zeev had never heard the Hebrew language before, and he did not understand what the teacher was saying. He also did not speak Russian and did not understand his classmates. After attending the Talmud-Torah school for less than 20 days, he was sent to a British school.

In December 1941, two days after the outbreak of the Pacific War, the school was closed by the Japanese occupying forces.

Zeev's father hired several tutors so that he could continue to have the courses that he took at school. Zeev had also a Chinese tutor who taught him in Chinese for two years and who he called older "Sister Martha".

At the end of a course, each tutor had to provide written evidence of Zeev's participation in the theme of the course, his level of knowledge, and that he was ready for an exam on the subject.

Zeev Rubinsohn joined the Zionist youth sports organization "Maccabi", which was founded in 1921 in Harbin by David Laskov. Before leaving Harbin, Zeev Rubinsohn worked from September 1949 to June 1950 in the pharmacy of the Jewish hospital. There he met his future wife, Najia, who was born in Harbin on November 25, 1927.

Najia's parents were born in Tomsk, Russia. Her father, Mikhail Solomon Markovic who was born in 1884 attended school until the 4th grade only. His father owned a hotel. Mikhail developed a good career in horse breeding.

Najia's mother, Anna Alexandrovna Gallier, was born in 1890 and was the daughter of the best merchant in Tomsk. She graduated from Maria High School for Girls in Tomsk. She also studied medicine at a college but did not graduate because her conservative father thought that children should learn to become workers. Then she married Mikhail Markovic and left her home.

In 1919, the couple moved to Vladivostok, where Mikhail worked as a timber merchant. The new economic policy of the Soviet Union, allowed Mikhail to buy horses in Manchuria. He moved to Harbin without his wife and continued to sell his horses, but with little profit. At the beginning of 1927, Najia his wife crossed the border between China and the Soviet Union illegally and joined her husband in Harbin. The couple lived in Waterway No. 78 Street, now Anfeng Street, at that time.

Najia's uncle came to Harbin in the 1920s to breed horses. He had a good sense for business and live a good life. He and Najia's father Mikhail bred horses and pigs in their large-scale farm. The younger brother of Najia's mother also owned a lot of land but lost it when the new collective socialization economic policy of the Soviet Union came into effect. This campaign affected Mikhail Markovic as well, and all of his properties were confiscated and he was exiled to the famine devastated Yarkutia. There he spent 18 "Springs and Autumns".[121]

At the age of 9, Najia joined the Harbin youth organization Betar. Her studies in Harbin were very fulfilling. She first attended the primary school for 4 years, then for 3 years the Russian No.1 high school on artillery street, where the former Jewish middle school had stood. Najia graduated from the 1st Harbin Russian Language High School on December 22, 1943.

At that time, the Japanese occupation forces did not allow students to learn Chinese. They did allow learning Japanese and German only. Najia chose Japanese. In her class were 30 students, including 5 Jewish students, 2 girls and 3 boys, while the other classes had 6 Jewish students. After graduating from high school in 1944, Najia was trained with the Russian Red Cross Association and received her nurse diploma on March 31, 1946. From September 1944 to November 1947, Najia studied at the Department of Blood Diseases of the Red Cross Medical College in northeast China and graduated with a diploma in medicine.

During her studies, she interned at the central hospital of the Chinese railway company, in the departments of obstetrics, gynecology, internal medicine, pediatrics, infectious diseases, and venereal diseases. On April 22, 1949, Najia received the deputy diploma as a senior physician from the health authority in northeastern China. From 1944 to 1950, Najia worked at the Jewish hospital in Harbin. She worked there for 3 years as a nurse and 3 years as a midwife. Because of Zeev's mother's poor health, it was very difficult to keep up the work in the clinic. For this reason, Dr. Rubinsohn hired the pretty, gifted Najia as an assistant.

On November 13, 1950, the Rubinsohn family together with Najia's parents left Harbin on their way to Israel.

Joseph Glikman

On April 3, 2013, Karen Glikman wrote to her cousin Sherry Smilo that she was "Trying to figure out what went wrong with our family." Attached, she wrote, is my initial and incomplete attempt to understand what went wrong with the Glikman family of Harbin. In many ways, it seems we were victims of class more than anything else ... more than antisemitism, more than sexism even. There is a lot more history that I could go into from 1940 on, but it all relates to the same issue of the wealthier relatives maintaining a distance from the poorer relatives.[122]

She took Harbin as a pivotal point in her search for understanding why a richer part of the family, the American one,

Fig. 7: Joseph Glikman as a child in Harbin

denied those who came from Harbin the luxury of life they built for themselves. The result of Karen Glikman's voyage allows us to enter her family's world in Harbin.

Aaron Felger married Rose Bernstein and they had two sons, Solomon and Samuel. His great, great-grandson, Joseph Israel Glikman, said that Aaron served as a Captain in an elite unit of the Czar's personal army. He also said that he had light hair and blue eyes. Aaron's son's Solomon birth certificate lists Aaron's occupation as a "tradesman".

Samuel Felger married a woman whose name was Bluma Zaaz. She died giving birth to our grandmother, Chana Felger, on September 4, 1889. Chana was Joseph Glikman's mother.

In an interview, Chana remembered that "Samuel remarried. He was shown an attractive girl and he agreed to marry her. At the wedding, the bride wore a heavy veil. When the time came to kiss the bride, he discovered that they switched girls and his wife was an unattractive woman with a poke-marked face, however, Chana said that she was good to her. From this marriage was born Chana's half-sister Celia".[123] She could not say whether the woman was Leah and Rachel.

Samuel Felger was attacked by highway robbers during one of his trips north and was clubbed on the head and died shortly thereafter.

Joseph Glikman said that his mother was very proud to be a Felger. She said the family was very educated, good at business and musical. She claims that the famous violinist, David Oistrach, was a cousin of hers. Unfortunately, she did not end up in the Felger family ... she was given to her mother's Zaaz family. She was passed around from one family to another whenever someone needed "a cleaning girl". She had a miserable childhood and her life was not her own; she was basically a slave. They "sold" her to Ezra (Israel) Glikman for more money. Ezra had a passion for travel and alcohol.

Ezra was born in Odessa. His mother was a nice woman, but his father, Samuel Glikman was a hard-drinking troublemaker

Fig. 8: Joseph Glikman boxing in Harbin

who had the nickname of "Mendele Knock". Ezra had a brother Joseph and a sister Pessa who became a prostitute. Joseph was a thief and a gambler. During the Revolution, Joseph and another man, known as "Moishe the Jap", organized their own military gang and started to raid and rob villages. Joseph was killed during one of these raids.

Towards the end of 1923 or the beginning of 1924, the Glikmans left for Harbin, China traveling the Trans-Siberian Railway. They had three sons, Aron age 11, Sam age 7, and Joe age 2. Their daughter, Polina was born in April 1924 in Harbin.

Joseph's father was a butcher and owned a small shop at 20 Yamakaia Street. But it was Chana, the one who ended up being the breadwinner for the family. She came up with the idea of

Fig. 9: Joseph Glikman in Harbin

cutting up chickens and selling parts rather than selling whole chickens only. The idea was evidently very popular.

The family was living at 2 Birjevaya Street in Harbin in 1930. That year Aron, the oldest child, was sent to the United States. He was 17 years old, almost 18.

To supplement the family's income Chana decided to take in boarders, and all the good cuts of meat went to them. They got the best of everything.

Ezra sexually abused his daughter. Paula nicknamed Polina was a beautiful child and became a beautiful woman. Looking at the family dynamics it played a big role. She might have fared better in life if she was not so attractive. In any case, Paula grew up being groomed and pressured to "marry a rich man". She was a beauty, an amazing seamstress, and a wonderful cook. The problem was that she was also Chana's way out financially … she needed her daughter to marry a wealthy man because it was her only ticket out.[124]

Joseph Glikman left Harbin en route to the USA and arrived there on September 15th, 1939 at the age of 17. He traveled with Cy Kaufmann, the son of Dr. Abraham Kaufmann who was the head of the Jewish community. Joseph's occupation was listed as a musician and his nationality was first typed in as Russian and then scratched out and changed into "Hebrew". His ticket was paid for by his father, H.S. Glikman who lived at 70 Birjevaia Street in Harbin.

Chana and Paula arrived in the USA on October 2, 1940. Chana was now 51 years old and Paula was 15. Chana's occupation was listed as an embroiderer and Paula as a student. The manifest also said they spoke Russian and German; probably "Yiddish". Their nationality was listed as Hebrew. Chana paid the passage for herself and Paula. The document requires them to list the relative and address of the place they left and the document shows that they lived with Mr. Ezra S. Glikman at 26 Yamakova Street in Harbin. Chana's son, Aron, was their sponsor and it showed that he was living at 1930 Wilshire Blvd, in Loa Angeles.

As one can imagine, the story continues on and on, and as it moves further from the Harbin past it becomes irrelevant to our tale. To just tie the knots, it should be understood that the life of Chana and Paula in America did not produce the result that they dreamed about in Harbin. The well-to-do part of the family refused to accept them shuttering their hopes and imagined future.

Galya Katz

Galya Katz spent her formative 25 years in Harbin. Her life she wrote, was saturated with vibrant emotions and ever new experiences — at times joyous, at times grim, but always quivering and pulsating.[125]

During the Japanese occupation, especially as of 1938, we, the Soviet citizens, were deprived of the right to study and work. Students were expelled from schools, even conservatories. We were held in complete isolation.

With the end of the Japanese occupation in the second half of August 1945, all the doors flung open. My father, Dr. M.S. Volobrinsky, and two other physicians were released from the Japanese prison in the second half of August 1945. By a miracle, they were not shot or exterminated by typhus inoculation, as was widely practiced in the Japanese prisons. My sister and I were at last enabled to study and work.

On October 2, 1945, Galya Katz began to work for the Chinese Changchun Railway Administration as a translator. After having passed written and oral examinations by a special translations committee, she was assigned to serve in the Commercial

Department as a Russian-Chinese-Russian secretary-interpreter. Such examinations were held annually and were compulsory for all the translators. She became a link between the Soviet and the Chinese Administrations, and the Soviet specialists and their Chinese counterparts. A very sensitive position indeed.

In December 1945 the Harbin Polytechnic Institute (HPI) was reopened for all those who wanted to receive engineering and technical higher education.

The programs were tailored to train the future employees of the Railway administration and other strategic engineering and industrial enterprises of China. The HPI was initially headed by the colonel Ojigov of the Soviet Engineering Corps, and subsequently, lieutenant colonel Sedykh. The head of the tutoring department was Professor Grigorovich.

Galya's sister, Irina Moiseyevna Volobrinsky, was appointed to head the personnel department, which immediately began to mobilize the tutoring contingent of the HPI. Now, with the Japanese out, over 2000 new students, mostly Russians, but also Chinese, Jews, and other nationalities, filled the classrooms. The tutoring was in Russian, and those who did not know the language entered the preparatory faculty, established especially for their adaptation.

Galya Katz began her studies in the mechanical faculty of the HPI in 1945. Her studies were combined with working in the Chinese Changchun Railway administration. Those were long days of work and stress, and studying at the evening courses of the HPI.

The Harbin Polytechnic Institute was housed in a beautiful building on Pravlenskaya Street on the corner with Sadovaya Street, close to the CCR offices and the Jelsob—the Railway Assembly Hall, which included a prestigious club and a spacious concert hall. The campus territory accommodated administration premises, workshops, and laboratories. Galya remembered that classrooms were spacious and full of light, sufficient to accommodate a large number of students. The presence of the students in classes was compulsory. As studies progressed, a part of the students dropped off: some left the Institute by choice, some were expelled for missing lessons or falling behind. At the end of Galya's first academic year, her class lost half of its students. Not everyone was able to walk long kilometers because there was no money for tram tickets. Walking was difficult and dangerous especially on slippery sidewalks, in late evening, during the freezing Harbin winters. The curriculum was huge. To successfully graduate one had to pass at least 60 major examinations during the four years of studies.

The ever-growing violent Chinese civil war reflected on the work of the CCR. In May 1948 all Soviet specialists were ordered to temporarily leave and return to the USSR. The head of the Commercial Services, engineer-major Zaharchenko insisted that Galya, too, should temporarily leave for Russia. He knew what he was talking about: after their departure, a number of interpreters were shot by the Kuomintang. It was only by a miracle that she escaped this event.

In 1949 she was transferred to the Economics Department of the CCR, dealing with the circulation of goods, tariffs, rates, monthly index, price increases, amortization of the railway stock, inventories, and the like.

Galya was totally immersed in her studies and later in the position she got at the Chinese Changchun Railway Administration. She remained secretive not only about her personal life but also about the Red Army rule of Harbin which was as cruel or even much more than that of the Japanese. Nor did she offer any glimpse of the change China underwent in 1949 when the new Communist government established the new republic and forced all foreigners out of the country.

Galya Katz left Harbin in 1952 for Israel.

Chayim Tadmor (Frumstein)

Hayim (Chayim) Tadmor was born in Harbin. His parents, David Frumstein and Frieda Kaznitz, born, respectively, in Russia and in Ukraine, were married in Russia in 1913, and their daughter Luba, his sister, was born there in 1914. Hayim Tadmor's father arrived in Harbin in 1916, in the middle of the First World War, and his mother and sister came from Russia to join him in 1921. Hayim's father died when he was 11 years old. Most memorable was the story of his mother's arduous trip from Ukraine to Harbin in 1921, amidst the Russian civil war. The trip would have taken a week or so in peaceful days. but for her it lasted nine months. Thousands of people around her died of typhus, but, quite miraculously, she arrived in Harbin safe and sound.

Chayim was born two years later in Harbin in 1931. Like most Jewish residents of Harbin, the family lived in the Pristan area, close to the river Sungari. His father's trade was in furs, which he sold to an American firm on the West Coast. He would acquire them either locally, in Fudzezan (Fujiadian), or by traveling far away to northern Manchuria or even to southern Siberia on the Russian side. He must have known Chinese, which was essential for his trade, in addition to Russian, German, and English, in which he was fluent. Chayim's sister was sent to the popular Komercheskoye, the Russian high school, while he was sent to a Hebrew elementary school, the Skidelski Talmud Torah. His father was not an observant Jew and he did not ordinarily attend the synagogue. Yet he wanted his son to continue the Jewish tradition, minimal as it was in his life. Chayim's father died in the autumn of 1934, at the age of 54, and was buried in the Jewish cemetery of Harbin. His sister became an ardent Zionist and joined the Betar Zionist youth movement in Harbin. She sailed to Palestine as a pioneer in 1934, a short time before his father's passing. Chayim Tadmor and his mother followed her, arriving in Palestine in November 1935.

Socially the family had very little to do with the non-Jewish Russians. Their personal contacts were mainly with other Jewish families of a similar background.

Harbin, unlike Tianjin or Shanghai, did not have a foreign concession, but the autonomous Russian-speaking community there would have looked to an observer like a sort of concession. Naturally, negotiations with the municipality, the police, and all levels of government were conducted in Chinese.

The Talmud Torah school was established in 1921, at the peak of the wave of immigration of Russian Jews into Manchuria. It was named after Mr. Skidelski, the noted industrialist who owned the Mulian Manchurian coal mines. He and his three sons took an interest in Jewish education. They built the beautiful Talmud Torah on Konnaya Street in Harbin and also saw to its running expenses. The school existed for over thirty years, until the early 1950s.

From 1920 to 1924, the Talmud Torah had only three classes and accepted only boys, but by the time Chayim attended it a fourth class had been opened, and girls were accepted as well. Altogether, there were 105 graduates in the first ten years. The school

Fig. 10: Chayim Tadmor in a Harbin park

offered instruction in the Russian language, arithmetic, Jewish history, Russian history, geography, and English.

Many of the programs were devoted to Hebrew studies, including the written and oral study of Hebrew. The school celebrated the Jewish holidays and held daily morning prayers before classes began. Rabbi Levine, an old-fashioned orthodox rabbi, presided over the religious functions, but the Hebrew studies were in the hands of trained teachers. He learned his essential Hebrew in the Talmud Torah. His teacher was Mr. Pineles, a literary critic from Poland who stopped in Harbin for several years on his way to Palestine. He was to become a professor of Hebrew literature at Tel Aviv University.

In the Talmud Torah, Hebrew was taught in the European, Ashkenazi style. Just before leaving for Palestine, he had taken some private instruction from Mr. Nadel, a teacher at the Talmud Torah, to help him convert to the Sephardic pronunciation.

Chayim was 12 years old when he and his mother joined his sister and her family in Palestine, and there he went directly into the sixth grade in elementary school.

Tadmor's fascination with history goes back to his childhood in Harbin, especially the history of China, whose classical periods, up to the Boxer Rebellion, he learned from his sister's high school textbook. Ancient history, the beginnings of civilization, always had a special appeal for him.

For Tadmor, the history of his family reflects the socio-cultural trends characteristic of the Jews in Harbin. His father, a western businessman, was typical of the local middle class; secular in his behavior and immersed in Russian culture.

His mother, daughter of Orthodox Jewish parents in Ukraine, was also secular and immersed in Russian culture. Emotionally, however, she was still attached to her revolutionary brothers in Russia and given the choice, she would gladly have joined them.

Tadmor's sister rejected both of these contrary trends. Convinced that immigration to Palestine was the only solution for the Jews, she became an ardent Zionist. Tadmor admits that he was influenced by her and her friends more than by his parents.

On 2 November 1935, the eighteenth anniversary of the Balfour Declaration, he and his mother arrived in Palestine. It has been his home since then.[126]

Shimon Fix

In February 1928, six years after the passing of his father, Shimon Fix felt compelled to express his emotions about his memories of his parents. He wrote this letter to his brothers Shabsa and Volf, and his sisters Hava and Rivka. They were in Proskurov, Ukraine, far away from Harbin.

Harbin, 21st of Sh'vat, 5688

February 2, 1928

It is not a letter that I now send to you, and not a page from my diary that I write to you, but a mournful page, torn from the depths of my soul to be sent to you, my dear family. If I controlled a pencil that had the ability to capture the pain that I feel in my soul the same way an x-ray machine has the ability to capture the illness of the body, then of course my letter wouldn't come out as pale in its substance as it will be in your hands, but I am writing to you anyway, as best I can, about my memories of our parents.

Fig. 11: Shimon Fix at his desk – Harbin 1925

Today it is exactly six

years since the Almighty Judge called our papa back to Him, affording him peace from this world's hassles. Today it is exactly six years since we were left without a father, and in life's difficult minutes we don't have our father to hear our sorrows, and there is no one with whom to share our moments of joy. Since the beginning of my time in foreign lands, no matter what I was experiencing, I always felt that there, far away, in Proskurov, there was an eye that watched over me, was cheered by my joys, was saddened by my troubles. No matter what I took on, no matter what I decided to do, I felt that there, in Proskurov, there was some authority over me to which I must be accountable. And it was terrible at first to have to answer only to my own self.

When I got the first telegram from Volf about Papa's death, I was overcome by a sharp horror that he is already no more, but I remember a subconscious feeling telling me that the sharpness of this pain would be temporary and that gradually it would dim. But this was not to be. Our invisible, unseen papa always and everywhere faithfully watches over me.

I have a packet of Papa's letters, yellowed with time, in front of me. Today, the sixth anniversary of his death, I took it upon myself to read them over. I read them and reread them, fell into them, and all the more sharply I feel and experience grief — over whom we had and whom we lost.

He seemed to feel the closeness of death and grieved that his children were far from him and that there was no hope of seeing them. Speaking in one letter about the timelessness of that period of time, Papa writes: "Who knows what tomorrow prepares for us. Who in case of death of the children will close our eyes with his hand."

Our papa was tormented by an awareness that brought sorrow to the great poet Heine Henrich in his poem that lamented that after death:

"Keine Messe wird man singen,	"No Mass will be sung,
Keinen Kadosch wird man sagen,	No Kaddish will be said,
Nichts gesagt und nichts gesungen	Nothing said and nothing sung
Wird an meinen Sterbetagen."	Will be on my days of death."

Prophetic words waft from the lines of Papa's last letter, where he wrote to me: "My Son, who knows if we are destined to ever "see each other with the eyes of the flesh in this world, or if we will meet only in the world to come with eyes of the spirit?"

This letter, due to the circumstances of that time period, was en route to me for almost three months; I received it when Papa was already no more. This letter was posthumous, though while I was reading it, I was sure that its author was still alive. Yet he was already in a better world, leaving us, brothers and sisters, scattered and strewn in various corners of this lump of dirt called Earth. Maybe when, at that time when I received and read his posthumous letter, at that very moment, our papa lay across from the door on the floor (according to the code for absolution from sins) and at his head candles burned and the synagogue workers went around the house with a jug, calling out: Charity, mitzvah, and charity.

But the stiffening body of our papa was a protest of the dead against these living cries, as if saying, "Nothing will help, and I don't need anything now except an inexpensive shroud and a patch of soil.

In terms of the number of years, I am the oldest of us, brothers and sisters, and was connected to our parents the longest. I lived by them for 20 years under one roof, and for 28 years, though I lived far from them, not one week went by without an exchange of letters. Close to 3,000 letters went between us and now, when six years have already passed without Papa and three years without Mama, I feel that with their departure from life, a piece of my life also departed. We were left alone, as "They," far away. Only memories of them are left. And these memories take unbalance the mind towards a state of disequilibrium. Let's, my brothers and sisters, remember those who genuinely loved us more than themselves, and let us, all the days of our lives, feel that: Ihil Shimonovich and Rahil Leibovna died, but Papa and Mama are alive in our hearts and will live until that time when we ourselves will be relieved of the hassles of this world, and until then on the anniversaries of their death — Kaddish: Exalted and hallowed be God's great name… Shimon

A September letter from Shimon Fix to his son Sasha (Alexander) who is in the US gives a first-hand account of the magnitude of the disaster and the way the flood of 1932 affected people and properties:

"On our street in Pristan generally, it began on August 8 and still hasn't finished. You want to have a clear image of this… take a rowboat and let's ride together on it through Harbin and you will take a look at the city, how it is reflected in the expanse of water that covered its streets 2 meters high and in some places more. Forgive me for taking you out the back door of our house, i.e., through the kitchen into the backyard. The front door, the one facing 7th Line (later renamed Liteinaya Street) is blocked since various things and household goods are piled up in the front entranceway and on the stairs. These are belongings from neighboring one-story homes. Besides, water has already reached above the 8th step of the stairs and it's impossible to stay dry while getting from this water to the rowboat. Now the water has receded a little. This situation lasted about a month. Things are improving, but we still ride in rowboats. Somehow we managed to create a pier for our rowboats in the backyard. And this was good because before we made this adaptation and before we acquired the rowboats (and it was very difficult to buy one because demand was very high and supply was almost nonexistent) we, the inhabitants of our courtyard, or rather of our upper floor, felt very unhappy, like people who found themselves on a deserted island in the open sea far from all living things. On the upper floor of our house, as on a high cliff above the raging sea, all the residents of our courtyard found shelter: the tenants of the first floor (Sasha, you are familiar with the Plat family and the Verblovski family, the sister and brother-in-law of the Shriro brothers), the tenants who live in the annex, the guards with all their children and the rest of their households, the maid, the dogs, the cats, the chickens, the goods, and the other animate and inanimate inventory. All in all 26-28 people were on our second floor. It was a mix not just of tribes, social classes, and dialects, but also of non-speaking animals. A true Noah's Ark, with the only difference being that we aren't swimming, but rather standing still, like a high cliff in the middle of a vast watery expanse... The water in the courtyard and on the street is high enough that even speedboats go on it, so our rowboat can withstand the maximum load. Just don't row too hard with the oars; we don't want to frighten the fish—let them splash around in the waters of our yard. For children they are entertaining, and for housewives they are economical—their own, not purchased. It is true that this tour of 7th Street by rowboat presents a gloomy picture. It will be difficult for us to go by boat to Diagonal Street and its side streets and to Chinese Street (your Wall Street or 5th Avenue) because given their insufficient experience, rowers inevitably collide with one another. On those streets, there is a lot of traffic of rowboats and motorboats. See how the water engulfed the city and the suburbs as if squeezing it with tight rings, flooding Pristan, Nakhapovki, Chinhe, Fudjiadian. In the last, water destroyed over 2,000 houses, including 100 stone houses. Many houses were completely demolished and carried by the current far out to the Amur River; others fell onto their sides; some were simply destroyed. From some houses, the only remaining, barely noticeable signs are the roof and some pipe parts. In some neighborhoods, there are absolutely no signs of the old life — there is only one unbroken sea. Water, water, water, as before the creation of the world, everything is covered by a flat expanse of water… These desolate waters make a very painful, depressing impression, don't they? As much water as there is — there is as much in human tears, and grief is a bottomless river… For now — the picture of destruction is terrible…"[127]

Harbin, November 20, 1932

Dear Sasha and Tanya![128]

I have described for you a picture of the flood. At the current moment, I am in the mood a little bit to write more and I want to use it to share my personal impressions and observations during this time of timelessness. This will require several letters because it is impossible to exhaust all of the "cold observations of the mind" that accumulated during this memorable span of time.

Starting with the first days of August, Harbin began to worry. Ominous rumors began to spread about the Sungari's approaching assault on the city.

The population divided itself into two opposite camps — believers and nonbelievers in the coming flood. One with exact statistical data showed that a flood is impossible; others with valid calculations assured that "rivers do not flow backward" and that if the Sungari continues on the same forced march as it was going, then flooding is inevitable. Many of the unbelievers turned into believers once some of the collectors sent their first spits into Pristan. The religious ones and the elderly then lifted their eyes to the heavens, and the free thinkers and young people turned their gaze to the second and third floors of buildings.

One more day—and all accepted the inevitability of flooding. And those and others began to pack their belongings and when on the streets and in the yards the soil became moist—began transferring their possessions to the nearest second floor to keep them safe, and with the same safety in mind, all the residents of our first floor, all the tenants of our annex, the watchman with all their children and housekeepers and all their inanimate and animate inventory moved into our house. Among the last were little dogs—Jeck and Johnny.

Where are you now, little four-pawed poets and philosophers?

The new situation, the overcrowding of the premises, the extraordinary aquatic surroundings seemed to hit them hard, and their restless nervous movements and wandering eyes seemed to ask: "What is this; what happened?"

These little dogs, one white, the other red with large eyes reflecting a deep thoughtfulness, took turns jumping up to the windows to peer into the distance they had never seen before. For the first time they saw the roofs of neighboring houses and the tops of trees, and the sun seemed so close to them, but at the same time it did not warm them as much as it used to below on dry ground and there was even a chill emanating from it as if it was being cooled by the cold flow of the water element.

And the water element, full of courage, lay upon the ground and, as in an iron vise, squeezed everyone and everything—the tall many-storied buildings, the squat fanzas, the tall trees, and the tender garden flowers. And it seems that this stream of water, coming to us from distant countries, wanted to show its wide scope and for that purpose throw its power with generosity and without calculation of breadth or distance.

Jeck and Johnny are as if studying the new situation. They

busily run from one room into another, back and forth, running around and getting mixed up under our legs. Now they sense — by the sound of oars striking the water — that a rowboat has swum over. Jeck, more impatient than Johnny, quickly goes to investigate. He runs out of his master's room into the shared dining room and into the kitchen, from the kitchen to the balcony, from the balcony down the stairs to the arriving rowboat. There he finds out all he needs to know, calms down, and returns running back along the same path through the kitchen into the dining room and back to his room. It is obvious that his nerves are stretched. He quivers at every rustling sound and, besides that, he constantly takes note of every inhabitant whom he has known since the time when he started living in the courtyard back when it was dry. He, I think, knows all the residents by name, while the residents have difficulty remembering the names of the dogs. Jeck is the more pensive one, the more sharply feeling of everything compared to Johnny. At times some kind of heaviness befalls him, he stops being interested in those around him, stands in the corner of a room, or goes out on the balcony, pressing himself against the railings, pressing his tail between his legs and with his big eyes begins to ask, "What, exactly, is going on around here, what is all the noise and commotion about, and why did all this happen, and why did everyone run upstairs?" But soon he will shudder as if trying to shake these empty questions off his canine head, and he will run into the room where his owner is. There, after all, he is always nicely welcomed. Along the way, he bumps into a resident who, himself stressed out by the circumstances of the place and the time –gives him a kick, later regretting the injustice of his action. No better are all the other temporary tenants of the house; they step on his legs and from them, he must listen to impolite shouts, "scat!" But it is fine. Jeck is not vindictive and after a few minutes, he is ready to give his paw and caress his abuser.

A whole month went by. The water started to retreat. Summer days also started to retreat and shorten. The blue sky started to twitch, covered by a leaden layer. Evenings became longer and cooler. The residents of the house no longer scattered on the balconies and roamed around on boats, but rather came together in rooms.

Another two weeks and the water were entirely gone from the surface of the ground, leaving only sludge and mud. Some of the residents left. It felt freer in the house. A little more time went by and of the temporary residents, only the owners of Jeck and Johnny remained. One fine morning they were amazed by a surprise that they apparently did not expect. Their owners began packing their belongings, taking them out to the yard, and putting them on a cart. The master and mistress and their children each carried out baskets, packages, and packs and arranged them in the cart. The children also sat down in the cart—on top of the things—the coachman whipped the horses, and the yard, as well as the interior of the house, emptied. They also took Johnny in their arms and left with him. Jeck, however, remained inside, hiding in a corner to give rein to his reflections. He couldn't for the life of him understand why things are being done this way, why these people, living together until now, were dispersing. He felt some kind of sharp pain from all that had happened, pressed himself against the wall, lifted his fourth leg, and standing on three legs, plunged into his thoughts. What is this, why did so much water spill, where did it come from, and where did it go, why is there so much instability in nature, why isn't there calm, why was it so warm before, and why did it become cold, why is there no enforcement of orderliness? And question after question crowded in his brain about the imperfections of the world's enforcement of the laws of orderliness and about the lives of people. He could in no way find answers to all that was not understandable, all that happens under the moon.

Soon the daughter of his master found him in his forgotten corner; with a shout she brought him out of his reverie and chased him to his new apartment. With that my observations of him ended. Where are you, little Jeck, four-legged philosopher and poet?

Papa

Hugo and Erna Zydower

Hugo Zydower and Erna Friedland came to Fürstenwalde after they married. They had a son Alfred, and 18 months later in 1931, their daughter Anna was born. Hugo stripped goats and sold the fur and Erna was a homemaker.

Anna was nine when Hugo and Erna left Germany in 1940. They took the train for 10 days through Russia on way to Shanghai. The Joint Distribution Committee brought sandwiches and gave them coupons to have tea and stuff, but they could not go to the dining car and had to stay in their compartment.

On the way, they spent one night in Harbin, which, Anna recalls was very nice. They had cots and were a little freer to walk the streets. They got into Pristan and were amazed at the sight of buildings that were the same as those they left in the old country. They saw many people with European faces and there were also some Chinese. They thought that all of China was just like that. Erna didn't speak English and Anna had just learned some. In German, you call a bathroom "closet" [klosett]. Everywhere we went, Anna wrote, my mom had to go to the bathroom. And she was so upset and said I don't know why there are so many bathrooms here — closets — and you can't get in. But it wasn't, it was closed.[129]

Mara Moustafine – Zaretsky – Onikul

Mara Moustafine was born in Harbin, into a family with Jewish, Russian, and Tatar Muslim roots and came to Australia as a child in 1959.

Four generations of Mara's family lived in Harbin and Manchuria for over fifty years. On her mother's side, they were Jews from Byelorussia, who arrived in Harbin in the early 1900s. On her father's side, they were Russians and Tatars from central Russia who fled the 1917 Bolshevik Revolution and the Russian Civil War. They lived through extraordinary times: the Japanese occupation under the puppet Manchukuo regime in 1932-1945; liberation by the Soviet Red Army in 1945; and the first ten years of the People's Republic until they left for Australia.

Harbin was a multicultural and cosmopolitan city, with many nationalities and religions living side by side. Jews were active in the commercial, cultural and public life of Russian Harbin. They also participated actively in Harbin's municipal affairs—making

Fig. 12: Mara Moustafine with her parents. Harbin 1940s

up 12 of the 40 members on the city council in 1909.[130]

In most families, the pattern of migration was that one member of the family would come first—to test the opportunities in the new homeland—then others would follow—brothers, sisters, parents, uncles, aunts, and cousins.

This pattern was followed by Mara's family from Byelorussia—early settlers on both sides. Mara's great grandfather, Girsh Onikul followed his brother and cousins to Harbin from Moghilev in 1909. Instead of staying in Harbin, he moved on to Hailar, a small trading post by the Amur River on the edge of the Mongolian steppes, where he was an agent for Singer sewing machines and later had a small dairy business. His wife, Chesna Klebanova, joined him the following year, with her son and Mara's grandmother Gita. Other relatives followed.

Mara's grandfather, Matvei Abramovich (Motya) Zaretsky, arrived in Harbin from Kopis in 1912 as a teenager and joined his older brother, Ruvim, who had come in 1906 and by 1909 set up the family meat business "Zaretsky and Zalmanov". His sisters and parents followed. They had a small kosher butchery on Yamskaya Street and a retail outlet at Harbin market. By 1921, Motya was a partner in the business, responsible for cattle purchase and slaughter. In 1924, he set up a cattle trading partnership "Myasotrud" meaning "meat work" and headed its Hailar office for 8 years. It was during this time, that he met and married Mara's grandmother. Although their parents on both sides were observant Jews and her grandparents were married by a Rabbi under a chuppah in Hailar and observed the high holidays, like many Russian Jews in Harbin at the time, Motya and Gita were secular.[131]

During the turbulent civil war years, while its political status was in limbo, the CER zone was a staging ground for the anti-Bolshevik White Guard and Cossack armies. With this came a rise in antisemitism, as the Cossacks regarded all Jews as Bolsheviks who perpetrated the revolution. For Jews living in areas close to the Russian border, like Hailar, life became especially dangerous. In 1919, Mara's great grandfather Girsh Onikul was captured by one of Baron UngernSternberg's[132] men, he miraculously escaped alive.

Life for Jews in Manchuria deteriorated seriously after the Japanese occupation. The Japanese associated closely with militant fascists antiSoviet Whites, such as the Russian Fascist Party (RFP), whose ideology of antiBolshevism and nationalism was laced with virulent antisemitism. In the early 1930s, Russian thugs linked to the RFP engaged in a campaign of kidnappings, extortion, and murder against wealthy businessmen, mainly Jews, masterminded by the Japanese military police, the Kempeitai.[133]

For Mara Moustafine's family, as for many others, the Japanese occupation proved to be a breaking point. Her grandparents and mother stayed on in Harbin, where her grandfather had recently built a two-story apartment block and joined his brother in a new firm "Brothers Zaretsky and Co". However, her grandmother's parents and siblings — the Onikuls — decided to seek refuge in the Soviet Union in the mid1930s. It was an ill- fated choice. At the height of Stalin's Great Terror in 193738, they were among the 48,000 Harbintsy who were arrested as Japanese spies — some 31,000 were shot; and the rest were sent to gulags — labor camps.

As a mechanism to control the Russian population in Manchuria, in 1934 the Japanese established the Bureau of Russian Émigré Affairs in Manchukuo (BREM). seemingly under Russian control, it was headed by a succession of White Army generals and run by members of the Russian Fascist Party (RFP) and their sympathizers.

All adult émigré Russians were required to register with the

BREM. Only then could they receive identity papers, residence permits, employment cards, and travel documents. Those who did not were denied employment and education for their children.

Mara's grandfather insisted that being stateless — "a citizen of nowhere" — was too risky in the face of Japanese aggression and his family remained 'Soviets'.

As a result, Mara's mother Inna was excluded from school and had to study at home with a tutor. Later, when contact between 'émigrés' and 'Soviets' was forbidden she could no longer study music or participate in concerts at Madame Gershgorina's music school. Nor could she belong to either of Harbin's two Jewish youth organizations — Betar or Maccabi. At first, she would walk with her friends to meetings or sporting events to share a little of the excitement, then must turn around and go home. Eventually, even this was stopped as émigré parents were warned there might be consequences if their children associated with 'Soviet' friends.[134]

But even émigré status did not save her grandfather's brother, Ruvim. In 1940, the Japanese arrested him and took over his retail business at the Harbin market. Ironically, they kept her grandfather on because of his experience in the wholesale business, making him an adviser in their meat monopoly association. Only in 1943 was he removed by BREM officials, who invented a case full of bizarre antisemitic and anti-Soviet innuendo to secure his removal.

In 1956 Mara Moustafine's family started to make plans to leave Harbin. By that time, her parents, both graduates from the Harbin Polytechnical Institute's new Faculty of Oriental Studies and fluent in Mandarin, had spent several years as technical interpreters working with the Sugar Refineries Construction Bureau.

Preempting the nationalization of private enterprise, her grandfather and his partners had already liquidated their meat and livestock business. Since 1951, Motya's main occupation was as director and manager of cash transactions at the Jewish Bank in Harbin. He later took on the additional role of a shochet, performing the kosher slaughter of animals for the dwindling Jewish community, and served on its audit committee.

Mara Moustafine's family departed Harbin for Sydney in 1959. By then, the Jewish community in Harbin had dwindled to less than two hundred Jews.[135]

Moisiei Borisevich Albin

Moisiei Borisevich Albin (later known as Moisés) was born in Zhytomyr, Ukraine, in 1895, and was given the name of his maternal great-grandfather, Yaakov Moshe Bialik. Yaakov Moshe, who died two years before Moisés was born, raised the orphaned Chaim Nachman Bialik, the national poet of Israel. The poet reportedly signed the ketubah for Moisés and his wife, Evgenia (Xenia) Subkis who was born in 1899 in Odessa, the daughter of Osip Shmuel Zubkis, a jeweler, and his wife, Fanny Goldenthal.

Moisés and Xenia owned a prosperous shoe business in Odessa and lived with their son, Boris, in an upscale apartment on Deribasovskaya Street. Because of the upheavals and persecutions in Soviet Russia, their business partner, Ivan Ivanov, fled to the West through Bulgaria around 1927. The Ivanov family was never heard from again, so Moisés together with his older sister, Sonia, and Sonia's husband, Isaac Krajmalnik — some 20 years Moisés senior — deemed the eastern escape route the less perilous one.[136]

Isaac Krajmalnik's second son, Mordko (Mitya), was the first one sent to cross the dangerous Sino-Russian border to Harbin in 1927 or 1928 while still a teenager to set a foothold for the family in Manchuria. His older brother Pesaj (Pedro) Krajmalnik was sent around the same time to Mexico to see if there were possibilities for resettlement there as well. Isaac and Sonia's youngest son, Lejb (León) remained with his parents. The older Krajmalnik boys, in their late teens and early twenties, were the pioneers who were sent from Odessa to far-distant corners of the world, China and Mexico, in the hopes of finding a safe haven for the family.

In 1928, having been arrested once in Odessa and with Mitya already in Harbin, Moisés had his valuables placed inside the soles of his shoes made at his factory, traveled to Vladivostok with forged papers. From Vladivostok, he was smuggled across the border to Harbin. His wife Xenia and young son, Boris, followed, later that year. They traveled at night to reduce the chances of being apprehended. In Harbin, soon after his arrival in 1928, Moisés partnered with Fyodor (Fedya, Theodor) Volkov, a none Jewish exiled White Army cavalry junior officer, in a wholesale dairy butter and cheese business. Moises and Xenia were active in the life of the community, with Moises acting in an amateur Yiddish theater group.

Moisés and Fyodor Volkov did well by distributing milk products among dairy stores in Harbin and other towns in the region. They lived in very comfortable homes and enjoyed the best of things Harbin could offer.

But by 1933, prosperous Jews like the Albins were being kidnapped and murdered in increasing numbers in Harbin, so the family together with Mitya, departed for Yokohama, Japan in 1934 and from there sailed to Manzanillo, Mexico, arriving there in 1935.[137]

Isaac Davidovich and Asne Zoll Bedones

Among the professions that were brought to Harbin by the newcomers was shoemaking. It was in a time when shoes and boots as well as any other footwear were done by hand. Many of the Chinese were wearing shoes that were called Zuyi (Busie) meaning clothes on feet. The ethnic minorities in the area were wearing shoes made of animal or fish skin.

Cloth shoes were the most popular and were a typical representative of Chinese culture. They were comfortable, simple, durable, and flexible. Today they are called kung fu shoes.

Foreigners wore leather shoes. These had a thick sole that was attached to the main leather form with nails.

Isaac Davidovich Bedonis and his wife Asne Zoll Bedonis left Kurshan in Lithuania in 1915 and traveled on the Trans-Siberian Railway to Harbin with their daughters Sonia and Dvaira. A third daughter, Gitel, was born in Harbin in 1919.

After settling in Harbin, Bedonis, who was a shoemaker, opened a small shoe factory. The family story had it that he was in business with a Chinese person, he spoke Chinese, and they made boots for the Russian officers stationed in Harbin. Another person, Eddy Lynn traveled with the family from Kurshan and worked together with Isaac Bedonis in Harbin. He was so good at his trade that years later when he was already in Indianapolis USA, he crafted a beautiful pair of small boots for his firstborn

Fig. 13: *The Bedonis (Berman) family in Harbin*

Fig. 14: Davidovich-Bedonis – Lewanda-Estrin Funeral Harbin 1925

grandson.

Sonia, the oldest daughter, never went to school in Harbin. She studied at home with a Russian tutor. Their extended family in Harbin included the Davidovich, as well as the Lewanda-Estrin and Berman families. The Bedonis family left Harbin in 1923 on way to Japan. They sailed from Yokoyama to San Francisco on the SS "China".[138]

George Lisniasky

George Lisniasky, brother of Evgenia Lisniansky Vasserman, was a watchmaker. He learned this trade in Harbin where this occupation was quite popular and continued as a watchmaker when he migrated to California in 1925 with his wife and first son Benjamin. Benjamin who became a world-famous composer changed his name to Lees in 1930. Lees (Benjamin) was born on January 8, 1924, in Harbin. With his family, Lees immigrated to San Francisco when he was a year old and moved to Los Angeles in 1939. He started piano lessons at age 5 and began composing at 15.[139]

Fig. 15: David Vasserman Harbin 1928

Fig. 16 – Rosa Evgenia Fania Vasserman
Harbin 1920

Aleksandr Cherniavskii

Harbin could be a violent place at times. There were many political ideologies there that caused disagreements and vicious rivalries among the foreign residents. After the Bolshevik revolution and the flight amass of those who were loyal to the throne, there was a clear division between the right and the left in Harbin. There were ideological clashes in the academic circles, at workplaces, at literary meetings, at the railway workshops, in churches, and in the parks.

In the winter of 1920, the Radbil family came to Harbin to join the father's family. The entire Radbil family, including uncles, aunts, and their children with wives and husbands, met the new comers at the Harbin Railway Station.

Among the relatives was mother's grandfather Radbil, a leading Harbin architect, her grandmother, her sister Sophie, her sister's husband Dr. Samuil Cherniavskii who was the publisher-editor of the newspaper Novosti zhizni [News of Life], and their two sons Volodia [Vladimir] and Aleksandr.

In the summer of 1920 twenty years old Aleksandr Cherniavskii, was savagely murdered by a raging mob in the courtyard of the St. Nikolay Cathedral on a hill in the New City that overlooked the train station and Pristan. This event became widely known and led to an indignant response in the entire world.

Aleksandr was active in student political circles of the far-left direction. His father's newspaper was a liberal left publication, yet at the same time defending the interests of Harbin commercial circles. Both father and son were ardent supporters of the Russian "social experiment". Groups of students, to which Aleksandr belonged, organized meetings and debates about world events, and about the ways their groups could put their political program into action. They published a radical newspaper named Vpered! [Forward], calling Harbin residents to join the "glorious revolution."

The majority of the Russian political groups in Harbin consisted of supporters of restoring the Tsarist regime in Russia. They considered the Russian revolution to be a misfortune for the Russian people and the murder of the Tsarist family an unforgivable crime. They blamed the Jews for overthrowing the Royal family.

On Sunday 27 June 1920 in St. Nikolaevskii Cathedral a funeral service took place for victims of atrocities committed by Red partisans in Nikol'sk-Ussuriisk, and a huge crowd of parishioners, all Orthodox WhiteRussians, filled the entire square in front of the Cathedral. A group of students, including Aleksandr, penetrated the crowd. There was a fistfight, and the students retreated, but Aleksandr Cherniavskii was surrounded and thrown onto the pavement. When the fight ended and the crowd dispersed, he was found dead.

Fig. 17: Little Cherniavsky in Harbin 1926

Newspapers described in detail the tragic event and demanded the finding of the murderers. The meaningless murder was condemned by most political groups. The Jewish community accused the crowd of antisemitism and demanded criminal investigation and punishment of the murderers. Ten thousand people, including representatives of communities and organizations of all colors, attended the funeral of Aleksandr the victim of mass bestial hysteria.[140]

Shimon Fix

Shimon Fix was known for his good handle of numbers, his devotion to Jewish literature, to the Hebrew language, and especially to his wits and extraordinary Jewish humor. That is, the quality of being amusing or comic, which appeals to a sense of the ludicrous or absurdly incongruous especially as expressed in his writings or speech.

One who read the stories written by the great Jewish writers of that era, among the Mendale Mocher Sefarim and Sholom Aleichem, could understand the way Shimon used his pen when describing people, emotions and events.

Harbin, June 10, 1939[141]

Yesterday's visit by Joseph (Ispa) reminded me of the story

"The Lucky Man" in Jewish Life. He came in a good mood and, pleased with himself, informed me that he has found good use for his "capital," acquired as a result of three concerts in Harbin, Tientsin, and Dairen. That he is a "bourgeois," with a capital of several hundred gobi, was sniffed out by his friends, and he was showered with several tempting proposals that his money not lay inert, without movement. Incidentally, one of the friends needs a loan to buy a ticket, another immediately needs to pay off an old loan to some ornery creditor. How not help out? And he, Smetanin-Liudie, is a person by nature accommodating and compassionate, and answering with a refusal he considers "embarrassing" and "awkward," — so, he tells me, — he already gave his firm promise, and, so as not to leave people languishing in anticipation, he now hurries to them to deliver the promised

money. Only in passing did he stop by to see me, to find out if there were any letters for him — good that our house is on his way.

Having listened to this, I said to him that the financier in him is diametrically opposite to the pianist in him, and suggested that right away he read the story, "The Lucky Man" in Jewish Life, and while he was occupied, I took his savings book from him. He was confused, said that it is very embarrassing for him, and asked if it was really possible in reality for people not to return

Fig. 18: Mira Fix at home. Harbin c 1925. (courtesy of Prof. Jean Ispa)

money given to them even without a receipt, but on their honest word. I just answered him with two words: "Saintly naiveté," and to rescue him from his "awkwardness," I gave him permission to go and say that his circumstances have changed and that he may shift all responsibility from his young shoulders to me, who is damaged by the experience.

Shimon Fix:

Yesterday I received your letter, Mirusya, about your meeting with Nissan. It's vividly written. But what spilled out to me was what was unclear in your letter, probably because it was hard for you to catch in a short momentary meeting. In his defense, I must tell you that you were mistaken in your memory of the substance of the comments in Jewish Life about him. There, I remember well, it was said only that he travels around and that his words heralding the truth according to Evangelic Lutheran teachings fire up the hearts of his listeners. That he points out the laughable aspects of Jewish religious garb—about that nothing was said. To evaluate his personality, it will be interesting to see how he will fulfill the promise he gave you regarding the visa. In any case, the fact that he sent you a telegram asking you to come, that he was proud of you before his congregation, shows that nature gave him good impulses. But was it also given to him to do what is right? When he was working with me in Baku, I considered him an extraordinary fellow. If he had gone in his grandfather's, Reb Heshel of Volozhin's, footsteps, he might have occupied a greater position in the Jewish World than he occupies now. Maybe he would have become the Paris rabbi or become the director of the restored Volozhin Yeshiva in New York, just as his grandfather was a lecturer at that Yeshiva in Volozhin. Mighty oaks leave mighty offspring. But the family of the Volozhin oak was sown far across the sea-ocean by the winds of life, and it grew sprouts and sent down roots in a foreign meadow. There grew a new tree and on its branches new birds appeared who sing new songs . . . .

By the way, I mentioned aspects of Jewish prayer garb. Every day these past few days I have to put on my tallis and tefillin. Five or six days ago the son of our neighbor Shteingardt, remember, a chubby 16-year-old who just this year graduated from YMCA, fell ill with either angina or scarlet fever and after a 2-day illness, died. There, in the apartment of the deceased, a daily minyan is arranged, and to fulfill my duty as a neighbor, I go daily to pray and to add to the minyan. Incidentally, Shteingardt's house is officially registered in this deceased son's name and now the father has to inherit the property from his son. This abnormality is especially painful. The father, on the first day, in nervous agitation, wanted to, and nearly succeeded in, throwing himself out of a second-floor window — he was forcibly restrained. And now he stands every day at the bimah in front of lit candles and prays to the All-Benevolent to forgive him for his sins, — "Lord God, God of my fathers, forgive my sins, that I have sinned, that I am all-around guilty before You. You are after all a God of virtue, a God of forgiveness, a God of mercifulness towards all who call upon You."

So Shteingardt prays aloud, "Shemoneh Esreh," (the 18 prayers) and he considers himself guilty before God! And he asks for forgiveness! But what about his broken heart? What about his only son, ripped from him? The dark memories that will follow him for the rest of his life?

No, something is not as it should be. It's not, maybe, that we are guilty before God for neglecting to fulfill some Commandments, but maybe that we made a mistake even accepting the Torah, when other peoples, according to Talmudic legend, flat-out refused to take upon themselves this burden. Maybe, if the Torah had remained in Heaven, then on earth things would be better, there would be no separation between Judaism and Lutheranism.

Forgive me, Children, for the liberties I have taken. God of course is righteous and his judgment is righteous, but it is hard for me to make peace with such a reality, that a father inherits from his 16-year-old son.

The above-described sad events, the heavy send-off at the place of eternal rest, the daily prayers in the home of the resting one, brought me the following vision during sleep. I dreamt that I had died. Lying spread out on the ground, covered with a black shroud, surrounded by burning candles. The synagogue's choir boys are reading psalms over me. Reading, reading, tiring, their heads drooped and they fell asleep. And I made use of this situation—began looking through the freshly delivered morning newspaper, "Zarya"—and had the great pleasure of reading for myself an obituary concerning my own death, in which the obituary's author colorfully describes that, as they say, an

Fig. 19: Mira on a tree stump in front of
Fix house. (courtesy of Prof. Jean Ispa)

Fig. 20: Basil the Chinese cook.
The Fix house is on the right

honorable Harbin old-timer, who for many years directed a large transport agency, and in recent years was occupied with literary work, has died. Jewish Life has lost a valued colleague, and so on. My reading was interrupted by Cantor Zlatkin's slow chanting:

El Malei Rachamim — God full of mercy…

And I in full heart cried out to him: "Don't disturb me. I'm reading!" and — woke up. So, for now, I am still alive, and given that, am enclosing a check from Yokohama Specie Bank (N 1262) for 60 d. $.

Harbin, June 14, 1939

My Dears![142]

Starting from Passover, except for the first two days, I felt, to put it mildly, in a state of some malaise: my seasonal illness — bronchitis. It seems that I caught a bad cold, and I had great difficulty breathing, so much so that I even decided that it was time already to run over to my dear-medic — feldsher Provatorov with his attributes and equipment — cups, medicines, shots, I refused the last of these, and so on and so on.

Now all this is in the past and I am on the path to getting better. True, Provatorov says that I should postpone writing to you for 2 or 3 days, but I already lack patience. Do you know the story about the peasant who was sentenced to 100 lashes with a whip for some sort of crime? When they were executing this punishment and the number of lashes had already exceeded 50, this peasant lifted his head, pulled some bread out from his pocket, and started gnawing on it. Everyone was amazed. To the question as to how, in the midst of being lashed with a whip, he could even think of eating, the peasant said, "What? Why? Just because you are going to be spending the whole day crisscrossing my body with a whip, — I won't have eaten?

So am I.- And so what if my raspy breathing lasts, God knows for how long, then I won't write? If only there weren't such a bad spring here then my malaise would pass more quickly, but as is known to you, here the spring is terrible. Pillars of dust swirl all day and all night and obscure the sky. Look outside through our window: here our neighbor homeowners, also coughing from swallowed dust, are going around, inspecting their "estate" — what kind of damage did the wind do last night, where are chimneys broken, where did stucco fall off, and so forth. Here visible through the window are three wandering geese, blown in by the wind. They wander around pitiable, sadly, gloomily stretching their long necks forward, raising their heads and eyes to Heaven, their honking as if announcing their protest and complaint that it was their fate to have been born here near the Gobi or Shamo, from where so much desert dust is carried, rather than on Waikiki Beach, where they could be swimming and diving, and even if a wave picked them up, it would be like being pushed up on a swing, and then it would be the opposite, from one's soul only one cry could escape — "delight!"

In any case, I still reside on the shores of the Sungari and therefore maybe I should have delayed writing this letter for a couple of days, but I was very touched that you sent me a postcard via airmail.

Here I took a little break, or more accurately I had to since my dear-medic came to check on my health — by the way, each of his "check-ins" gets paid for in rubles. I asked him how I can get out of my situation: on the one hand, "Yetzer H'ara" evil inclination, pushes me to write, but on the other hand might not writing stress my still-weakened system? The verdict of dear-medic was as follows: drink a glass of coffee and a wineglass of cognac. I did just that and now I am writing to you with the support of these two companions. Actually, writing about nothing in particular. Just to chat.

Do you remember "Vasilii?" This reminded me of this fact:

You, probably, remember, amidst our photographs, the picture of a stately woman in a large wide-brimmed hat. Her name is Celia; she is the daughter of Leib Beshkin. She used to tell about how, after she met her man they were betrothed to one another, those present decided that they should leave the young people alone so they could get to know each other more closely and intimately. And so, it was arranged that the two of them would set off on foot in the direction of the Rizhskaya Train Station — this was almost 2 kilometers from the apartment. The whole way they walked in silence, not spilling a single word. In this manner, they came to the railway tracks where freight cars are hooked together in preparation for the remainder of their journey. In silence they decided that this was a natural end-point and, still silent, decided that they should turn back. They did so, and the whole way back they walked just as silently. It was only when they were right at the apartment building that the recommended fiancé spoke: "Did you see that on the train cars it was written: '40 horses and 6 people?'"

Osya Platt is still at a crossroads. For now, he can't go anywhere. He is studying with Kistrutsky — every day he has an English lesson and among other plans, has distant plans to maybe sooner or later land in America.

Yesterday, I interrupted my jottings because Mr. Smetanin (referring to Joseph Ispa) came over and interrupted me. He told me about the incredible difficulties he is having organizing a concert, but these are all gradually being overcome. He is preparing a packet of posters, notices, programs, flyers, and so forth for you, so I won't start describing them. I'll chat with you a little more and with that, end this letter. By the way, my health is better today. What helped, I think, is not the medicines, but the "gogol-mogul" poured into me according to Berta Solomonovna's recipe. I also have to give credit to the new tenant,

Natalia Solomonovna Levitina. She attended to me like a sister of mercy: she went to the market to buy chicken for me, pressured "Vasilii" to cook well and frequently came to me to ask how I'm feeling, if I'm better, etc. Sometimes this burdened me. Of course, if it had been Tatiana Naumovna, her expressions of care would have been intolerable, but this one is immeasurably more sensitive than she. That is why I was surprised that she didn't understand that her questions were over the top, excessive. In any case, one can't deny her [Levitina's] sincerity, though she says that she gave me all this on credit, given she thinks that sooner or later she will fall ill—this apparently happens often.

Here for you is a picture of today's meeting this morning on the kitchen's threshold:

No sooner had she and I exchanged "good morning" than:

She—It seems you are in a bad mood today?

I—No, I'm OK.

She—You look somehow out of sorts.

I—No, I'm OK.

She—But it seems to me that you still don't feel very well.

I—No, I'm OK.

She—Does anything hurt?

I—No, I'm OK.

She—Maybe you are tired?

I—I am in a good mood, I feel great, nothing hurts, I am not at all tired. And—goodbye, I am in a hurry to write a letter to my daughter. Excuse me.

Abram Mihailovich Kochanovskii (Nelly's father) is seriously ill. Recently he moved back from Qiqihara because of his illness. Misha immediately took him to Peking to the Rockefeller Institute. There they examined him and sent him back home. Now he lays bedridden in the Shifrin's home. Last week I went to see him and am thinking of visiting him a second time this

week, if the weather improves, permitting me to go out. When I was there with him last time I left with a heavy feeling, though during the minutes when he feels better, he tries to joke around as before. My impression is that the Angel of Death has taken a firm seat on him from above, has set a bridle tightly in his mouth, and resolutely holds the reins.

Now I've gotten to know his son-in-law Shifrin better. He made a good impression on me. That my impression is correct is evident if only by the fact that he nervously flinches when Tatiana Naumovna starts talking with the tongue of Yente Telebende.

Our milkmaid has a son, an 18-year-old fellow. He rode by motorcycle to the mountain. At the viaduct, he ran into a car or bus and the bump threw him off his motorcycle. As a result, he lays in the hospital. The bridge of his nose is broken, his face is disfigured. His mother's state of mind is the same as mine was when Sasha had the same kind of meeting with a car right before his exams at Commerce School, also at a viaduct. I think he still has a little scar under his left eye. "Each time at this same place."

Why hasn't Tanya written in a while? She should know that it's because of her that I worked hard studying English so that I could read her letters. And I continue to learn from her letters because she writes well, with a good literary style. In English, I am illiterate only halfway: I don't know how to write, but I can tell what is well-written and what is poorly written. Tanya's letters belong to the first category.

Kiss Ninochka. I would have liked to write to her, but I can't right now. The cat is snuggled up tightly against my arm, making it impossible to write. Will write another time. Papa

Harbin, March 26, 1939

Darling,[143]

Yesterday the sun came out a little; there appeared the smell of spring. Coincidentally, Mr. Liulkin agitated me to buy a different spring hat. I told him that though I would not commit myself, I was not averse to considering it if, at a reasonable price, I could sell last year's hat. We looked outside and, in fact, saw and heard a junkman: "Old things buy." I took out my hat, and showed it to the "merchant." That one looked at it and asked, "Duōshǎo? [How much?]".

"Five tsien," answered I.

"Meiyou [No, I don't have that]," responded the Chinese man. — "One tsien."

Then, so as not to err, the Chinese man took the hat in his hands, turned it inside out, rudely crumpled it and cleverly said, "Such rubbish buy meiyou [not]" flapped his hand and left. Unintendedly, I remained with my [old] hat. But it's fine; fortunately, again we've been pulled to cold weather, so this issue can be postponed.

Yesterday on our line's sidewalk, I bumped into the measured marching steps of the Old (in the literal sense) Guard,

Fig. 21: Mira Fix with friends on a sleigh. Harbin 1938. (courtesy of Prof. Jean Ispa)

as represented by Madame Pechnikova and Madame Levitina (our new tenants). The latter, it appeared, was happy to see me and told me that this day God had led her to witness some evil business: one of the Japanese men, in our house, having bathed, emerged from the bathroom in Adam's suit. Madame Pechnikova shared Madame Levitina's outrage, and in a chorus of questions they asked for my advice — what should they do if this happens again? I said that in such situations they must be guided by the Biblical directive, "an eye for an eye," that is, one should obey only the sixth. Specifically, said I, — keep a watch out for when this gentleman passes through the corridor, undress, and stand side-by-side in front of his eyes in Eve's suit — that will be your revenge. But they, it seems, did not understand the bite in my advice.

Harbin, July 25, 1939

The city of Harbin, 9th of Av (Tisha B'Av) 1939/5699.

My dears! A moment of silence![144]

Do you remember that terrible day, exactly three years ago, when at 5:00 in the morning, a messenger came to call us to the Jewish Hospital? Do you remember that our Mishka the dog, who never ventures from our yard, wouldn't leave us, running after us right up to the hospital building? Mishka, with his animal instinct, sensed death. Only we, with our human blindness, didn't comprehend yet the dreadful seriousness of the moment.

I remember how, arriving at the hospital, I pulled the doctor aside and asked him to tell me the true situation. The answer was: "Serious, hopeless." I came up to you, and to the silent question in your eyes, I answered, "Serious, but not hopeless." I lied. The truth arrived in a few hours. And today, on the third anniversary, I went to look truth in the eye. Of course, I didn't see anything. Just a little mound of earth, overgrown with grass — but how many memories it awakened! You, children, are tied

Fig. 22: Evgenia Fix by the Sungari River. (courtesy of Prof. Jean Ispa)

closer to Mama in blood, but spiritually—so I think—she and I are more closely tied. Each of you lived with her 17—18 years, of which the first third should be discounted, for the first years are years of pre-consciousness, whereas I spent 40 conscious years with her, from 1896 to 1936.

I remember her as a 16-year-old girl, a dreamer tearing herself from Volozhin's provincial ways. She sought "enlightenment, education." These were the soaring words of the Jewish street in those days. Back then I gave her the name "Hope Dreamer," and that is how I addressed the envelopes of all of my letters to her. Individual episodes of our life stand before my eyes. At times it feels to me that this was very long ago, while for you, children, this tale probably seems from times prehistoric. And so, many, many years ago, in times for you prehistoric, when the author of these lines was himself still a youth, cheek fuzz just beginning to break through, I remember her as my youthful, life-loving, sparkling peer. We played in the city garden, she taking off into a run around the big fountain, and when I would catch her by her braid or by the edge of her dress, she would cry out, a ringing shriek like a little trapped animal. Then she became a woman, a mother, a cultured person, and most importantly, a good person.

Over 40 years have passed since that time when, playing in the city park in Kovno, we sang: "Little birds fly high, and we even higher." Now fate wills her peer to stand over the little mound that covers her dust. Where did they go — the wide hopes of Hope Dreamer to spread her wings and rise higher than the birds? Why is man born with clenched fists, but dies with open palms? Because, at birth, man is thinking that, as the sweep of an eagle in flight, he will take all into his hands, but when he dies, he opens his hands — here, take this, he says, I am giving you back all of your world. I came with nothing and leave with nothing, and in the middle of this "with nothing" — a big hunk of vanity of vanities.

Today is the 9th of Av, by custom a day of broad attendance at the cemetery. While I stand over Mama's grave, I see in the distance of group of people, and the Kaddish service for a dear one reaches me. Some kind of professional Jew with a wedge-shaped goatee is walking around the cemetery together with the relatives of the dead, his voice that of a bleating goat, pronouncing the words of Kaddish.

It was my turn. "Will you allow me to lead Kaddish for your deceased spouse?" he asked in ingratiating tones.

"Not necessary."

The Professional looked at me with surprise, but I, so as not to sound like a renegade, explained that the deceased has a son who does all that is necessary so that his mother's soul may rest. And to myself, I thought — what point is there in reading these tired old words of Kaddish, in pronouncing some kind of words in Aramaic that we do not understand, that have no connection to the specific situation, that were born in a distant time somewhere in Babylon, created for a forgotten event? To think that one can pay one's debt to the deceased in this way –profanity. But this philosophy also does not bring relief. Only this is true:

"Short is man's life,
And narrow is the corner
Of the earth
Wherein he dwells."
"A moment of silence...... Papa."

Alexander I. Pogrebetsky

Hobbies such as stamp collecting were quite popular among members of the Jewish community. One unusual hobby was that of Alexander Pogrebetsky who collected Chinese and Asian banknotes.

Alexander Iliych Pogrebetsky was a Russian economist, financier, and businessman who was head of the board of directors of the Chinese Eastern Railway Company and an authority on numismatics.

Alexander Pogrebetsky was born in Irkutsk, Russia in 1891. He trained as an economist and financier.[145] Pogrebetsky was director of the Department of Finance of "Centrosoyus" for the district of Irkutsk, Zabaikal, and Iakutsk provinces and Mongolia. Later he was the interim finance manager of the Office of the Government of the Far East and a member of the Finance Commission and the National Constituent Assembly of the Far Eastern Republic (existed April 1920 to November 1922).[146] He was a member of the Irkutsk Political Centre[147] an independent political group in Irkutsk during the Russian Civil War.

Around 1920, he relocated to Harbin, where he became head of the board of directors of the Chinese Eastern Railway Company. He wrote financial articles for the Russian-language Vestnik Man'chzhurii (Manchuria Monitor). Around 1935 he moved to Tientsin, where he was part owner of a private bank.

He then moved to Shanghai, where he traded as the China Trading & Investment Company.

He was closely involved with Jewish organizations during his time in China. He was a council member of the Jewish People's Bank in Harbin (1925-34) and on the council of the Jewish Commercial Bank (Harbin, 1929-34). He was a member of the Tientsin Jewish Club "Kunst" and the Shanghai Jewish Club.

Around 1948, Pogrebetsky emigrated to Palestine. He died in Tel-Aviv in 1952 of liver cancer.[148]

Pogrebetsky spent much time searching for banknotes and was able to create an important collection of Chinese and Asian banknotes and coins. He published one of the first books on Chinese banknotes. In the 1960s or 70s, part of the collection was donated to the Smithsonian Museum in Washington D.C.. The rest of the collection remained in family hands until 2015 when it was sold in two sales by Archives International Auctions.[149]

Shimon Fix

Harbin saw good and bad times. When life was stable people were planning vacations and trips to summer resorts for the coming summer months. Winters were deadly cold but this did not stop the inhabitants of the growing city to look for cultural events and dining in the many types of restaurants that were open for gastronomical pleasures in the heart of the Pristan part of Harbin.

For Shimon Fix the summer presented outdoors fun. In a 1930 letter to his son Sasha, who was by now in America, he writes that at the beginning of the summer, he was expecting to go to a dacha, "but circumstances are such that for now, we are all staying home in the city. I had wanted to reserve a room in Ertsedzyantsah so that from time to time we could go there to relax, but for one decent room, they charge 200 yen. Expensive. Besides, this summer it is not hot at all here and our little garden is blooming gorgeously. There are the ridges of flowers that you planted. We call them "Sasha's ridges."[150]

Shimon Fix did not write but only suggested in just a few words about the impending changes that loomed over Manchuria as the Japanese were ready to invade the region. What is very interesting is that in all his letters, he never mentioned the Japanese occupation of Harbin, nor the impact it had on his life.

Rinia Zyskind (nee Slavutin)

Rinia Zyskind, nee Slavutin, was born in Harbin Manchuria on February 10, 1925, and there she and her family stayed for 10 years. She enjoyed school but only attended 4 classes — lower prep, middle prep, higher prep, and first grade. It was a Russian school where a hot lunch of borscht, piroshki — "katas", an egg-shaped ground meat pie covered with thick baked dough, was served.[151]

"We had a big family of aunts and uncles and met every Sunday at Grandma's place where we went by horse and carriage. I remember my grandmother as an old woman, hard-working with a stooped back — she died when she was only 56. Grandfather went blind and I remember as a very little girl taking him for a walk. These were maternal grandparents. I never met the paternal ones.

At home life was busy. There was always someone living with us — Grandma, and as she was religious we had a kosher house. Sometimes one of mother's sisters stayed with us.

The sicknesses I remember were measles because I had big complications with my eyes and ears and was in a lot of pain. Also Scarlett fever — I was about 5-6 years old then. Since it was very contagious, I was at home but isolated in one room and only a professional nurse was allowed to be with me. The rest of the family only waved through the window. Don't know how long it lasted — it felt like an eternity, but I was very sick.

Father had a stationery shop — everything for school but not books. The shop burned down in 1935. Since the Japanese came to Harbin — they were arrogant and cruel — and there was not much of a future for white people — father decided to move to Dairen.

Our home in Harbin was small and cozy. I don't know how we all fitted there. There was a big wood stove in the dining room, one that was built into the wall up to the ceiling. Something you see in movies about Russia. I used to love standing next to it warming myself. The kitchen also had a wood stove. I don't know how they used to make such beautiful cakes. There were no frigs or even ice chests but everyone had huge cellars full of home preserves: pickled cucumbers, red and green tomatoes, sauerkraut, jams — all varieties, beetroot for Pesach borsht, and many more. I remember my mother making her own noodles for soup and laying the dough on a bed to dry so she could roll it up and cut it."

The jam-making was a big event. We all went to the orchards on a Sunday and picked whatever and brought back bags that weighed about 40 pounds each. Picking of

Fig. 23: Zyskind — Luba nee Bododavkin Berman. Harbin, outside Jacob Slavutin's stationary shop

plums stayed clearly in my memory. The taste of these enormous plums was very good and we could eat them until the stomach ached. Then we came home by the horse and carriage. The preserving was done in bulk and put into enormous tins. Then the Chinese man would come and solder it up for winter. It was always so delicious. And nothing ever went bad.

For Pesach, there was a great activity and for weeks there were dishes to be changed, cakes to be baked. 500 eggs were bought for the 7 days—sometimes it was not enough. Sponge cakes took 25-30 eggs and there were many sponges made.

Shopping was done at home. Chinese peddlers brought live chickens, fruit, and vegetables across their shoulders in baskets hanging from both ends.

It was a good life until 1935.

Our vacations were always in summer. The whole family moved for three months to the other side of the river[152]. Always the same house, the same landlord, the same daughter to play with us. We all loved those times.

Father commuted in the evening over the river being rowed by a Chinese man, always the same company—they were called "Lev" the lions. In winter the Sungari River froze and we used to go skating on it. Also on this same river, the real Russian people cut out holes in the ice and took a plunge on Russian Christmas. It was a big celebration with vodka and everything else.

Father was going to wish the Russians Christmas greetings and he would eat a thick piece of butter so that he would not get drunk with all the vodka.

After Abe, my eldest brother matriculated he went to Dairen to look for work. Harbin was hopeless after the Japanese came. He got a job in a fur shop. Soon after we all went to Dairen.

Father rented a room in a hotel called El Dorado. It was a summer resort and the summer season was full for 3 months. But the rest of the year most of the rooms were empty and business was slow. My mother worked very hard those few years we were there. She helped the chef in the kitchen who had a violent temper — it was nothing for him to throw a pound of butter into the fire out of spite. Poor mother was supposed to keep quiet.

Nathan my second older brother and I went to the American school and it took us one and a half hours each way and we changed trams. The nuns were very good to us and never tried to convert us. These years were extra happy for me.

Our relatives came to stay with us for most of the summers — Grandma and Aunty Sara from Harbin. And the cousins Toochinsky kids from Shanghai. Our hotel was not far from the beach but to get to the beach you had to walk through a park and in Spring it was full of blossom trees which made a lovely unforgettable picture.

I don't remember how many years we lived there. Then we moved and were closer to Luba, Vera and their families. The financial situation was not great and I remember when we waited to visit Luba one Sunday while we were still in the hotel, but on counting our money one penny was lacking for the 5 tram fares and we could not go. That hotel was in a place called Hashigaura. Then we moved to Nanzan Roku and that was walking distance to school.

The school was small — about 200 hundred students but the atmosphere was one of a big family, a very friendly family.

When the family moved to Shanghai, we found a flat — a tiny one of two rooms, tiny kitchen and bathroom, one bedroom, one lounge, and not only the 5 of us lived there but most of the war also Rivas family of four. The men occupied the floor, and mother, Vera, Riva, and I slept in a double bed and across the bed with our legs hanging over into chairs.

It was very difficult but we all survived.

Abraham Shichman

Storytelling is the interactive art of using words and actions to reveal the elements and images of a story while encouraging the listener's imagination.

History, however, depends on the story which should be as close to the reality of the time as possible. When the story is told it should minimize the distance between the reader and the space and time of the occurrence of the story.

Storytelling is the thread connecting history, memory, and imagination, piecing together alternate truths, unraveling forgotten memories, and making meaning for the teller and his audience.[153]

Hayden White writes of history as the telling of a story, a representation, and interpretation of the past, utilizing language to help people make meaning for their world.[154] He introduces the notion that the power to shape history has been removed from the hands of the historians and placed with the people who lived through the event — the silenced victims, the defeated — and their descendants.

The representations of history, he says, repeat, in almost every detail, the processes of fiction. … History, memory, and language intersect so precisely as to be almost indistinguishable: the 'origins' of history, as recovered through memory, are encoded in language, and each of these three moments becomes a condition for the others.[155]

Zvia Bowman's grandfather Abraham Shichman was born in Odessa in 1876. He died in Nathanya, Israel on June 6, 1962. Her grandmother Sophie (Sluva) Stukina was born in Odessa in 1885. She died in Beijing on March 3, 1962. She was buried in the Tianjin Jewish cemetery.

They had two children. Zvia Bowman's father Isaac (Yitzhak) Shichman was born in Harbin on October 17, 1908. He died in

Jerusalem on June 19, 1988. His sister Fruma was born on July 4, 1910, in Harbin. She died on January 27, 2002, in New Jersey, USA.[156]

Zvia Bowman's grandparents moved from Odesa to Harbin following the pogroms of 1905 in Russia and Ukraine. They took the Trans—Siberian railway to Harbin and settled down in a small adobe house on 15 Konnya Street in the Pristan district of the city (today, Daoli District). The street name was changed from Russian to Chinese to Waigouwudao Jie around 1925. It was then changed again to Dongfeng Jie.

grandfather Abraham Shichman would go back periodically to Russia and bring back caviar, fine clothes, and other items that were not readily available in Harbin. However, after the Bolshevik Revolution of 1917, he was not able to travel to Russia anymore. His savings in Russian rubles became valueless and the family had to find a different way of making money. The enterprising grandmother, Sophie Stukina, always liked nice clothes and hats. She opened a shop selling Western dresses and coats in Harbin.

Zvia's father, Isaac Shichman, was learning Russian and Yiddish in Harbin but his mother wanted him to learn English and French as well. She felt that Harbin was too provincial for her family. When Isaac Shichman was nine, his parents sent him to a French boarding school in Tianjin. It was run by Jesuit priests. They followed him to Tianjin a few years later and his grandmother opened two successful Western clothes shops in the British concession area of town.

Fig. 24: Isaac (Yitzhak) Shichman in Harbin

Isaac was a very bright student

and when he became a teenager, his mother sent him to the British School. Besides doing well academically, Isaac was also a very good sportsman. He excelled in swimming, boxing, rowing, and different ball games in his school. After graduation, he started working for a Jewish furrier firm. He was sent to Shandong Province to buy furs from the Chinese huntsmen. After weeks or months of buying, he had to oversee Chinese workers who would transport the furs back. There the furs were cleaned and processed before being made into fur coats that were sent to Europe or the USA.

Isaac was very popular among the young Jewish set and would regularly go to dances and parties. In the summer, many young Jews and other foreign residents would go to the Beidaihe seaside resort in Hebai.

However, their carefree life ended with the Japanese occupation of China in July 1937. Zvia's father and grandparents were stateless residents in China and could continue operating their businesses. In his thirties, Isaac opened his own fur and fine clothes shops. This coincided with more Japanese officers frequenting Western shops and buying Western dresses and fur coats for their wives or mistresses.

In 1943, Isaac hired a young Chinese accountant, Dora Wen, to work in his Beijing shop. Isaac and Dora fell in love and got married after the Japanese surrendered in September 1945.

With the Japanese occupation, Abraham Shichman the grandfather, who worked as an accountant for the Chinese railway company, lost his job.

In 1957, Isaac's shops were nationalized by the Chinese authorities forcing him to become a teacher of English and French in the Polish, Pakistani, and other foreign embassies in Beijing.

Harbin was always and remained the home. It was where the family gathered and started a new life in China of all places.

Zvia wrote that Abraham Shichman emigrated to Israel in 1947 and was hoping that her father and grandmother would follow him. Most Jews started leaving China in the late 40's and throughout the 50's. Zvia, her elder sister, and her brother all attended the diplomatic school at the Soviet Embassy in Beijing. They were finally able to leave China in November 1967 during the Cultural Revolution. Isaac obtained a visa to go to France but once they reached Hong Kong, he went to the Israeli Embassy and asked to go to Israel. They arrived in Israel in April 1968 and first settled in Nathanya before moving to Jerusalem. Zvia's mother was among the very first lecturers of Mandarin Chinese at the Hebrew University of Jerusalem. Zvia's family was the last Jewish family to leave China.

Keila and Dovid Waddel

The Trans-Siberian Railway and the construction of the Chinese Eastern Railway that pushed south into Manchuria presented a new route for the Jews who were fleeing pogroms in Europe. It was a new direction that took them east and to China. No one in his wilder dreams would have predicted that the sleeping dragon would conceal its streaming fires and let foreign people, barbarians as the Chinese referred to all strangers, settle in its space.

In this new and exotic, although almost barren region, they put their old stories into memories and created new ones.

What is apparent are the destinations all members of the large family chose in dispersing from Harbin and from China. Harbin seemed to be the magnet that pulled everyone into her, and then, at various times, people continued on to spaces and geographies that touched the four corners of the world.

Myra Waddel has tried to reconstruct his family's past by putting together bits and pieces of information he heard or came across in family stories.[157]

He starts with his great-grandparents, Keila and Dovid. The family is thought to have moved to Harbin in China in 1914 or 1915. Keila and Dovid died in Harbin, sometime in the 1920s. The cemetery in which they were buried is no longer in existence as it underwent "deep burial" as the Chinese say, between 1958 and 1962.

When Myra Waddel tells his family's past, there are questions he has but seldom answers. He is not sure, for example, what was the reason for his great-grandparent's move to Harbin. Was it World War l and/or the building of the Trans-Siberian Railway and the addition of the Chinese Eastern Railway? The railways, he concludes, would have made traveling between Irkutsk and Hailar and Harbin much easier.

Praskovja (Pasha), probably born in the 1860s, married David Binder and died in Harbin, to where they probably moved from Hailar, in 1937 or 1938. They died there—Pasha on February 16, 1948, and David a year later on April 28, 1949. One property they owned was burnt by the Japanese but they also owned other properties. They actually owned about half the street, including an apartment in which Boris and Chaya lived. Pasha and David were in their 80s when they died.

Rachelle, their daughter, was born in 1884, in Irkutsk, Siberia. She married Shimon Litvin and they had five children, two of whom moved to Israel, Leah and Chaim who was known as Tima. They moved there in 1963 with Rachelle, Tima's wife Rina, Chaya and her two sons, David and Yosef.

Rachelle and Shimon's eldest daughter, Bluma, who was a pharmacist in Harbin, returned to the USSR in 1937 with her husband, Mordechovitsch, and two daughters, Katie and Margaret. Mordechovitsch was imprisoned by the KGB. Bluma was forced to hide somewhere near Moscow but still managed to work as a pharmacist. One of her daughters, Katie-Keila or Margaret, not sure which, married an Armenian, went to live in his country and they had a son. Katie's son was Artur and Margaret's was called Valeri.[158] Bluma relocated to Israel but in 1967, during the Six-Day War, she panicked and returned to Russia.[159]

Rachelle's second daughter, Leah, also studied as a pharmacist in Harbin and then returned to Hailar where she married Leib Apatov, "the best

Fig. 25: Waddel – Tima Litvin & Abraham Usherovich

tailor of men's suits in Hailar". They had a son, David, and lived in the same house as her parents and Chaim. It was a large house with eight rooms, with a separate apartment for the Apatovs and they all lived there in harmony, So the story goes.

Tima, having been accused of being a bad influence on his classmates, left school at age 14 and started working, first with odd jobs, then reselling livestock. Very soon, he knew enough Chinese and Mongolian to go into business for himself. His uncle gave him three thousand rubles and he became involved in the wholesale buying and selling of cattle—he was a successful businessman.

Rachelle's youngest daughter, Dina, left China in 1958 so that she, her husband, Abraham, and her two children, Ilya-Ilusha and Sima, could live in Melbourne, Australia. They went from Hailar to Harbin, then to Tianjin, and then to Hong Kong on their way to Australia. Dina remembers her mother talking about life in Irkutsk.[160] Rachelle died in her mid-80s in Israel in March 1969.

Moshe, moved to Switzerland at the time of the Russian Revolution. It would have been at about 1917. He was a watchmaker and jeweler and married Maria, who was also born in Russia and who followed him to Switzerland. Moshe spoke German or Yiddish. They had no children. In 1946, Moshe wrote to Boris and, because Boris had died by then, the letter was passed to Dina who replied and continued to be in touch with Moshe and Maria for several years.

Boris (also known as Berl, which is Yiddish for a bear, was born in 1886/7 in Kolno. He married his niece, Chaya, in about 1921, in Harbin. They had two sons, both born in Hailar — David in 1931 and Yosef in 1933. They had a farm in Hailar.

Towards the end of 1932, the Japanese occupied Hailar and the Manchurian territory, and following a severe bombardment by the Japanese during the second Sino/Japanese war, their farm went up in flames.

When Boris was murdered by beheading in Hailar on August 9, 1945, Chaya and her two sons were left homeless and were forced to move to Harbin. There Chaya worked hard to support her children. Joseph graduated from elementary school and went on to trade school, where he learned metalwork and welding.

After the establishment of the State of Israel, the family decided to emigrate and, after many trials and tribulations, they left in 1950, to live in Israel. They sailed for three months in very crowded conditions. The ship carried soldiers, young children, the elderly, and the sick.

Riva had at least one daughter, Chaya, born in Irkutsk in about 1901. She probably had two others. Riva didn't leave Irkutsk. Chaya died in Israel on June 4, 1989, at about 88 years of age.

On August 9, 1945, there was a horrific massacre at Hailar

in Manchuria, of citizens of the U.S.S.R. This was done at the instance of the Commander of the Kwantung Army. Those murdered were not charged with any offense, but the reason given for the murders was that the people might carry on espionage or sabotage against the Japanese Army.

On this date, among those beheaded, were Boris, youngest son of Keila and Dovid, Shimon Litvin, their son-in-law, and also their grandson-in-law, Leib Apatov.[161]

August 9, 1945, was the day the Japanese surrendered!

John Block

The city of Harbin was largely populated by Russian people and those who were part of the countries that were under Soviet control. During the Revolution, remnants of the White Russian Army had fled to the city for safety, where they stayed and raised their families. Other refugees had come over the years. The city had grown into an international center.[162]

While there were many Chinese shops and stores, the larger businesses, department stores, and the city government were all Russian. The exception was the Mayor, who was Chinese. It should be noted here that the Chinese took over the city council only in 1926, 28 years after the establishment of the city. Some of the Russians had become Chinese citizens so they could legally remain there, even though racially they were Caucasian.

The population of the city of Harbin was largely Caucasian, though located right in the heart of Manchuria. There were Americans, English, Germans, and many others of European descent.

John Block remembered that his brother Jake and he liked to go to watch ice skating and listen to the skaters speaking English. They would stand by the railing and listen to them, then say to each other, "Someday we may be speaking that language."

When we arrived in Harbin, John Block writes, other people we knew were already living there; at least our parents knew them. One such person was Henry Schmidt, who had lived with us for several years in Siberia. He was one who worked for our family and had lived with us. He was to have been drafted into the Soviet Armed Services, a circumstance he did not relish. Just about the time for him to be inducted, he escaped into China and settled there. I hadn't known what had happened to him until we came to Harbin, even though most everybody else knew. He had fled first to the Amur region, together with his sister's family, the Isaac Warkentins, and with some other families. They escaped across the river into China and preceded as a group to Harbin.

"We arrived in the city at about nine in the morning and found Henry Schmidt there to meet us. He had already rented a house large enough to accommodate three of our families. We got settled right away in our new "temporary" quarters, but our stay in Harbin was to last just eleven months.

Having a house to stay in was a great relief for my sister, Anna, for she was close to delivering her fourth daughter. The baby was born on the very first night we were in Harbin. They named her Mary."[163]

Anna amazed us all by surviving that rigorous journey, and delaying the birth of the baby until then. There were two midwives among our traveling group, and they had stood by her during the rugged bus trip and now assisted with her delivery.

The next day our men hurried out to find jobs. We were surprised at how fast they found employment. Some of our men found jobs on a construction project, and even though I was only fifteen, I was hired along with the rest. It was heavy work, carrying buckets of concrete mix and sometimes pushing wheelbarrows of heavy cement. I worked there for about a week.

Meanwhile, Dad had spoken to our landlord about finding suitable jobs for "the boys," meaning my brother Jake and me. He was told there was a confectionery that had advertised for a delivery boy. He gave us the address and directions how to get there.

When we got to the street, it was lined with shop after shop. We thought we had found the right confectionery shop. Dad took me in there and asked if they had advertised for a delivery boy. It turned out they hadn't advertised, so we must have gone to the wrong address.

However, the manager interviewed us a little and said, "Yes, we can use a delivery boy."

So, after a brief interview, I was hired on the spot. On the same day, Jake was hired as a delivery boy at a restaurant. In the evening of the same day, I stood outside the big gate that was closed for the night. In the big gate was a small walk-through door that we used in the evening; I stood and watched the crowd on the street. To my surprise I saw my brother, Jake, coming toward me. He told me that he was working in a restaurant, but now was going home for the night since he had not prepared to stay there. I, too, would have liked to go home, but I needed to be ready for delivery early in the morning. I just encouraged him to move on before it got too dark. He was twelve years old in a strange city. I had reached the ripe age of fifteen.

I worked at the confectionery for more than nine months, at the lucrative wage of six yen per month, or $1.50 in American money; I think Jake received four yan. We got our food at our jobs and lived in a dormitory. I lived with another delivery boy and two men in a small room. We didn't get paid much, but at least we paid our way and weren't an expense to our parents.

After some time on this job, one of the boys quit, so I asked the employer whether they might hire my brother, Jake, who was now twelve. He was still working at the restaurant, delivering meals to people who called in orders. Mr. Azadovsky, the owner of the confectionery, was glad to hear about my brother and hired him. Thus Jake and I got to work at the same place, sleep in the same room, and, for the last three months, we worked together.

In the 1920s wages were very low, so for a family man, it was very difficult to make ends meet. Henry Rogalsky, my brother-in-law, worked in a sausage factory for 15 yan per month. It was hard for a family with four children. They had to draw on what reserves they had brought along from Russia.

I received a raise, from six to nine yan per month. Our boss and his wife were pleased with our work, which wasn't that easy. We had to rise early, before dawn, package up our merchandise, and get going. We delivered small orders to residences and larger orders — whole baskets full of things — to stores. In the evenings we delivered "bubliki" (something like bagels). They were strung up, one dozen to a string. We didn't need a fitness program to keep us in good shape because all of our deliveries were made on foot. It wasn't easy, but it was interesting. We would walk long distances around the city.

Besides the early morning and evening deliveries to stores, we delivered cakes during the day as orders came in. The Russian people give gifts on special days. In the Russian Orthodox Church, children are named on the eighth day after birth, at which time they are baptized by immersion. Therefore, they commemorate "name days" instead of birthdays. It is customary to send gifts, often cakes and wines.

Their cakes (torte) were much like our cakes here. They came in a thin cardboard box, under which we placed a plywood board to help us balance the box on our arms, carrying it on one arm and balancing the box with the other hand. Since most of these were gifts, they usually were a surprise. People felt good about the gift, and we felt good about getting a tip for the delivery.

We learned to facilitate the receiving of a tip by asking the receiver for the plywood board. They took the cake at the front door and carried it off to the kitchen or dining room while we waited for the board. When they returned to give the board back to us, they usually brought a tip with them. If we didn't ask for the board, it would have seemed natural for us to simply hand them the cake and leave without a tip. After all, we had walked a long way to bring them a present. Mr. Azadovsky discouraged us from asking for the little board because he did not want to appear cheap, but for us it was rewarding. Mrs. Azadovsky was very kind to us. She treated us more like friends instead of mere delivery boys.

One of the senior clerks in the business, Vera, had been a professor of German at the Moscow University before the revolution. She always encouraged us in our work. It was she who usually sent us on our way when we were delivering special orders. She always made sure we knew where to find the address and in many other ways showed her concern for us. In fact, she treated Jake and me like her sons. However, she would not speak German to us. When her husband was killed in the First World War, she took a vow never to speak German again. It would have been much easier for us, because even though we, and our parents, were born in Russia, it was always a second language to us. We had always lived in a German settlement, and most of our schooling was in German. She would have liked to speak German but was true to her vow.

One Sunday afternoon, balancing a large cake on my arm did not work out very well. I held the box on one arm and fumbled for the paper with the address with the other. Suddenly the weight on my arm shifted and the cake landed upside down on a walkway in a park. I scooped up the mess and returned to our store, terrified. I did not know how I would explain this. I thought my boss would charge me for the cake; one whole month's wages were down the drain. To my good fortune, Vera was at the store and I could report to her. The shop was closed, it was a Sunday afternoon, but a cake had to be delivered. They always had cakes made and on hand so she told me to go find the cake decorator who lived just a few blocks from the shop, and ask him to come and decorate another cake. Mr. Popof was a kind and considerate man. He came, frosted another cake, and I was on my way again. This time I knew where to go before I got out onto the street. My pride was hurt, but there was no other cost to me.

Adjoining Harbin is a large Chinese population where foreign languages were not known; thus knowing Chinese was essential. One Sunday afternoon as I was delivering a cake and was trying to find an address close to the all-Chinese city, I had difficulty finding the address and wandered across a small bridge, thinking the address might be there. I suddenly found myself surrounded by people who were curious about what I was carrying in the white box on my arm. To my dismay, I soon found that no one understood what I was saying. In Harbin, most Chinese people did not understand Russian. I soon concluded the people for whom I was looking did not live there, and I retraced my steps. Back on the other side of the bridge where people understood my questions, I found the right address. It was a different world across that bridge.

During that summer there was a border conflict with Russia and many Chinese troops came through Harbin. They occupied the high school to which I was delivering food. All school personnel moved, except one teacher and his family who stayed living in an upstairs apartment on one end of the two-story building. To get to his apartment, I had to go through the building. At the gate, the guard looked into my basket of fine bakery wares. I was always afraid they would take it away from me, but they just lifted the white linen cover and looked, but did not take anything.

The hallways were usually crowded with military personnel. One morning I had to go through a classroom filled with sleeping soldiers; all had their rifles lying at their feet. I had a few shivers but walked through on the path between them. When I got back to the store and told my boss about my experience, he said it would not be necessary for me to go back there. He picked up the phone to inform the teacher that he would have to come to the store to buy his bakery goods.

Mr. Azadovsky obtained permits for us to walk on the streets in the evening and early morning hours. One evening I had gone to see my parents and stayed a bit too long. It was dark when I returned. I had to cross an open field, perhaps a block wide. All of a sudden I heard someone shout, and next I heard the click of the lock on a rifle. I froze on the spot and lifted my hands in the air, though he could not see me in the darkness. My tongue seemed to cleave to the roof of my mouth, but I managed to say the few words of Chinese I knew, "I house go." and hoped he would understand.

He must have, because he said, "Zoo," which I knew meant "go." I went, and soon came to lighted streets and passed other military guards without incidents.

We had told our boss that we were there only temporarily; we were waiting to go to America. He laughed and said, "You people! You say you are going to America. Let me tell you, I have friends here in the city who have been waiting for five or ten years. They have the money, but they haven't left yet."

We protested that we were different from the others, to which he replied, "You haven't got the money, so how will you go? Besides, the American quota is full.

Many people have waited a long time, you'll never make it."

Our family had enough left to live on, but some of the people, especially the younger families like my sister and brother-in-law, Henry Rogalsky, and the Abraham Klassens, were pretty much dependent on just what they earned. What he said was true.

But what he did not realize, and could not know was that we believed that God was on our side. Humanly speaking, not only was the prospect of going to America slim, survival where we were in Harbin was difficult. Yet somehow even the young families got by. In the late 1920s we did find a way to immigrate to America.

Shimon Fix

Shimon Fix writes:

Harbin, April 23, 1940[164]

I am tired of receiving invitations from other people's tables. For this reason, I decided that this year I won't accept any Passover Seder invitations, but rather go back to the old ways and invite guests over for Seder. Truly, it is more pleasant to receive guests at one's own home than to be a guest. I decided that I will call friends and acquaintances. Those who, so to speak, aren't lazy, will call back, and "like a flock of ravens they flew in — why not visit, why not partake?"

We had a gay time. But during the reading of the Haggadah, the narrative of Egyptian slavery and our deliverance from it, my mind was frequently overtaken with contemplations about that long-gone era and its similarities with the present. I couldn't help but compare this ancient history of the Jewish people to its contemporary story. What, after all, is the difference between the Egyptians' intrigues in relation to our ancestors, as compared to the (Japanese) dirty tricks going on now? Essentially nothing.

Essentially it was childlike amusement, archery, in comparison to today's pirates from the sea and our local bandits!

I looked over my creditors and debtors and discovered that I am in debt to Tanya. I haven't answered her letter. But I have had so many hassles connected with Joseph's departure, that my lack of reply to her must be viewed as an involuntary omission. By the way, I will try, sooner or later, to pay off my debt regardless of my accounts with other debtors.

Report—For the House of Shimon Fix, in Harbin on the 7th Line No. 5. For the months of June and July in the year 1940. Paid in June:

June 1 From	Kabaysi Inoske for Apt. No. 57 from July 1 to July 31 Gobi 35.00
" " "	Takanaga for Apt. No. 58 from July 1 to July 31 Gobi 25.00
" " "	Okuba Takamasi for Apt. No. 59 from April 23 to June 23 Gobi 41.00
" 3 "	Kabayasi Inoske for Apt. No. 60 from July 3 to Aug. 3 Gobi 23.00
" " "	S.Sh. Vigdorchik for Apt. No. 61 from July 3 to Aug. 8 Gobi 37.00
" " "	F.C. Pechnikova for Apt. No. 62 from June 1 to June 30 Gobi 25.00
" " "	K.K. Mavridi for Apt. No. 63 from June 1 to June 6 Gobi 25.00
" 10 "	Sin-Chan for Apt. No. 64 from May 10 to Aug. 10 Gobi 150.00
" 17 "	Kabayasi Inoske for Apt. No. 65 from July 17 to Aug. 17 Gobi 85.00
" 22 "	N. S. Levitina for Apt. No. 67 from July 10 to Aug. 10 Gobi 15.00
" " "	From her, her debt to you Gobi 5.00

" " "	Matsuzaka/Apt. F.C. Pechnikova/for Apt. 68 July 1-July 31 Gobi 25.00
" " "	Matsuzaka for Apt. 69 From Aug. 8 to Aug. 31 Gobi 25.00
" 23 "	Hashimoto for Apt. 70 From Aug. 8 to Aug. 31 Gobi 150.00
" 28 "	Okuba Takamasi for Apt. 71 From June 23 to July 23 Gobi 25.00
" " "	L. I. Vertsman for Apt. 72 from July 28 to Aug. 23 Gobi 42.50
" " "	Loan repayment from B.B. Gurevich Gobi 23.78

Gobi 1759.15

Shimon Fix rented rooms at his 2-story house near the New Synagogue. There were 15 tenants in all, out of which 6 were Japanese, and 2 of which were Geishas.

S.H. Soskin – Paul Soskin

Harbin was a refuge place for most of the people who came there. But it was also a space of opportunity for those who were able to see the potential of fertile Manchuria and its black soil.

By the end of 1902, there were 300 Jews and 10 Jewish-owned shops in Harbin. It was then that Simeon H. Soskin arrives in the new town and started his local enterprises. The Soskin family were famous Jewish entrepreneurs, whose main businesses included flour factories and import & export companies. The Soskin family owned coal mines and set up factories in Harbin. They brought large sum of capital they accumulated from their businesses in Odessa and other parts of the Russian Empire.

The Soskin Residence was in a large villa on Jingwei 4th Street,

Fig. 26: Soskin's Home in Harbin

in Daoli District, not far from the old and new synagogues. The villa serves now as the Harbin Association of Civil Engineering and Architecture.

The Harbin Zionist Group was formed in 1909 and V.X. Soskin was elected its Chairman. In 1922 Simeon H. Soskin bought the Kasatkin Oil Mill in District 8 and started the Soskin Oil Mill. The new mill had 60 spiral oil presses with daily output of 4.26 tons of soybean oil and 41.40 tons of soybean cakes. In 1925 M.P. Soskin succeeded Dr. Bertha Schwartz-Kaufman as president of the Harbin Jewish Women Charitable Society after her death. In 1928 the Soskin Flour Mill was bought by the Northeast Official Silver Company and renamed No. 3 Dongxing Electric Grinding Mill.

Fig. 27: Soskin in Harbin

The story of Paul Soskin,[165] is especially interesting. He was born in Kertch, Crimea, on February 23, 1905, to Isaac Soskin and Manya Galperine. Isaac was manager of the family grain business on behalf of his father Hariton Soskin.

Isaac and his family left Kerch in 1917 for Harbin, due to the family business going bankrupt in the wake of the collapse of the Tsarist regime. The family were ardent Zionists and the growing antisemitic attitudes of the white Russian faction was also a factor.

Harbin was the hub of the Chinese Eastern Railway which linked the Trans-Siberian Railway with the Russian Far Eastern port of Vladivostok.

Isaac's younger brother, Simeon, had found a great deal of success in Harbin since arriving there in 1902. Simeon, who was a poor scholar, had fallen out of favor with his father, Hariton. He had been set to work in the family business under Isaac, but his extravagant ways reflected poorly on the reputation of the family. Hariton decided it would be best if Simeon were to make his own way in the world. In Harbin, Simeon had found success in the timber business which had thrived due to the demands created by the Russo-Japanese War. Simeon poured his profits into further investment in the local cereal industry and was by now becoming an international business figure.

At Simeon's persistent invitation, most of the Harinton

Fig. 28: Paul Soskin with his parents, Isaac Soskin and Manya Galperine

Soskin's family from Kerch had already emigrated to Harbin. In Harbin, Isaac was also to find success. He was made a partner in Simeon's company and helped found The Jewish Bank of Commerce.

In October 1923 Paul left China to enroll in a study for a degree in architecture at The University of London. After qualifying as an architect, he traveled the continent 'studying styles in European cities.'

On the 3rd of October 1925, Paul was in Hollywood where he witnessed the filming of the famous chariot race in 'Ben-Hur.' What impressed him also was the 3,500 paid extras that crowded at the Circus Maximus which was swelled with invited dignitaries and other interested members of the public.

In 1928 The Soskin family left Harbin due to increasing anti-Semitic activities spurred by an influx of disposed White Russians and a downturn in economic activity. After leaving China, Isaac and Manya first went to London. In 1932 Manchuria was overrun by the Japanese and any Soskin assets left there would have been rendered worthless.

Paul became a British citizen and established himself in London. He became a director of Simeon's company, British European Film Corporation. Ltd., London.

In August 1934 a new company, Transatlantic Films, was formed with Paul, as managing director.

At that time new quota regulations were being put in place which should have increased the number of British-made films made. In anticipation of this new production companies were set and studios were built.

Paul made a deal with British and Dominion to produce a series of films. With his uncle, he formed the 'Soskin Productions' to make these films.

Simeon Soskin invested nearly all of his savings into building

Fig. 29: Paul Soskin on the set of "Two's Company" — January 1936

a new film studio, the best in Europe — Amalgamated Studios in Elstree.

By now the Soskins of Harbin pictured themselves a film moguls.

In America, he spent the holidays with actress Gloria Swanson with whom he was having a serious relationship and there was talk of marriage.

In January Paul was due to return to London with a deal from Columbia to make rent space at the new studios. The deal with Columbia appeared to be dependent on MGM's intentions to use the studios as their production base.

In August 1937 the press found out that Paul Soskin had run out of money. In 1938 Paul Soskin was forced to liquidate his company, Soskin Productions, and in 1939 McAlpine called in the mortgage on the studios and sold them.

In 18 months he lost in British films a fortune of more than £300,000, which took him 18 years to amass as a grain and general merchant in China, Mr. Simon Soskin, at 60, was determined to start again—but not in films.

Mr. Soskin told the story of his rise and fall. "I came to England from Harbin in China with more than £300,000 in 1921. I lived on that capital. My nephew, Paul, had taken up the production of films, and they talked to me of a site at Elstree. For £10,000 we bought the site on which the derelict Amalgamated Studios now stand. I was to be the director with no fixed salary or remuneration."

"Studios—were built. They cost £300,000 at the start. And then," the grey-cropped mustache was given another twist, "they needed more money." "I raised loans and advanced the money till the final cost of about £600,000 was met.' "But not one film was oven produced not a camera turning has ever been seen on the floors of those eight studios where every star that matters was to have been engaged since 1936."

This sixty-year-old, who, was a power in the Far East, declared "Finished? No. I am going back to the export merchant business where I became an expert in my old town Harbin. But films? Not for anything."

In 2020 the Harbin government announced plans to turn the Soskin villa into a Jewish Museum exhibiting Jewish daily life and living Jewish home relics. The museum is scheduled to be opened in 2023.

The Sandler family

Life can be full of happiness and joy or exactly the opposite — sad and miserable. While there were Jewish families in Harbin that enjoyed the tasty flavor of high life, there were those that experienced misery and were deep at the bottom of everything. People who were looking for a way out from a certain situation or condition could find comfort in believing posters and other propaganda devices that life somewhere else may be much better.

Winters were seasons of pain and turmoil for those without the means. And in summers they could only look at those who enjoyed the season's offerings and hope for the next one that will let them share the pleasure they have not been part of.

For the unfortunate and the naïve believer, Stalin's propaganda was as comforting as the dreams they had about sunnier places.

Stalin's propaganda created socialist realism focused on glorifying the motherland and presenting a dream, an idealized version of life that did not exist. It could be found in many different types of artworks, including sculptures, paintings, poetry, and novels, as well as in the description of daily life.

The "little memoir" to which Rafael Medoff referred, is a list of the Sandler children with brief descriptions about each of them. It is a sad family saga. It is mostly so because like many other Jews in Harbin, they fell into the trap of Stalin's propaganda and returned to the Soviet Union which they assumed was a paradise by then.

The reason the family assumed that Rachel was in Harbin when she was killed is that we believe, in general, that the Sandler family members went back to Russia only in the late 1920s and 1930s. The family consisted of two parents and nine children. The father died in Harbin in 1928, and the mother went back in the 1930s. One sibling, my grandmother Lea, went to America. Yosef died from his wounds in the 1905 pogrom. One sibling,

Mula went to Russia in 1933. And one, David went there in 1922. We don't know the dates when the other five siblings, including Rachel, went to Russia. But since they all died in Russia, they clearly all did go back at some point. Except, perhaps, Rachel.

On the one hand, it would seem unlikely that she would have gone back when it was Tzarist Russia since that was what they were all escaping from; and it seems unlikely they would have gone back during the turmoil of the war, because of the hardships and dangers of going there then.

At some point, Rachel got married and had two children. We don't know the names of her husband or her children. I guess it's possible that for some reason her husband needed to go back to Russia and they all went along, before or during WW 1 or the revolution. It's one of the many mysteries that we are pursuing.

My oldest sister Sasha died in Moscow. Her husband was killed by Stalin. They had 3 children: Zaima was wounded in the 2nd W.W. and after the war died of a heart attack. Sasha was 36 years old. Rachel lived in Moscow and has two children. I do not knowall their names. The youngest Maya was on the front in 2nd W.W. and is listed as missing in action.

My brother Mulia was a soldier in the Tzarist army of the 1st world war. He was a prisoner of war in Vienna. After the war, he hitchhiked to Harbin, where he married and had 3 children. He died in Moscow of cancer at the age of 80. His wife died in her sleep at the same week. The first boy was wounded in the 2nd world war and died in Moscow from his wounds. The two daughters are engineers. They are married, have children and live in Moscow. I do not know their names. They have never admitted that they have relatives in the U.S.

My brother Yosef was wounded in a pogrom in Russia. He fought with the guerrillas by joining a self-defense group. A few years later he died.

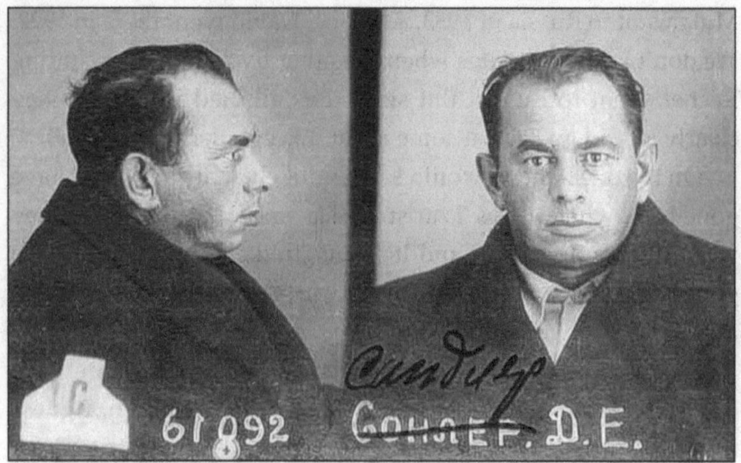

Fig. 30: David Sandler KGB Photo

Brother David who was born in 1895, was tortured and executed by Stalin. He had a wife Feera and they had two children: Natasha in Israel, Leva in Moscow married to Varvara, and has two children. They are completely Russified.

Sister Rachel was killed by robbers with two of her small children in the period of the 1st W.W.

Luba married in Moscow. Her husband died in the time of evacuation in 2nd W.W. They had 2 children: Leonid a captain of a ship in the Far East, who recently retired and is back in Moscow. He has two married daughters. Nellie, Luba's daughter, divorced her husband and has two married sons. They live in the Southern Part of Russia. My sister Luba lives there too. She had a stroke and is paralyzed on one side. Sima visited her not long ago. She has an unmarried son, aged 30, and grandchildren, her daughter's children, who recently married.

Bella lives in Moscow with her husband and two children and two grandchildren in the same three-room apartment they have had for years. Bella is quite sick.

Rafael Medoff described his mother's life in Harbin as "My

mother—the worker."[166] She worked from early in the morning till very late in the night. She cooked, she cleaned, she washed clothes for a family of nine children. She sewed clothes and baked bread at night. In the summer she grew potatoes, onions, and other vegetables to store or preserve for the winter. In the winter when the days are short and the nights are long—the project was to make blankets and pillows down from geese' feathers. I remember sitting with her and other sisters around a large table in the dining room and plucking the features which resulted in down pillows and quilts. She was tall and beautiful. Her concern for the family was unbounded. She passionately encouraged her children to study and learn a profession. For me she selected dentistry. She was very pious and observed the 10 commandments so passionately. Every Saturday in the synagogue she was the leader in praying because most of the women couldn't read. Saturday was a very special day. She dressed in the finest and rested. No work, just rest and pray. Her Saturday evening prayer rings in my ears. Loudly she begged God for a week of "gesund un azlohe" (health and success). I still feel the pleasure I experienced in shining the candles for her on Friday "licht benchen." She enjoyed joining the grown-up girls in dancing, games, and having fun. Father didn't think it was proper for her to do it and affectionately called her "staraya dura" (old bull). Every Friday she performed a mitzvah—a deed, like taking care or doing something for an orphan or a poor bride. When in Moscow she found herself without work she began to study the Russian language and read Russian literature which was forbidden by the Jewish orthodoxy. She wrote to me with pride that she read "Anna Karenina" and how she enjoyed it. On September 8, 1945, I received a telegram from Sima: "Our dear mother died" It was one month to the day after the USSR attacked Japan.

Rafael Medoff described his father as "The Amish". Tacit man, withdrawn, and hard working. He was more like an Amish man. Always on the watch for the children should do the right thing according to Mosaic law. He was especially concerned that the children should show respect for my mother as he set himself as the example. I can't remember witnessing an argument between my parents. I remember father having arguments with my older sister. He never showed direct emotions, but when I left home for the University in Siberia he couldn't hold out and after two months came to see me and I was very glad to see him.

Before my eyes are very vivid the picture. My parents having tea in the wee hours of the morning. Father would prepare the samovar and place it on the table in the kitchen. They would drink tea, talk quietly till the gang got up readying for school. And work began. He was an entrepreneur. When his sons were threatened with arrest by the Tzarist police he ran with them to the Far East. After two years he moved the whole family there to Harbin. He was very pious and active in the synagogue. I was told that when he died, the whole city turned out to his funeral. He died 10 years before my mother.

Tzvi Hirsch Aronow

Simone Clay's[167] grandfather Tzvi Hirsch Aronow and his daughter, Astna Guinshesna Aronowa fled from Ukrainka, in Ukraine after the first Russian revolution. They took the Trans-Siberian and what she called the Trans Manchurian to get to Harbin.

My grandmother met my grandfather Szulim Szrajer shortly after and they were married in 1907.

Uncle Gershon had his Bar Mitzva in 1928. They had two children who died during the Harbin cholera epidemic of 1911. I don't know the names of these first children. Then, they had four more children:

Goda was born in 1912 and died in 2006. She married Abraham Portnoff—who died in Shanghai, and then, Icek Szmulevitz. They lived in New York.

Chana was born in 1913 and died in 1978. She married Donald I. Craig, and lived in Kokomo Indiana, in the USA.

Haim Gershon was born in 1915 and died on February 6, 1943, in Auschwitz.

Dvora (Dweira) was born in 1918 and died in 1975 in France.

Ren'e Chauveau was a nurse in the Red Cross. She notified the family when my uncle Haim Gershon was sent to Auschwitz, and she is the one who also notified the family of his death. In Auschwitz, my uncle was part of the orchestra, and he also performed in the home of German officers.

Szrajer, Dwejra, my mother, married a Frenchman, my father, Jean-Louis-Emile Monnier. We are four children: 3 born in Shanghai, and my youngest brother who was born in Damascus, Syria.

The family left Harbin for Shanghai in 1934, for several reasons, the main one was the Japanese occupation. My great-grandfather had just passed away in Harbin, and the body was moved to Shanghai.

Haim Gershon Szrajer, was born on November 1st, 1915. On the occasion of his Bar Mitzvah, Haim's godfather offered him a violin, and it became obvious that my uncle was a prodigy. So, when the family moved to Shanghai, Haim was sent to Paris (around 1936, with a Polish passport) to study at the music conservatory.

In France, he supported himself as a cantor and as a violinist, and when the war broke out, he joined a Polish unit then, and when France surrendered to Germany, the Polish unit was dismantled.

My uncle, being a foreign Jew, was arrested and sent to Pithiviers in 1942. While in Pithiviers, he met two sisters, Renee Chauveaux and her sister Madeleine.

Renee was a nurse who had been working for a physician she greatly admired. She was married, and her husband—Jean Chauveaux—spent the war as a prisoner in Germany, and she was wondering what was happening with the Jews that were being arrested. After they met my uncle at a cafe where his group had been taken by the gendarme in charge, they brought packages of food to my uncle and his friends, and often they would sit outside of the fence—with people who lived in the area—to listen to the orchestra. Eventually, Madeleine became engaged to Max Schwartz—one of the musicians. Then, one day, when they came, the group was gone. They learned that the young men had been sent to an unknown destination in the east—Transport 4 from Pithiviers to Auschwitz which left on June 25th, 1942. Since Ren'e was working for the Red Cross at that point, she was able to find out that my uncle was in Auschwitz. At the time everyone believed that prisoners were sent to the east to work, but subsequently, Ren'e learned that the records of the camp showed that my uncle had died of typhus, and she contact his family in China.

From people who were in the camp with my uncle and later returned to Paris, we learned a different story:

Upon his arrival in Auschwitz, my uncle was assigned to the orchestra, and he also performed for guards and officers in their homes. We were told that the daughter of one of the officers asked her father to help my uncle who was quite handsome, and this cost him his life. He was murdered on February 6, 1943.

In 1934, the family moved from Harbin to Shanghai in three groups.

First, my mother, Dvora, and her sister Hannah were sent to Shanghai because friends of the family had opened a clothing store and the two sisters found employment with them. The grandparents, Szulim Szrajer and Astna Guinshesna Aronova, and my uncle followed, and then, Goda who was born in Harbin in 1912, her husband, Abraham Portnoff and her mother-in-law. Eventually, Abraham Portnoff died of cancer, and Goda married Icek Szmulevitz around 1945. He was born in Wielun in Poland, in 1902 and died in New York in 1971. His first wife and two children were killed when the Germans invaded Poland and somehow, friends of his, helped him reach Shanghai.

In Shanghai, Hannah who was born in 1912, and died in 1978 in New York, married an American, Donald Craig, right after the war, and they moved to Kokomo Indiana.

My mother, Dvora, who was born in 1918, and died in 1975 in France, met my father in 1942. My father, Jean-Louis-Emile Monnier, was born in 1918, and died in 1973 in France, was in the French navy at the beginning of the war. When the French surrendered, he joined an American ship, and that is how he ended up in Shanghai—where he joined the French police and studied to become an electrical engineer.

In Shanghai, my father met my mother. The French consul married them in early 1943, just after the family learned of my uncle's death in Auschwitz.

Most of the family left Shanghai in 1949.

Having no visas, Goda, her husband, their twin children and my grandmother were sent to a displaced person camp, near Munich in Germany: Iro Camp in Wildflecken. They spent a year in that camp. Hannah (Ania) and her husband came directly to the USA.

Since my family had French passports, we left Shanghai in 1950 and went to France.

We spent a few months in Brittany, near Rennes, where my parents bought a house in the town where my father was born. Then, the family spent 5 years in Damascus, Syria, were my father occupied a position as a chief electric engineer at the Centrale Electrique of Damascus.

My third brother was born in Damascus. He was named after my uncle, and he is now a physician in Paris and is an orthodox Jew, as we are, my family and I. The doctor who delivered him was the same doctor, Dr. Charles, who had delivered the first three children including me, at the Hospital Sainte-Marie, in the French concession of Shanghai.

We left Syria in 1956 during the Suez conflict and settled in France.

Szulim Szrajer and Astna Aronova had two little children who died during the Harbin 1911 epidemic.

It seems that the journey of survival a Jewish family takes is part of its daily life story. The concerns, the deaths, the newborns, the changing geographies, all have their music. It is the sound of a heart bit, sometimes it has its highs, and then it drops. It is fate that could not have been anticipated. The goal is to avoid a straight line at all costs.

Kalman Sloustcher

Liora Dankner's[168] grandfather Kalman Sloustcher son of Moshe, who grew up in a traditional family in Minsk Belarus, left his home and family at the age of 18, escaped from the Russian red army, and came to Harbin.

Liora said that her grandmother Rosa Levitin came from Yarkutzk Siberia to Harbin together with her sisters and brothers following their parents, who were looking for work in the town.

They got married in the 1920s. They lived at Politseskaya Street and then on Commercheskaya Street. My grandfather was working at the Jewish bakery.

They had two children, Ahron who was born on August 4, 1924, and Susana who was born on September 21, 1931.

Her uncle studied at the YMCA and was active in the "Betar" youth movement.

Since her childhood, my mother was playing the piano and danced ballet. She was the favorite student of the pianist teacher V.L Gershgorina the director of the Harbin musical school.[169]

Fig. 31: Sloustcher ballet performance. Harbin 1940s

On December 31, 1945 my uncle Ahron married Lisa Pastarnk who came together with her parents from Odessa to Harbin.

At the year 1946, her father G.I. Pastarnak who was a businessman, was arrested by the Soviets and was sent to a working camp in Siberia for many years. Her Mother Rosalia died and is buried at the Harbin Jewish Cemetery.

Only after 20 Years Lily and her husband who became American citizens succeeded in releasing Pastarnak and brought him to their home in San Francisco.

The father Ruven levitin is buried at the Jewish cemetery in Harbin.

The Burak–Vickers families

Anne Atkinson[170] recreates the story of the Burak–Vickers families who traveled from Berdichev in Ukraine, through Manchuria and Harbin, found themselves in Shanghai, and from there crossed the high seas into Australia. It is a story of long journeys, changing geographies, and in the process also the changing of identities.

…Our great grandparents were born in the towns of Berdichev and Sudilkov in times of great upheaval for Jews in Ukrainian Russia. Both towns were in the area of Hassidic Judaism, with Berdichev known as the `Jerusalem of Volhynia', and home to several prominent Hassidic leaders in the late 18 century. They included ` Rabbi Levi Yitzhak of Berdichev, a prominent Hassidic leader, and Rabbi Yitzhak Ber Levinzon, a famous advocate of Jewish Enlightenment.'

Both Berdichev and Sudilkov were located in the central area of the Pale of Settlement. The Pale was the term given to the region of Imperial Russia acquired through political and military conquests between 1791 and 1835. Driven by strengthening anti-Semitism, it was the only area in which Jews were permitted to live. In the 1890s it was estimated that almost 5 million Jews lived in the Pale. The area was also the scene of numerous outbursts of violence, or pogroms, against Jews.

By the time my great grandfather, Shulim (Solomon) Khaninovitch Burak was born in 1878, 41,617 inhabitants of Berdichev, or 80% of the population, were Jewish with Yiddish the predominant language spoken. His family appeared to have lived a comfortable life, even though, throughout Solomon's childhood, the economic position of Jews in the Pale was threatened by increasing restrictions on Jewish commercial activity. This resulted in waves of Jews, previously self-employed, emigrating or finding work as wage earners in manual trades. By the 1890s, the political and economic environment encouraged the development of a Jewish Socialist Party, known as the Bund, in Berdichev. The Bund was `devoted to Yiddish, autonomism, socialism, and secular Jewish nationalism'.

Very little is known about the family that Solomon Burak was born into. His father might have been called Khanin Burak as this was one of the familial names given to Solomon in accordance with naming custom. There is no record of his mother, not even her name. One family story is that Solomon's father owned a theatre in Berdichev. During one performance, a fire broke out which destroyed the theatre and killed hundreds of audience members, including Solomon's entire family — his parents, sisters and brothers — leaving Solomon as the only family survivor. The story is confirmed in several online entries[171] of a large fire at a circus performance in Berdichev in 1883. Atkinson brings one item that provides a summary of the catastrophe.

Circus Ferroni Fire
Berditschoft, Poland
January 13, 1883
A fire broke out on January 13, 1883, during an evening performance of Circus Ferroni in Berditscheff Russian Poland.[172] A stableman working in the stable adjoining the circus was smoking a cigarette while lying on straw, and the straw ignited. A fellow laborer ran for a pail of water. He left the door open which created a strong draft that fed the flames. The circus building was made of double wooden walls with straw filling the space between the boards to act as insulation from the cold. The circus building caught fire and, inside twenty minutes, the whole circus was in flames. Owing to the extreme cold weather, water was scarce. A fire engine was delayed in getting to the fire because while en route it broke through some ice. Official

figures state that 268 people were burned to death, 80 were mortally injured, and 100 were missing.[173] Many children were crushed and suffocated in the jam of people. Both stable labourers who caused the fire died in the fire. 27 horses and 11 trained dogs also died in the fire.[174]

Solomon was five years old at the time. An uncle and other relatives took responsibility for him, providing him with a comfortable childhood, a good education and ensured a livelihood as an adult. His adoptive father was a jeweler and watchmaker.

Our great-grandmother, Bella Lazarevna Haendler was born in Sudilkov in 1878. Similarly, next to nothing is known of great-grandmother's family either except that her father was a merchant, named Lazer Hendeer. Her mother's name was Zipe Kuzenow.

Like Burdichev although a much smaller town, Sudilkov was in the center of the Pale of Settlement where most Jews were Hassidic and spoke Yiddish. The 1897 Census recorded a population of 5,551 of which 50% were Jewish. Of these, 38% gave their occupation as merchants and lived in the center of the town. Printing was a significant industry and Sudilkov was renowned for publishing rabbinic literature. Manufacturing and fur production were also important industries. Members of the Haendler family ran two large fur factories.

While we know nothing of our great grandmother Bella's childhood, or her brothers and sisters and her parents, notes left by her granddaughter, Dolores, give the impression that she had a very comfortable tand loving childhood. She was well educated and raised to respect and value her Jewish traditions. Apparently, she took pride in keeping a spotless house, a kosher kitchen, and practicing various Jewish rituals and customs wherever and whenever she could.

Solomon and Bella almost certainly met through a professional matchmaker. They were married in February of 1898 in Sudilkov when they were both 20 years old and lived with or near Solomon's family in Burdichev. Nine months later, in November 1898 their first daughter, Ida, was born. Sometime within the next two years, the family moved to Kiev, and their second daughter, Rebekka Katya, our grandmother, was born there on 9 August 1900. In 1902, Fiera (Esther) was born and then, Lucy the youngest daughter arrived in 1904.

The family lived in Kiev until 1908.

Ida and Katya started school in Kiev but this was interrupted when the family moved to Harbin. The move was instigated by increasing restrictions placed on Jews and increasing outbreaks of anti-Semitic violence in Kiev. The Buraks were further encouraged to migrate when one of Solomon's uncles established a button factory in Harbin, which Solomon was expected to manage.

There is no mention of the route the Burak family actually took from Kiev to Harbin in 1908, in which months they made the journey, and how long it took. Atkinson presumes that, as most stages of the Trans-Siberian railway and the Trans-Manchurian railway were built by 1908, the majority of the journey was by train and most probably undertaken in spring through to early autumn months. The speed of the journey was not helped by the fact that the railway employed a single line so that only one train at a time could use the tracks. This meant that there were many hours or days wasted waiting for a free line.

The pace of the journey was also reduced by having to find alternative ways to travel when there were gaps in the lines. There was one area south of Lake Baikal that was not linked by rail until 1916 so coach, cart, and sled must have done this section. Depending on the season, most of the time the track was muddy and rough. In winter it would have been impossible or at best, exceptionally difficult and dangerous for the Buraks to have plowed through the snow and ice on sleds.

When the Buraks arrived in 1908, Harbin was a rapidly growing town with a truly multicultural, multiethnic, and multireligious population. By 1913 it had 68,549 residents representing 53 nationalities and speaking 45 languages. After the 1918 October Socialist Revolution, the population further increased with over 100,000 defeated Russian White Guards and Russian refugees. Harbin had the largest Russian community outside the then Soviet Union. It had Russian schools, newspapers, churches, and synagogues for the large Jewish community.

Apart from the bitter cold of extreme winters and the outbreak of a catastrophic epidemic in 1911, the Buraks settled into a comfortable life in Harbin. The Burak household with its indulgent father, strict mother, and four vivacious girls and their pet Samoyed dog seemed a happy lot.

They lived in a brick villa in a street in which houses were fairly close together and for a time they had servants to help with the work in the house. The girls went to Russian school dressed in serge dresses, black stockings, and high-buttoned boots with big, typically Russian, bows in their hair. Solomon managed the button factory which was the first job he had held, and Bella kept a spotless house, a kosher kitchen and ensured that Jewish customs, such as Friday Shabbat rituals, were observed.

Bella was a fanatical housewife — cooking, cleaning, polishing, and dressing the girls in stylish outfits, a habit that lasted all their lives. They were a close family. Ida was the eldest and very beautiful. She had previously had rheumatic fever and was the closest of the sisters to her mother. The girls were all expected to help with work around the house—except Rebecca who refused point blank and locked herself in the bathroom where she spent hours reading.

Katya was angular, bright, and very clever. She was especially fond of reading, sports playing basketball, math, and science in primary school. In high school, she read the Russian novels and plays that were so popular then and excelled in her studies for which she was presented with a scholarship and gold medal. She was a defiant girl, with her outbursts and rebellious spirit a trial to her conservative orthodox mother.

Of the younger girls in Harbin, unfortunately, nothing is known. Atkinson imagine that they enjoyed primary school, helped Bella in the house, and had several hobbies that might have involved needlework and knitting, playing games, and reading. They might also have learned to ice-skate on the river and enjoyed being pulled around on sleds.

Equally unknown is any information related to the button factories in Harbin, in particular, the Burak button factory, except that in the 1920s Bernard Darel's family owned a button factory with an apartment attached in Harbin.[175]

The Harbin winters were freezing. The cold was so severe that the temperatures averaged 30 degrees below zero for six months of the year. Rebecca remembers that milk was sold in frozen bricks. Fresh pears were frozen and sold in the market to be thawed in cold water. They had a special delicate flavor and were very popular for the Spring Festival. Dumplings were also frozen and preserved in bags to eat when ready.

Pelmeni, a Siberian dumpling made from flour, water, and egg paste, kneaded and rolled out into small rounds and filled with finely minced meat and onion. It was cooked in a meat broth and was served as a dumpling soup, or separately with sour cream, vinegar, or mustard. It was made in autumn and stored in the cellar and eaten throughout the winter.

Katya was an exceptionally bright student and in high school, when she was barely sixteen years old, was offered a gold medal, a scholarship, and entrance to a university of her choice. She chose the University of Tomsk in Siberia to study medicine which she commenced in 1917, when she was still 16.

Ida also went to the University of Tomsk to study law and to keep `an eye on Katya'. Both Ida and Katya loved the freedom of student life away from the limitations of family life.

The life in Tomsk suited Katya. She studied hard, sang political and traditional songs, danced, debated the politics and politicians of the day, and was a good student. Her Russian Reports from those three years showed progress in all subjects.

She talked about cutting up cadavers — which started off her chain-smoking and continued till she was 52 when the scare of lung cancer and smoking was gaining publicity and she gave it away immediately.

Katya's scholarship provided them with a living allowance and they boarded with families, perhaps in large double storied wooden houses with ornately decorated carved facades. It seemed like an idyllic life for both of them.

Ida, her gentler older sister, met a handsome Hungarian horseman of light cavalry who was living in military barracks in Tomsk. His name was Marçi Diamant, but for official purposes he preferred to use the anglicized version, Martin. He was born in Budapest and was two years older than Ida. He eventually followed Ida to Harbin, and then to Shanghai where they were married. However, the strongest memory that Katya had of Marçi in Tomsk was that he regularly supplied the girls with sugar he had smuggled from his garrison.

Russia was undergoing momentous social and political changes and the effect of these changes on Ida and Katya was monumental. At first, the years of unrest far away from Siberia provided them with material for spirited political debate in a safe social environment. However, in 1919, after the gradual encroachment and rise in military activity in Siberia, the University was closed and Katya's dreams of university study and a career as a medical doctor were bought to a sudden halt. She and Ida were forced to return to Harbin. The last entry in Katya's record of studies was dated 18 October 1919, so it is presumed that they left Tomsk shortly after on the Trans-Siberian railway. It couldn't have been too much after that as the seemingly flimsy clothes Katya was wearing when she alighted from the train in Harbin would not have been suitable for Harbin's late autumn weather.

The increased military activity in Siberia and its effects in Manchuria, life in Harbin was becoming more difficult for the Buraks. The button factory was struggling to retain viability, leaving the family in uncertain financial circumstances. Solomon, again, called on his family for help. Solomon's father and brothers gathered as much jewelry as they could, including two diamond rings and several other small pieces and, through family members in Irkutsk, sent them to Tomsk for the girls to take to Harbin. Katya told a story of catching the last train from Tomsk to Harbin before the army closed the line to civilian traffic.

The Trans-Siberian carried soldiers backward and forwards and on one of the last journeys, my mother and her sister gathered whatever valuables the Russian relatives could spare for the factory had floundered and boarded the train back to Harbin. The medical course was terminated.

Ida took the top bunk and pretended to be sick, guarding the valuables under the blankets. Mother foraged for food at the stations, totally unafraid of drunken soldiers and their lewd suggestions. When they returned their father was disappointed at the things they had brought back.

The family was now poor and decided to leave for Shanghai, It was becoming a popular place for Russian exiles.

While in Harbin, the Burak family had befriended Joseph Maria de Figueiredo, also known as Joe. He was a Portuguese Catholic in his late 30s and married with a 12-year-old daughter. He was an import-export agent who was also studying journalism. His intention was to learn Russian in order to take advantage of the many stories of refugees fleeing over the Russian border from the Bolsheviks. It was most probably through her father, Solomon, that Katya met Joe and started to teach him Russian on her return from Tomsk. Although the association between Joe and Katya started out as a friendship of a family friend which included Joe's wife and daughter, it soon resulted in a secretive love affair between a young rebellious, and intractable girl and a middle-age man who appeared besotted with not only Katya but the romantic situation he found himself in. Thus started a turbulent and difficult time for relationships within the Burak family.

Katya met Joe through the paper. They ran away to a hotel — he had a revolver which she discharged into the wall by accident. Her father came and took her back and her family went to Shanghai on a job transfer and did well even bought a car.

KGB documents found at the Khabarovsk archives identify Joseph Maria de Figueiredo as a counterintelligence agent for the USSR.[176]

No doubt Joe was most likely prevented from seeing Katya and the family, although it seems this situation only lasted for a few months. In the meantime, the button factory was closed and Solomon returned whatever money he raised to his brother who had established it. In 1920 the family left Harbin, probably traveling in spring after the winter thaw, by steamer boat down the east coast of China to Shanghai. Katya remembered that despite limited funds, her sisters, Bella, and herself were dressed in the height of fashion in matching cloche hats, stylish coats, and shoes. The hats and coats were probably sewn by Bella who made most of the girls' clothing with the help of servants when the Buraks were able to employ them.

Anne Atkinson summarizes the family's Harbin period—The Buraks had migrated to Harbin in the beginning stages of its development and perhaps with an expectation that they could make Harbin a permanent home. They had seen it grow from a small town to a modern city, with an ever-increasing population because of the rush of Russian refugees escaping the political situation in Russia and perceiving Harbin as reflecting a vision of what life in Russia could have become had there been no communist takeover.

Fig. 32: Joseph Maria de Figueiredo (Joe) on the left. Courtesy of Anne Atkinson

However, now they were leaving Harbin for Shanghai which seemed to offer more economic benefits for the family and more promising futures for the girls. Shanghai was a `free port' that allowed entry to anyone not in possession of a passport or visa, including the members of the Burak family who, as Russian Jews, were regarded as stateless. No doubt Bella—as matriarchal head of the family—had realized the potential of the rapidly developing multinational population of Shanghai to provide her daughters with the means of safe social, economic, and political futures through marriage, even if this meant perceiving settlement in Shanghai as a temporary measure until the girls could migrate with their husbands to safer countries such as the USA, Canada or Australia.

Moshe Lichomanov

Moshe Lichomanov remembers his childhood in Harbin as having a place of honor among all his memories of the past. In his memoir, he remembers the innocent years of his first steps in life. He writes that he remembers every detail as if it had happened yesterday, although over 60 years have passed since he studied at the Talmud Torah, the Jewish school on Konnaya Street in the Pristan district of Harbin.[177]

I studied in distant Harbin for five years: two in kindergarten, and up until the third grade, he recalled. I had to halt my studies in April 1950, because we left Harbin. We immigrated to Israel in June 1950.

I remember well the teachers, friends, the tricks we played, and the punishments we received for them. It all seemed big and frightening to me then, probably because that is the way that children perceive things. We were afraid of the homeroom teacher, Galina Gregoriyevna, who instilled order and discipline in the class to a greater degree than usual for children of our age. We were afraid of the three-day suspension from school that my friend and I received for fighting and breaking a window in the classroom. For me, it was the end of the world. Today, I smile when I remember those things. In my heart of hearts, I even secretly thank that "witch" of a teacher, to whom I owe my current excellent command of the Russian language.

I also have vivid memories of a teacher of Jewish studies named Nadel and his warm Jewish heart. He hurried to calm my mother and me when the school administration decided to suspend us for only three days—not the permanent expulsion from school announced by the "witch."

On each Jewish holiday, there was some kind of ceremony and musical play, in which children from all grades took part. Nadel could also sing and play the piano, and used to direct the musical plays at the school. I was a musical child. I loved to sing. I learned to play the violin and loved listening to music on the record player.

The years after WWII, which ended in the summer of 1945, were stormy years for the community in Harbin. It began with the entry of the Soviet army into Harbin and release from the tyranny of the Japanese regime, and ended in the tragic destruction of families caused by the exile of Jews, headed by the community leader Dr. Kaufman, to labor camps in Russia. My father, an immigrant who left Russia illegally, was very apprehensive at the time and avoided socializing with the Russian soldiers who came to have their pictures taken in the photography studio that he managed, which was named "Stalingrad" in "Novi gorod" district (now Nangang district).

I remember the frightening story he told us about a drunken Russian officer who came into the studio and asked to be photographed. My father led him to the counter on which sample pictures of all sizes were laid under thick glass. The officer saw a picture of a Chinese girl in one of the samples and began to accuse my father of keeping a picture of a Japanese woman — an "enemy of the people" — in his store. My father's explanations that this was a Chinese girl, the daughter of a Chinese employee of the studio, were of no avail. The officer drew his pistol and fired at the picture through the glass on the table. The glass shattered into fragments all over the floor. My father was sure that the second bullet would be aimed at him. Fortunately, the Chinese employee managed to calm the officer, and get him away from the studio.

I also remember happier events from the same period. When the Russian soldiers came, "Churin", the largest department store in the city, was filled with merchandise from the USSR that had been absent from stores during the entire period of the war: "Lincore" and "North Pole" chocolate bonbons, toothpaste, shaving cream, shirts, sweaters, handkerchiefs, socks, needles and thread, and so on. The new Soviet movies and the popular war songs gave the feeling that a new and better era was about to begin.

As a boy who loved to sing, I quickly learned the new songs, and even performed in a big auditorium before a large audience in a benefit evening of young artists organized on behalf of needy children. I did not suffer from stage fright. I stood on the stage and sang "The Cannons" and "Katyusha" in a loud voice like that of Joselito, the Spanish boy singer.

I was brought up in a traditional Jewish home. My parents observed the Sabbath meticulously and forbade my sister and I to write, let alone to travel or perform any kind of work on Shabbat. Every Friday night, I went with my father to the "new" synagogue, where a place of honor near the stage was reserved for us. My father inherited this place from my mother's uncle, Yaakov Lifshitz, a renowned photographer in Harbin in the 1930s.

On the major holidays, we would run around inside the synagogue. We also went into the women's section on the second floor to play tag. Once we saw several ladybirds crawling on the railing of the women's section. One push, and the beetles landed right on the table of the cantor, who was standing and reciting the morning prayers at the time. That was my first sin. On Yom Kippur, to our shame, we threw a few firecrackers on a shed belonging to the Chinese servant, who lived in the synagogue yard. That was a big sin by any yardstick.

Anti-Semitism existed in Harbin, mostly among the White Russians, who also transmitted it to their children. I first encountered this phenomenon in a summer camp of the Soviet Club where my parents registered me. I met a Russian boy there name Fyodor, and we made friends immediately. He asked me where I studied. I answered that I was studying at the Jewish school. "What, are you Jewish?" he asked me in surprise. I told him I was. "That's impossible," said Fyodor. "You're such a nice guy. You can't possibly be Jewish!"

The Chinese children, on the other hand, were unable to distinguish between Jews and Russians. For them, both were "Lamoza"[178]. At the end of the school day, I walked home with two other boys who lived in the same neighborhood: Mona Yezersky, who lived on Samannaya Street, and Victor Agranovsky, who lived on Yamskaya Street. I lived on Korotkya Street, meaning the short street, and I used to continue walking home by myself.

On the way, I sometimes met anti-Semitic Russian boys, who started throwing stones and shouting, "Beat the Jewboys," which they undoubtedly heard in their parents' house. We didn't take this quietly; we would throw stones back at them. Sometimes, Chinese children would also join the fun by throwing stones at both us and the Russians. They shouted "Lamoza, lamoza," which made me realize that for the Chinese, we were the same: both Russians and Jews were "Lamoza." That was some consolation to me.

In the summer, all the Jews used to move to the other side of the Sungari River, where there were wooden summer homes, grazing pasture with cows, and lots of fresh air that was lacking in the hot, dusty city. For children, it was paradise. We ran and played tag, got a tan, and swam in the river. We were always warned, however, not to step on the "landmines" left on the paths by cows.

Every morning, my father would cross the river on a boat on his way to work, and cross back on the way to our family in the evening. There were all sorts of channels along the river, and a large island called the "The Island of the Sun." On Sunday, when my father did not work, we would sometimes wander along the riverbanks to quiet places, and spend an entire day picnicking bathing, and fishing.

My father liked to play the piano. He also had a record collection of classical music with selections from well-known operettas, such as "The Czardas Princess," "Countess Maritza," "The Merry Widow," and others. Of course, we also had a record player with a wind-up handle and needles; these were the best Japanese equipment available at the time. I had a good ear for music when I was a boy. I learned all the tunes and could identify the musical segment by the label on the record. Of course, I couldn't read yet what was written on the label. This was used to show off to relatives and friends of the family.

I remember a sad case in 1944, during the period of Japanese rule in Harbin, when I was four and a half years old. I was walking with my mother on a street where electric streetcars drove. Suddenly, we saw a crowd of people and a streetcar standing still. The people standing there told us that the streetcar had run over a Chinese boy, and a Japanese policeman who came on the scene saw that the poor child's stomach contained rice, which Chinese were forbidden to eat. Only the Japanese masters were allowed to eat rice. Instead of helping the victim's unfortunate mother, the Japanese policeman began beating her and arrested her for the crime of giving her child rice to eat. There was no limit to the cruelty of the Japanese to the Chinese in those days.

I remember another event, in which I was almost run over by the cars of a freight train. There were railroad tracks at the end of" Kitaiskaya", the main street, along the banks of the Sungari

River. My father, my sister, and I once went for a walk along the river. When we reached the railroad tracks, we saw that a long freight train was blocking the way to the river. Like a foolish child, I ran forward and tried to pass between the cars, and then the train suddenly began to move. Hearing the shouts of my father and sister, I ran back at the last moment and was saved from certain death.

In late April 1950, my entire family boarded a train that brought us to Tientsin on our way to the land of Israel. Harbin stayed behind with all our memories, and a new future lay before us.

Dina Vincow (Lichomanov)

Dina Vincow, sister of Moshe Lichomanov, recollected her memories of her days at the Skidelsky Talmud Torah school.[179]

For many of us Jewish children born in Harbin "Talmud Torah" was the starting point of our learning and a determining factor in our lives. My memories of "Talmud Torah" belong to a different, later period. I attended this school between the years 1939 to 1947.

I was told that I am going to be attending kindergarten. My mother brings me to a large sunlit room with low tables and stools. Apparently, I am happy to stay there and let my mother leave me there without a fuss. The classroom of our kindergarten is the largest and the brightest of all classrooms, the one on the first floor with its windows facing Konnaya Street. The most memorable people for me in this room are Moreh (teacher) Yechezkel Nadel, or as we were accustomed to address him — Ademoreh, putting two words together — Adon meaning Mister, and Moreh meaning teacher, and a teachers helper, Luba Slutzker, a young beautiful girl, whose hand we were all fighting to hold when we were asked to form a circle. I like making little woven mats from strips of colorful shiny paper and love to use sticky glue.

Yechezkel Nadel wrote many plays in Hebrew. In 1949, for example, he wrote the play "On the Crossroads". This play was written in Harbin, China. It depicts events that affected the lives of people in Manchuria between 1906 and 1949. The places where the events take place are Riga in Latvia and Harbin in China. There are scenes in border towns across Russia's Siberia. The play starts with a conversation about the nature of the Chinese people.

"The Chinese, says the young man, are a special people that are very similar to ours (the Jewish People). Thousands of years ago these people had a very high culture and civilization. The scriptures of Confucius are no less in their meaning and message than ours'. David: Even today they have an advantage over the Europeans..."

Nadel was the teacher of the first and the second grades. He was serious but not condescending. He treated students with respect. He had two eyes of different colors, one blue and one brown.

It was a special time when Nadel taught the narrative of the holidays: Passover, Purim, and others. He did it in Russian. He was a master storyteller, telling each story in several sessions, and students could not wait to hear the next installment. In teaching the Bible, Nadel mixed the biblical text with interpretation and legends.

One year, on the second day of Passover, students were invited to visit Nadel and his wife Rachil Isaakovna, who was the math teacher, in their apartment. The Nadels lived on the second floor behind the main school building. I also felt very privileged. We were given some refreshments, played games with walnuts, and had a good time.

We also were doing some serious learning: Ademoreh takes me aside and lets me read in a book that teaches the Hebrew alphabet. I read words like" booba"- doll, "sal"- basket. Apparently, I am learning to read in Hebrew. We have posters with pictures hanging on the wall. One of the posters has pictures of animals, another one of musical instruments. Ademoreh is pointing to various items and names them, we repeat after him and are learning Hebrew words.

Music was an important part of our learning. We had a small organ that requires pumping with feet to make the keyboard play. Our teacher Nadel plays and we stand around and sing Hebrew songs with words that we do not really understand, but we absorb them with ease.

On some of the holidays we had special stage performances, and we rehearse skits and choral presentations. For my first "Chanukkah" stage appearance, my mother helps me memorize some lines in Hebrew. Neither she nor I knew what we were saying, but I remember the wonderfully festive mood of the Channukkah celebration and the blessing for the lighting of the candles on the stage as little Shurik Feingold sings them. Somehow this memory always comes back to me each Chanukkah time.

We were so involved in the story that Nadel told us and we loved to hear the song of Passover when Moses is standing at the burning bush. We are told: "And then he heard...." This is when we hear the bell that announces the end of the lesson period. We are begging our teacher to go on with the story, but he tells us that we have to wait until the next day to hear the rest. Everybody sighs with disappointment but is looking forward to tomorrow. In teaching us the Bible books, Nadel mixed the biblical text with commentaries and legends.

I recall listening to a speech given by Dr. Abraham Kaufman

on our school stage. I was quite young at the time but I knew that it was about the Land of Israel. My mother, who also listened to the speech, was full of admiration for the speaker and commented again and again about what a wonderful orator he was. I also remember that he came to our house as a doctor. My two-year-old brother was very sick. He was treated by another doctor at the time and was getting worse. Dr. Kaufman diagnosed him as having pneumonia and took care of him.

The school stage brings up many memories for me. There were many occasions when I stood on that stage throughout my years at school.

It is winter and, while we are waiting for our mothers to come and pick us up, we put on our coats and our rubber boots over our shoes with the help of one of the two Chinese men who worked for the school as the janitors and caretakers: "Vasilii" the tall and slim guy, and "Ivan", the short and chubby one. They take care of us and of the building, serve us hot tea at lunchtime as we sit at long tables and eat the sandwiches we bring from home. There is a single slice of bread that is served to each of us. I think it was done in case someone came to school without a sandwich from home.

At home, we did not keep kosher, but I carefully instructed my mother not to give me anything that is not kosher for lunch. My peers are watchful and would make my life difficult if they would see something of that nature.

There is noise in the lunchroom, everybody is talking at once, but not for long. We hear our teacher Slutzker rushing into the room with words of admonition: "Sheket udmama!!" (Quiet and silence). We quiet down for a while. After lunch, the older kids are called upon to read the short version of the food blessing. Only on rare occasions do they call me to participate as well.

The lunchroom is also the main hall where we spend our

recess in the wintertime. I watch the older boys exercise on parallel bars and other sports equipment like the rings. They seem to be so grown up. The school had six grades at this time so they must have been about twelve or thirteen years old.

In those first two or three years, we learned to read and to write Hebrew. Obviously, we did the same in Russian. While in kindergarten, we were briefly exposed to some English by Mr. Elkind, but then came the war. The study of the English language was now forbidden in the Japanese-occupied territory. Instead, we began learning Japanese with Dinda San, a Korean woman who was probably not the best of teachers. In her culture, she was accustomed to disciplined students. We, a small group of Jewish children, apparently did not meet her expectations in that regard, and she showed us her dissatisfaction. We, in turn, paid her back by misbehaving and doing mischiefs. Even though I was a timid soul I got into trouble with her at times. The motivation to study Japanese was somewhat lacking, but despite it, I learned to read "katakana' script. Aside from the lessons in the Japanese language, we all memorized the words of the Japanese and the Manchukuo national anthems. We also observed a daily moment of silence in memory of the Japanese soldiers that died in the war.

The war marched on. In the last couple of years, we became strangers in the school building. We sat in freezing classrooms. I remember having to wear our coats and gloves during the lessons and, on a few occasions discovering that the ink froze in the inkwell. We did not know then how lucky we were to live in that remote corner of the world named Harbin where we only had to deal with the shortages of material goods and not the disaster that befell all the European Jews.

Sometimes at the beginning of the fourth grade, I became sick with what was at first diagnosed as a strep throat infection but turned out to be diphtheria. A few other children came down with the same sickness. One of them, Difa Fonaroyova died. For me, the aftermath of diphtheria resulted in many months of "complications" from the disease. I missed a good portion of the school yet went on to the next grade. The one thing that I did not makeup was learn to read the more advanced Japanese Hiragana script. Luckily, by the time I was in the fifth grade the war ended and a whole new era began for us at our Talmud Torah school.

It was 1945. The Soviet Red Army came to town. For it to continue to exist the school now had to restructure its curriculum in accordance with the Soviet school model. New teachers were hired. They were educated Russian émigrés who were well qualified to teach subjects like Roman History, Algebra, Geometry, and Russian Grammar. The number of students per classroom was very small at that time. In the fifth grade, we had only 5 or 6 students. We were getting an excellent "private" education. Our Russian teachers were caring and dedicated. I remember sometimes wondering about how they really felt about us, Jewish kids, thinking of the anti-Semitism that was associated with the White Russians. One of them, Boris Ivanovich, was a former White Army officer. But I only remember their efforts to educate us, and I hoped that they enjoyed their work. I do not remember the name of our history teacher anymore, but I do recall that when her husband died during the school year and our whole class attended his funeral at the Cathedral in Noviy Gorod. There was an open casket and it made a strong impact on our young minds.

A very special presence was that of Galina Gregorievna — our teacher of Russian language and grammar. She was such an energetic, enthusiastic and dedicated person. She was very strict and completely determined to make us literate in Russian. What I learned from her served me well later on in life when I was a student at the University of Washington, I myself was given a chance to teach Russian to American students.

Our education in Hebrew continued despite the pressures of the new curriculum. Teacher Slutsker was strict and most of us behaved in his presence. In general, I think that because we were such a tiny group of children, we were somewhat spoiled and did not learn proper behavior in a classroom. Talmud Torah of my time was a very protective and had a pampering environment for us.

In the Hebrew lessons of that period, I remember studying the book of Isaiah. We were supposed to memorize each chapter by heart. This was a difficult task. Teacher Slutsker let us get away with having an open book on the desk in front of us, so that when I was asked to recite the chapter, I would peek at the lines to keep myself going with the recitation. In addition to the Bible studies, at some point, we were reading the stories by Y.L. Peretz in Hebrew. This was a big stretch for us.

When we were in the sixth grade, the final grade of the Talmud Torah school at that time, all of us, parents and students, became aware of the fact that in the Soviet educational system primary education consisted of the completion of seven grades of school. It made good sense, therefore, for our school to add another grade. We, the students, were strongly motivated to lobby for it. For us, it meant staying another year in our familiar and protective environment and having the advantage to further our Hebrew education. But how could this be accomplished? We became aware of the fact that it was a matter of funds that the school did not have. Before that situation, I personally never knew how much my parents paid for my schooling but had a vague notion that the tuition in our school depended on the financial status of the family. Now we all became aware of the fact that our school existed largely because of the generosity of the community philanthropists. So we were advised by our parents and our teachers to turn to the individuals who could help us. By this time, I think, there were just the four of us: myself, Mark Goldberg, Shurik Faingold, and Alik Fainman. We had to convince the community leaders that it was a worthwhile project to which they were asked to contribute. We prepared a program of part entertainment, part speeches of appeal. In the entertainment part, we wanted to show how much we have learned and in the appealing part, we expressed our desire to learn more in Hebrew studies. I remember standing on our stage and delivering some convincing arguments about our request. I was very nervous and I am not sure who was in the audience that day. I wish I could remember the names of the individuals who so kindly responded to the four Jewish kids who asked for a lot of money so they could have another year of the very special education that Talmud Torah had to offer. The event was a success and we were given that chance.

The building of our Talmud Torah school is no longer there, but I can still see it very clearly in my mind: the way we entered it through the yard and the back door, the dark walls of the corridor, and of that corridor, the classrooms and the room that the principal German Yakovlevich and the teachers used, and finally the main hall and the stage. It all looked very big then but probably was not that big after all.

Shimon Fix

Shimon Fix wrote:

Harbin, March 19, 1940[180]

"All beginnings are difficult," and I don't know from what to start, but I have faith that in the process of writing, the material will come to me.

By the way, the radio from your room (the room now occupied by Rkubi-san, the Japanese) just crackled with an overview of this past weather season. It says that in N. America, in the course of this past winter, 150 people died from the cold, getting caught in snowdrifts, snowstorms, and freezing temperatures. Well, given this statistical figure, what do you say in defense of your propagandistic doctrine that there one doesn't need a fur coat?

And also the radio tells about some kind of mild earthquake in an unknown place –admittedly a while ago, in September — in New York enough so that even the tops of some buildings shook. Did you feel this or did you also, like I, learn about it from newspapers? By the way, on what floor do you and Sasha live, and on what floor do you work?

In Harbin, it barely snows; so — this winter's end is unusual in the almost complete absence of snow. But since the last half of last night, there has been an abundant snowfall that has completely changed the look of the street, and this "manna from heaven" continues to fall without interruption. The inhabitants of the first floor of our house noisily and gaily ran outside and began to make snowmen. They put one snowman in front of the door of our apartment. I remembered the Russian winter of 1915 when I was sent on a business trip to Nizhny Novgorod. There I had to walk through snow that here "the old-timers won't remember," that is, they live so as to forget. I lived there alone without the family because the job was temporary, but mostly due to the circumstances of "right to live," Mama and the children stayed in Mogilov.

When the job in the company ended, I, with my co-workers in Nizhny Novgorod:

"In the dead of night
Loaded the bold troika

Ate and whistled and like an arrow
Flew over the snowy depths."

The other day I had a strange experience, or more exactly, a funny adventure, which reminds me a bit of the tragicomic experience that I recently read about in an English newspaper. It was about an incident in an American court, it seems in New York. The newspaper, reporting on this incident, calls it a judicial mistake (in quotation marks). The story can be drawn thusly: The accused was sitting on a bench—accused of stealing a pair of trousers. Evidence pro and con were brought forth, the evidence from the prosecutor was heard, and finally, the defense attorney, who with colorful words was able to convince the jury, tipped the scales in his client's favor, and he was acquitted. After the acquittal was announced, and the courtroom began to empty of the officials— the judge, the prosecutor—and the public, the accused continued to sit motionless on his bench; he didn't even stand up. The lawyer told his defendant that the judge had acquitted him and he was free to go home, but the accused continued to sit, not rising from his place, and openly following the accuser with his eyes until the latter left. Only then did he get up to leave. At the exit, it turned out that the accused, when dressing for the trial, had mistakenly put on ...... the stolen pants.

Recently I had the following experience. I woke up at night and couldn't fall back asleep. I was in a battle with the wall clock. First it was 3:00, then 4:00, and finally 5:00 a.m. I wasn't in the mood to daydream, and I didn't want to think. Therefore I crawled out from under my blanket, put on just a suit jacket for warmth, sat down at my desk, and under the blue lampshade of our table lamp started jotting some scribbles. Wrote and crossed out, scribbled and smudged, not noticing that it was becoming light—the time was about 7:00 in the morning. Our tenant,

Madame Levitina, saw the glimmer of light from the electric lamp through the faramin[181]. She was curious, and since she is always such as stickler for economizing on electricity, with the intention of finding out why, at this hour, the light was on, she knocked on the door, and asked, "May I?" to which I spontaneously, without thinking, automatically answered in the affirmative, "You may." She came in, started to approach my table, and I, forgetting my nighttime "toilet" (or more accurately, my lack of toilet), barefoot in night slippers and, most importantly, in the full brilliance of my nighttime attire, got up to greet her. From this nighttime apparition, she squealed so loudly that other tenants, now awake, came running into my room—Okuba and Feinburg (whose wife is now visiting in America). The scene of our mutual misunderstanding was like the scene in the last act of Gogol's The Inspector. The scene was tragicomic, no less than the tragicomedies of the American Bxxxkokrada.

By the way, about S. Levitana. She is a very nice person. She contributes a lot to the management of the kitchen, keeps an eye on the house when I'm away, etc. Keeps notes about household expenses ... always in English. I'm sending you a sample of her notes. If she were younger, say by 10 years, I wouldn't hesitate to entrust her with the management of the house after I leave for America. But now she is too weak. For this a strong nobody [is needed].

Between pp. 8 and 9: Mme Levitana's list:

The 23th of February receipted 5 goby.
Expenses:

ham	32
eggs	30
milk	8 ½
caviar	7

fruits	42
milk	8 ½
eggs	22
vegetable	18
крупа grits	15
cream and lard	20
luhan	7.66
ham	32
Xxx	16

On back of list: Transport—The 27th of February

Milk	8
an egg	.102
2 eggs	.20
milk	8 ½
an egg	.10
Axxx eggs	22
milk	5
fruits	29
eggs	26

Across (or rather down) the list in large letters in pencil: оплачен (Paid)

You probably know Madame Alkunovich (from the women's clothing store on Kitaiskaya St.) Last Friday evening I went to the synagogue I saw a boy who looked like Alkunovich and next to him, a young man reading Kaddish who turned out to be the son of the deceased, who had come temporarily from America, the former schoolmate of Sasha's at Commerce School. He was under the supervision of Serzova. He, not Sorzov, but the young Akunovich, was reading Kaddish for his mother, his expression full with the humility of a lay brother of a cloister.

The other day I read in the newspaper that a ship, "President Quezon," leaving America for Shanghai, sank along with the mail. If one of your letters happened to be on that ship, there will be an intermission in the receipt of correspondence from you.

Recently I met Mme. Messe on Kitaiskaya Street. She asked how Sasha was doing, calling him Shura. Her son was Sasha's schoolmate. The father, that is Mme. Messe's husband, is chronically ill, and frequently has episodes when it is necessary to take him to the hospital at night to ease his suffering. The mother is also not in full health and to add to that, they are poor. Their son lives in Tsingtao. He's a businessman and supports his parents with packages and spending money. The result is that they have a decent life. Mme. Messe wants her son to connect to Sasha for some sort of business plan. If Sasha receives a letter from the young Messe, let him know that I gave his address, but I don't vouch for him. I don't even know what they are talking about.

It's somewhat strange to me that Sasha aims to once again sit on a school bench. The main thing is that I can't understand his choice to take classes in American literature. If Tanya did this, I would not be surprised: her letters are sprinkled with literary talent. But in Sasha I don't feel this. If he were to take courses in wood carving, wood burning, then I would tell myself that he is being pushed towards it by the invisible force of his grandfather (on his mother's side), but in terms of literature, his other grandfather (my father), as unfortunate as it may be, apparently spared him of his inheritance, giving all his literary riches to his granddaughter, Mariam Shimonovna. But we shouldn't be sad about this. If, as they say, a husband and wife complete each other, then in this regard he received an excellent complement in the person of Tanya. Of course, as a capable person (a compliment to Sasha, like a ricochet, falls back also to me) he of course can improve himself in this respect, but it is unlikely that he will achieve excellence.

Now the radio is reporting on a directive from the authorities that everyone must get vaccinated against smallpox. Therefore, now I also issue a directive, to my department: ---- Sasha! Make Mira get a smallpox vaccination. ---- Mira! Make Sasha get a smallpox vaccination. About Ninochka I issue no order. Her parents will take care of her.

Every once in a while I feel a need to talk, or more exactly, to write, in Hebrew, but I don't have enough people with whom I can do this. While my papa was alive, I could fully satisfy this need. After his death, this need could be satisfied only partially — during Mama's trips (with you) to the dacha, and then you would claim that I was writing in an unknown language that made you have to ask Mama, "What is written there?" In any case, now that possibility has fallen away, and I remember that Lev Yakovich, I think, told me that Alex Yakovich Lishchiner knows Hebrew, and I would like to use him, that is A.Y., as a sounding board.

All last night it hailed fluffy snowflakes, and in the morning the streets were of fairytale-like beauty. Our apple tree in our little garden was a beautiful sight in the morning. It stood in white transparent attire, sparkling snowflakes on its branches. Around mid-day, the snow started to melt and it soaked through our roof into the attic (over the winter some little holes or cracks appeared in our roof), and from the attic to the ceiling. As a result, in several places, the plaster in the dining room ceiling was damaged, got chipped, and resembles the blush and pallor on a woman's face the morning after she has spent a stormy night.

I am remembering the following incident: It was during Passover in 1896. Mama — then a high school student in Kovenska M. Filin Okei Girls' High School — came to Dvinsk to stay with her uncle, Leib Beshkin, for the Passover holidays. I was working for him for Rostrans. On one of the days of HaMoed, I invited Mama to take a walk with me along the shore of the Dvina River. We got carried away in conversation and found ourselves about 2 versts outside of town. Noticing a little café with a sign saying "Dairy Bar" in a garden, we, without thinking, entered and sat down at one of the tables. Without asking, the server, a Russian peasant fellow, immediately put the dish of the day on our little table—milk and two buns. When I mechanically reached for the glass of milk, Mama screamed, "Mr. Fix, what is today?" "Passover!" I answered in a frightened voice, and we jumped up and retreated, afraid to even look back behind us. The path from the dairy bar through the garden was sprinkled with sand and the whole time while we were running away, we couldn't shake the question, "What will they say?" Just think—the granddaughter of the Volozhin Yeshiva Lecturer and Spiritual Rabbi in Paris on her mother's side, and granddaughter of Rebbe Reb Shneur Zalman on her father's side, is taking a walk outside of town with a young man and is visiting a Russian dairy bar during Passover . . . Our hearts were filled with one wish: that a strong wind would kick up and blow away all traces of our footprints from the sand in that garden. Our hearts worried and fluttered, just as they pounded, knocking and trembling, when, four years later, while on a walk towards, as it was called in Dvinsk, the Petersburg Station, for the first time Mama and I shyly said to one another, "We." That was in the year 1900. Your Papa

Alexander (Shura) Galatzky

It was not uncommon for families to be separated for long periods of time. After all, people were looking for safe places that could offer security, employment, and a better life for their families. In many cases, one could find a mother and her children waiting to hear from the father who was in a faraway place trying to save enough money so that he could bring his wife and children. This was applied to Harbin when some members of a family left their homes in the countries under the umbrella of the Soviet Union and arrived in town either to inspect the conditions there or prepare the grounds for receiving the rest of the family. In other instances, men went from Harbin to either Europe, America or a destination in South America looking for opportunities there and then, when the time was right, reunite with their families in the new geography.

Alexander (Shura) Galatzky was born in 1912 in Poltava, Ukraine, then part of the tzarist Russian Empire, and died in south Florida in 2005. He was the only child of Benjamin and Nadia (nee Paltzeva) Galatzky.[182]

At the time of the Bolshevik Revolution in 1917, Shura's father was working in the U.S. where he had a brother and a plan to send money to his wife, so that she and his young son could join him there. Unfortunately, amidst the chaos of the period, his hard-earned savings were "lost" in transit, and Benjamin realized he could not spend another few years saving sums to bring his wife and child to him. He decided to reunite with them in Harbin, Manchuria, where an established Russian community, including a Jewish community, had developed since the early 1900s.

Nadia, a young woman in her twenties at the time, was left to her own devices to plan and negotiate the passage for herself and their son. Shura remembered the trans-Siberian train journey that took several months and required his mother to barter the few rags and goods she carried and plead with the various contingents of soldiers, revolutionaries, and opportunists for food and safe passage eastward. In letters written later in life, Shura recounted how, at around the age of 7, he and his mother arrived in Harbin and were reunited with Benjamin after several years. Shura looked up and asked, "Are you, my father?"

Life in Harbin offered the Galatzky family some stability and gradual upward mobility. Benjamin became a bookkeeper for cattlemen. The pictures Shura kept from the period show a nicely appointed apartment. Letters tell of being able to rent vacation properties across the Sungari River.

Shura kept diaries throughout his school years in Harbin. His entries speak of very normal boyhood concerns, friendships, rivalries, crushes on girls, writing plays for the school theater club, going to Betar meetings for Zionist youth, and having the occasional run-in with Russian nationalist youths. He received a solid education at the Harbin Commercial School, had his Bar Mitzvah in the community, wrote poetry, studied art, and took piano lessons.

As his high school graduation approached in 1929, he and his parents had to decide where he should go to the university. In Shura's diaries, he writes with some sentimentality that all his friends were scattered across the globe "forever". Graduation pictures show well-dressed classmates posing for professional photographers with handwritten words of friendships to be cherished and remembered.

It was ultimately decided that Shura would travel with one of his close friends, Boris Lesk, to Paris, France to study. The two boys, 17 and 18 years old, left together from Dalian by boat to Shanghai. They continued their

Fig. 33: Alexander Galatzky and his mother in Harbin

journey over a couple of months in steerage aboard a ship that was transporting French colonial soldiers to various locations. Pictures, a passport, and a visa booklet record the boys passing through Ceylon, Singapore, Hong Kong, Malaysia, the Suez Cannal and finally Marseilles. From Marseilles, they made their way north to Paris.

Shura spent 10 years in Paris, first learning French, then getting admitted to the Institut de Chemie, and ultimately earning a Ph.D. in Chemistry in 1934. During that time, he was unable to travel back to Harbin to see his parents, who, following the Japanese occupation of Manchuria in 1932, found their living conditions deteriorating. At some point thereafter, they made a decision to leave and resettle in the U.S. Meanwhile, Shura was a stateless Russian Jew living in France on the eve of the Nazi occupation. Luckily, he was able to get visa papers to the U.S. in 1938, leaving Paris to join his parents in New York.

Once in the U.S., Shura Galatzky became Alexander Galat and lived the "American Dream." He married Helen Grankin in 1940. They eventually had three children and made their home in Westchester County, where Alexander worked in his own laboratory and invented and patented processes and drugs which were sold to the large pharmaceutical companies. In addition to inventing the patient-friendly testing strips for diabetics marketed as Clinitest by Miles Labs, other notable work included a novel treatment for chronic urinary infections marketed as Urex and Hiprex by Riker-3M, a synthetic caffeine process developed for Coca-Cola during World War II, when caffeine was in short supply, and anticaries process for Procter and Gamble.

During several decades of work up until his death, he devoted himself to perfecting injectable, soluble, and transdermal aspirin. His later years also included artistic creativity, and his unique oil paintings on acrylic were exhibited in gallery shows in Florida.

An epilogue that Alexander Galat's daughter Bonnie Galat wrote tells that "My father's 1929 Commercial High School class held several reunions, all in Israel. The first took place in 1970 and brought together at least 15 of the Harbin "boys" who came from Australia, Japan, the U.S., France, and Germany. Pictures show them toasting each other and remembering their professors, for whom my father wrote a poem to recognize a debt of gratitude they all felt for having received a top-notch education in such a remote and unlikely place as Harbin, Manchuria."

A letter from R, Tsiroulsky in Harbin to Alexander Galatsky in Paris gives light to the way people spent their time and how young people dealt with romance, the matters of the heart. The envelope, dated 1932, shows that the letter went from Harbin to Paris via the USSR.

Mr. A. Galatsky

12, Boulevard Poissonniere, Paris

Ronya Tsiroulsky, 76, Rue Commerce, Kharbine-Chine

Shura, dear!

I'm sitting down to write you a letter in the most unexpected manner. I wanted to go to the movies and instead am writing you… I received a letter from you a long, long time ago… I don't know why, it even implored me to reply to you (that, which you wrote living "in a small village on the French Riviera — Côte d'Azur").

I heard from your family that you are supposed to come home — when this will come to be and whether it will be soon or not, I don't even know, in any case, I want to see you and am interested in who you have become. Mosya (Moshe) wrote me that he saw you when he was in Paris, and that outwardly you had changed very little.

Oh, how I now dream of Paris, of the fact that it is impossible for me to now go study there. Especially now that I have reached, more or less, the prime in my work, I feel lacking in exercises with teachers, given the situation I am currently in, regarding trends in art (which I can only follow through articles and pictures in journals/magazines), from the works of the great masters, and from the entire art world at large.

At the moment, I am painting a full-length portrait of Mira, the approximate size of which is 2.5x1.5 arshin[183]. This work keeps me very occupied. As a matter of fact, I started to really love painting portraits. Upon your arrival, I will make sure to paint one of you. We just have to make sure to come up with something more original for the portrait. I don't imagine it will take too much effort!

If only you weren't so lazy, and would write me more often. There are many, many things that interest me in this way. I will not ask any questions, as it is both exhausting and uninteresting. Questions limit the margins of a letter, and I am all for freedom and spontaneity.

I am currently in Harbin (Kharbine). I did not, as I initially thought, go to Shanghai. I am more than happy with my choice of house (if choosing between Harbin and Shanghai).

I came to my senses and am learning English (oh, what a bore, especially taking into account the little love I have for learning languages!)

It's cold here now. I go ice-skating infrequently. Other things constantly preclude me, such as illness—'I had a cold for the longest time', and another time some extravagant youth in the middle of some unsafe skating flew into me from the back with such force that he and I both flew forward, and after this incident I have already spent two weeks avoiding skating, such was the unlucky extent of the flight.

What entertainment do you have available in Paris, besides

cinema? After all, I've heard that it is prohibitively expensive to go out to the theater or a concert, even more so for students.

Do you have friends? Lesk, it seems, has undergone total Francization, according to Mosya's letters. Are you two still friends? How does that old saying go—old feelings don't rust, I believe? He, most likely, is not planning to come to Harbin.

Tell me honestly, are you very homesick or no? I have always been plagued by the thought of this longing for the homeland. Although if I were abroad simultaneously with you, then you, I believe, would be able to minimize and help me with my grief, as a good friend -?

Are you familiar, even if indirectly, with the artistic life of Paris, do you ever go to galleries? If so, please share with me your impressions. Although I doubt that this would interest you much now.

My letter doesn't seem to be coming together like I had hoped. I do not wish to simply write about events that concern us, and yet writing about something distractedly is something I cannot do. I seem to have lost your overall essence, I think you will help me find it once more with your next letter. Speaking of which, you had promised to send me postcards from your "blessed village in the south of France". Where are they? Hurry, hurry my friend, you are a poor keeper of your promises!

I will end on this note.

Au revoir, to use your language

Ronya. I await your quick reply[184]

The Dinaburg family

The saga of the dispersion of the Dinaburg family from Rogachev at the beginning of the 20th century was repeated in Jewish families throughout the Pale of Settlement for more than a decade. By 1915 more than two million Jews had emigrated and settled in new homes around the world.[185]

The exodus of the Dinaburg children did not follow any preset plan or pattern. Each one took a different route and by 1913 all eleven had left home. For many, the Chinese town of Manzhouli, on the border of Russia and Manchuria, provided the first step in their journey to their maybe final home. As the economic climate stagnated in Manchuria, several grand uncles and grand aunts were able to arrange passage to North America. The others chose to move to Harbin, the booming hub and administrative center of the planned extension of the trans-Siberian railroad by the Chinese Eastern Railway into Manchuria and then eastward toward Vladivostok.

Those that settled in North America had their first and only family reunion in Toronto, Canada in May 1946. Henry Strage, son of Michael Strajevsky and Sophia Dinaburg, writes that he was fortunate to attend the reunion. Fittingly the venue was the home of the oldest child in the family, Uncle Abraham. It was a moving experience for all.

Granduncle Abraham, the oldest son, born in 1880, was conscripted into the Russian army to serve for a period of twenty-five years. The story of his escape or, more accurately, his defection from the Russian Imperial Army is one of the family's treasured legends. As a young inexperienced recruit, uncle Abraham served as an orderly to an officer somewhere in the far eastern corner of Russia. One day he was given a five-ruble gold coin and commanded to go and buy some vodka for the officer's dining rooms. It was a cold night and he saw an opportunity, albeit risky, to escape from the twenty-five years in the Army. He decided to take his chances. He dressed warmly, pocketed the coin, and never returned. He knew that there was a small Jewish community somewhere far off in Manchuria on the border with

Russia and thought his brother Michel might live there or in a similar small Jewish enclave nearby. If he could get there, he would be beyond the reach of the Soviet authorities, which, he knew, dealt very harshly with deserters. Uncle Abraham gave the gold coin to his grandson, Mark Lebo.

Manzhouli suited Uncle Abraham as a safe haven with both religious tolerance and economic opportunities. Several years later he decided to immigrate to North America. He died in Toronto Canada at the age of 77.

When Uncle David arrived in Manzhouli his brother, my grandfather, found a job for him in his now established general store. Uncle David took over most of buying of goods for the store. In Manchuria, camels were the most economic form of long-distance transportation and it was not unusual for a whole caravan to be found near the rear of the store. Many long trips away from home eventually persuaded Uncle David to take his family to the booming metropolis Harbin where he joined some friends in a textile enterprise.

While the serenity, security, and comforts of Manzhouli provided a practically ideal environment for the Jewish families fleeing pogroms and Czarist restrictions something important was missing. There was only a very limited opportunity for economic activity or stable employment. There was no industrial life with the exception of small usually family-operated establishments.

At the same time as the small flow of Jews from Russia began, a major event occurred which

Fig. 34: Sophia (Sonia) Dinaburg, daughter of Michel Dinaburg and Gita Dinaburg

was to change the economic viability of the whole of northern China and Manchuria. In 1898 the Chinese Government granted Russia a twenty-five-year concession to construct an extension of the Trans-Siberian railroad through Northern China.

Harbin's unique location and almost guaranteed future economic prosperity provided an opportunity that attracted both newcomers to the region as well as those who had already settled in small towns in Manchuria with limited opportunities like Manzhouli.

Harbin provided the Jews with an unbeatable combination of forces of not only providing unique economic and financial opportunities but also a friendly, dynamic and welcoming environmental umbrella under which to construct, develop and expand their community and all of its associated infrastructure both religious, social, and cultural. Prosperity meant that what was once a small village became an oasis of excellence in a whole range of cultural activities. Theatres, concert halls, and music conservatories enriched the lifestyle as did libraries, schools, health facilities, a home for the aged, a soup kitchen, modern hotels, and fine restaurants.

With the growing affluence, two spectacular synagogues sprung up, the Main Synagogue on January 15, 1909, and the Hasidic Synagogue, known as the New Synagogue that opened on September 25, 1921, as well as the whole range of Jewish support activities, several mikvahs, a bespoke matzo making facility, social clubs, youth organizations, and an active young Zionist movement. At its peak the Jewish population reached more than 20,000 souls in the early 1920s, which represented one third of the city's population. Russian became the lingua franca and more than twenty Jewish magazines and newspapers were published in Harbin, all in Russian except one which was in Yiddish.

The Dinaburg families and others who came to Harbin via Manzhouli and chose to stay were rewarded with a rich lifestyle that exceeded their expectations. But the good life soon began to erode. The end of World War I and the Revolution in Russia saw a stream of White Russian royalists, and Bolsheviks settle in Harbin and with them, the first signs of anti-Semitism that was completely unknown to most of the Chinese population.

For the Dinaburgs a turning point in their lives was the brutal kidnapping of Aunt Ada's son-in-law Lonya Sherrell who was married to Ada's daughter Anta. The kidnappers threatened to cut off an ear or worse. Another kidnapping a few months earlier resulted in the death of the victim. Eventually, after a significant ransom was paid Lonya was freed but the incident was a clear wake-up call that things were changing for the worse. The exodus of three Dinaburg families followed. The first stop for them was Tientsin and then Shanghai. Eventually, the families settled in Australia and the United States. Today some of their offspring also live in the UK and Israel.

Henry Strage's grandfather together with his wife and unmarried sister Riva Rebecca made the decision that despite his leadership role in the Manzhouli community, it was time to move and join some of his brothers and sisters in Harbin. The Jewish population of Manzhouli gradually shrunk to a dozen families. "In Harbin, my grandfather continued to print newspapers and periodicals. Matters turned worse in 1932 when the Japanese occupied Harbin and the city was officially ceded to the puppet state of Manchukuo.

"The Jewish population of Harbin continued to dwindle and at the end of World War II, there were less than 2,000 Jews remaining including my grandfather who became active in the depressing task of protecting the remaining Jewish buildings including the synagogue, library as well as the cemetery. It was while he was in the synagogue one morning looking after some administrative matters that he was beset by some hooligans and badly beaten. Sadly, he never recovered from his injuries and died in 1946. In the following year, his widow Nadia came to New York where she lived with us on Riverside Drive for many years."

For many, Harbin represented a golden age and revival of Jewish life under the bitterly anti-Semitic Czar to the creation of what came to be known as the Paris of the Orient and the largest center of Jewish life in the Far East.

Myron Vladimirovitch Kofman

Olivier Thomas described his Kofman relatives as "leaders of the Harbin Jewish society."[186]

His grandfather's uncle was Myron Vladimirovitch Kofman was born in Odessa in 1867 and died in Harbin in 1932.

Olivier Thoma's Kofman relatives and his family that lived in Harbin consisted of Myron Kofman and his wife Vera Lvovna, maiden name Ring born in 1888 and died in 1952. They were married in Harbin in 1910 and had 3 children: Vladimir "Valia", Sophie "Sima", and Boris Mironovich.

Miron or Myron V. Kofman was the Tzar's sister Xenia Alexandrovna (1875-1960) lover. She gave Myron lands and houses in Harbin and granted him the title of "Honorouble Meshanin"[187], a name for Jewish people because he couldn't be a Dvoranin that was reserved for Russian people.

Myron Kofman had many brothers and sisters and some of them came with him to Harbin: Among them, Dobrishman, Gurfinkel, Gilevich, Leizerman-Gitman, were the most famous ones.

Myron's sister named Berta or Betia Vladimirovna

Dobrishman who was born in Odessa in 1864, died in Harbin in 1936.

An obituary that appeared in the local paper announced the passing of Boris M. Kofman at the age of 20:

> Last night at 10 o'clock, В.М. Кофман (Boris M. Kofman) suddenly passed away due to illness. He was born in Harbin and finished his primary and secondary education here. Later, Kofman went to Shanghai and entered Saint John's College. He was a sophomore and had always been studying hard.
>
> Kofman's classmates admired and respected him very much. His death was really a shock to them. Last Wednesday, he felt a little bit uncomfortable. Then, things got worse and worse rapidly. Last night at 10 o'clock, this man left us forever at the age of merely 20.

In 1932 the Japanese invaded Manchuria, creating the puppet state of Manchukuo. They sought to expel the Soviets by buying out the Chinese Eastern Railway in 1935.

When the Japanese came to Harbin, they immediately made alliances with the fascists Anti-Semitic White Russians and used them as their proxies in intimidation of the Jewish community, extortions, kidnappings, and murders.

Throughout the period pressure rose on the Harbin Russians, especially the Jews who were not recognized as a separate group, but put under the supervision of the White Russians—often antisemitic and strongly anti-Soviets. Chinese criminals in league with Russian Fascists and the Japanese secret police kidnapped for ransom but soon after murdered a number of Russian Jews in Harbin.

Myron Joseph Kofman was one of them. He was kidnapped

on March 11, 1932. The Japanese wanted to force him to hand over the family brewery business. After his death, the brewery was sold to Japanese interests for almost half the price, and the capital was reinvested in a block of apartments in Shanghai.

Myron Joseph Kofman owned the Central Pharmacy at the intersection of Vodoprovodnaya Street (the present Zhaolin Street) and Mostovaya Street (the present Shitouydao Street) He was kidnapped when Harbin was under Japanese rule and died after being tortured by a White Russian gang who works for the Japanese military police in March 1932. The pharmacy was purchased by Mr. Stechinsky.

Another kidnapping was that of Sherel de Florence Abel Moiseevich. The Sherell de Florance family moved from Harbin to Tientsin after the head of the family was kidnapped by 3 Russians and one Chinese who were working for the Japanese. He was released after the family paid a ransom of 25,000 Dollars, a huge sum of money in those days.

Peter Berton

Being almost European in architecture and following the European cultural trends, Harbin was a music center of her own. The city offered its residents a variety of cultural activities among them philharmonic orchestra and classical music, jazz bands, well-established music schools, concerts, operas, and operettas, and theatres of several repertoires, including a Yiddish theatre, as well as visiting world-famous artists.

Peter Berton was a young musician in Harbin. He was fascinated by classical music and with the biblical roots of Jewish music.[188]

The Bible is full of stories of music, he wrote. Music played an important role in the life of Jews in the Diaspora, even in the constricted environment of the Pale of Settlement in Tsarist Russia. Klezmer musicians were a feature at Jewish weddings. In middle-class Jewish families, children were given music lessons, mostly piano and violin.

As an only child, Berton was 6 when he and his mother moved from Poland to Harbin, one of the largest Jewish communities in the Far East. Berton's father, Claude, arrived and established

Fig. 35: Peter Berton with his violin Harbin c. 1930s

himself as an accountant and businessman, importing heavy woolens from Europe.

Berton remembered 1931 when he was 9 and Japan launched an attack on Manchuria. "The Japanese came in on tanks and the retreating Chinese armies on Mongolian horses were dropping firearms left and right," Berton recalled. "We kids picked them up and traded them. Can you imagine tanks against horses?"

In Harbin, Berton attended an English high school, modeled after schools throughout the British Empire. He then graduated from the Harbin Y.M.C.A. College, established by American missionaries.

He played the violin and graduated from The First Harbin Music Academy, where his teacher was Vladimir Trachtenberg, a pupil of the famous Leopold Auer in the St. Petersburg Conservatory. After music school, Berton sought graduate education in the U.S., but couldn't get a visa. His parents encouraged him to study the violin with the world-renowned Alexander Mogilevsky in Japan.

That's where Berton's world changed. He became fascinated

with the Japanese culture, art, and calligraphy. He explored many aspects of Japanese culture. Studying martial arts, he earned a black belt in karate.

After 12 years, in 1949, Berton's visa arrived. It wasn't a student visa; he came to the U.S. as an immigrant seeking permanent residency.

Wherever they settled, Jews actively participated in the development of cultural life, as teachers, performers, and also importantly as audiences.

The same thing can be said of Harbin, where Jews, who were mostly involved in commerce, were an integral part of musical audiences, especially when famous performers from abroad came to Harbin, such as Jascha Heifetz, Mischa Elman, as well as many non-Jewish performers among them Fyodor Chaliapin and Maurice Marechal.

Among the many talented refugees from Soviet Russia in Harbin were some first-rate musicians, actors, directors, and other members of the Russian intelligentsia. Many of them were Jews.

The First Harbin Music School was the premier music conservatory in Manchuria and probably in all of China. This school not only served the needs of the European inhabitants of Harbin, but also had a number of Chinese, Korean, and Japanese pupils. The Director of the school was the Jewish pianist Valentina Leontievna Gershgorina. The Dean of the Faculty, literally the Chairman of the Artistic Council, was Berton's teacher and mentor, Vladimir Davydovich Trachtenberg, who was also the Concertmaster of the Harbin Symphony Orchestra and the leader of the Harbin String Quartet. Trachtenberg was a pupil of the violin teacher Leopold Auer, whose other pupils included Yasha Heifetz, Misha Elman, and Efrem Zimbalist. Trachtenberg also studied composition with the famous Russian composer Alexander Glazunov, who was, in turn, a pupil of Nikolai Rimsky-Korsakov.

In the last years of his sojourn in Harbin, Peter Berton served as an assistant to his teacher, who asked him to tutor young violinists for a year or so before they were ready to enter his class. Among these young violinists whom he started on a musical career were two Jewish boys, Garrik (Garry) Bravinsky and Hellmut Stern, a young refugee from Berlin. Hellmut went on to become an assistant concertmaster of a prestigious symphony orchestra in the United States, before returning to his hometown, Berlin, to become one of the principal concertmasters of the world-famed Berlin Philharmonic under the legendary Herbert von Karajan. After many years in the orchestra, Hellmut retired but stayed on as an administrator.

Jewish students comprised more than a third of the student body, and some of the most talented silver and gold medalists were Jewish pianists and violinists who went on to prominent careers in the Soviet Union, Israel, Australia, and the United States. Talented pianists Valya Ravve and Ruta Budnevich come to mind among his peers. Ravve also won first prize in the All-Manchurian Musical Competition in 1941. Another Jewish pianist, Tata Bursuk, won third prize in 1942. Tragically, Ravve was sent to Siberia by the Red Army when they occupied Harbin, while Budnevich married a Jewish clarinetist, Herbert Tishman, in New York and pursued a successful music career in the United States including concretizing with her husband as the Tishman Duo.

Joseph Ispa also went to the United States, but found it difficult to pursue a piano soloist's career. David Gootman had a long career in Tel Aviv teaching piano. Gena Bomash was the principal of the second violins in the Harbin Symphony Orchestra, which had a large number of Jewish members, including Peter

Berton himself as the first violin, the cellist Viesenberg, a refugee from Germany, and Isidore Tepper. The orchestra was sent on a one-month tour of Manchuria, Korea, and Japan in March 1939. Tepper went from Harbin to Australia, where he worked as a professional violinist, but also as an owner of a store selling musical instruments, much like teacher Trachtenberg, with his Cantilena musical store in Harbin. Tepper's son Robert became a member of the Sydney Symphony Orchestra.

More tragic was the fate of an exceptional violinist Lev Tyshkov, who in the early 1930s studied the violin with the then concertmaster of the Harbin Symphony Orchestra Nikolai Shifferblatt. Trachtenberg was then the principal of second violins. When Shifferblatt was offered the post of conductor of the national radio orchestra in Tokyo, Lev followed his teacher to Japan. He was making good progress and concretized with a prominent Japanese pianist Miwako Kai. Much to the outrage of Shifferblatt, who was a committed anti-Communist, Lev accepted an invitation to perform at the Soviet Embassy. Shortly thereafter the Soviets offered him a scholarship to the prestigious Tchaikovsky Conservatory in Moscow, and Lev made a near-fatal mistake of accepting the offer and traveling to the Soviet Union in the mid-1930s at the height of purges, arrests, and executions. Some months later, even more naively, he accepted an invitation to perform with his old pianist friend Kai at the Japanese embassy in Moscow. Shortly thereafter, he was arrested on suspicion of being a Japanese spy, interrogated, and shipped off to a Gulag labor camps in Siberia.[189] After Stalin's death, Lev was released from the camp but was forbidden to return to Moscow. As luck would have it, he ended up in Sverdlovsk (Ekaterinburg), where Boris Yeltsin was then the provincial secretary of the Communist Party, and de facto boss of everything. Yeltsin turned out to be a patron of music and Tyshkov became the assistant concertmaster of the local symphony orchestra and second violinist in the city's quartet.

There were also a number of other prominent Jewish music teachers outside the First Music School. In the early and mid-1930s, the Jewish couple, violinist Ury Goldstein and pianist Vera Dillon, were active in Harbin in another music school named after the famous Russian composer Alexander Glazounov.

Jews were also prominent in the lighter, pop music venues, such as the American bar, Gambrinus, and the coffee shop of the premier hotel in Harbin, the Moderne. Here, Jewish refugee musicians such as Wiesenberg, Spielman, and others, played regularly salon piano trio repertoire. Indeed, some of the refugees from Nazi Germany in the late 1930s were either professional musicians or amateurs who tried to make a living in the music field.

Jewish youth organizations, such as Betar had marching bands, on occasion parading down our main street Kitaiskaya Ulitsa (now Central Avenue).

Jewish women organized afternoon music and discussion sessions on Wednesdays called "Sreda" in Russian, which has the double meaning of Wednesday and of being among people.

Jewish musicians also played a part in various non-Jewish organizations and institutions. Berton was a member of the jazz band at the Y.M.C.A. College and also performed at the Gospoda Polska, a Polish service organization, once participating in a concert devoted to the music of Frederic Chopin.

Peter Berton died in Los Angeles on March 28, 2014. He was 91.

In all, these show the scope and breadth of Jewish participation, and on many occasions the leadership it undertook, in the musical and cultural life of Harbin, where Jewish musicians contributed heavily to the cultural scene of the city, as well as established the foundation for the Chinese contemporary western music.

Jason Joseph Isaac (Davies)

Many attempts to tell the stories of individuals have transformed the pasts of Harbin into mental geographies; sometimes imagined, sometimes reconstructed, and altered on occasions. These pasts have been packed into suitcases that moved from one geography, space and time to another; changing, taking on new colors, creating new identities and new stories, or hiding portions, while neglecting to note what was actually happening. These, in turn, formed an 'imagined history' and therefore a constructed present and especially a new and confusing future.

The story of Jason Joseph Isaac, the father of Rita Davies, is a most interesting one, as it can be a study of changing identity and its relation to migration from one geography to another and from one time to another in order to form a new story.

The case of Vera Alexandrovnya Dobrolovskaya who was born to a White Russian orthodox family in 1910 in Harbin and then moved to Shanghai in the 1930s, only to move again from there to Israel, then to Italy, and from there to Canada, is a most interesting study of what I have coined "Glocalized Suitcase Memories—Changing Geographies, Changing Identities, and Changing Pasts".

Vera's father, Alexander Dobrolovskii, was from Ukraine. Her mother, Panna was from Vladivostok. Both were Russian Orthodox and part of the anti-Semite White Russian community of Harbin. Rita Davies the granddaughter, now living in Canada, writes: "My Russian Orthodox grandmother was anti-Semitic as I heard her making comments about the Jews killing Christ. All this could not necessarily be reconciled and was buried instead."

Vera's 82-year-old daughter Rita who lives in Toronto Canada has been trying to construct the early story of her family with much frustration. Vera, her flamboyant mother who searched for different lifestyles, identities, and fortunes, had only left an imagined past.

Alexander Dobrolovskii, the father, was an officer in the Russian Tsarist military. "My mother thought that her father was the Chief of Police for Harbin. She said that in 1928 a man he had put in prison, then shot and killed him following his release... I have always found the story odd, even as a child,"

Fig. 36: Alexander Dobrolovskii

writes Vera's daughter. Perhaps the circumstances of Vera's father's death were difficult to accept, or it was his lifestyle of drinking that led to his death. Over time, she made it palatable by imagining a more noble reason and making him a heroic Dostoyevsky figure..."

In Harbin, Vera attended a Russian school. Later she went to a convent and returned to the city at the age of 18. In the late 1920s, she married a Catholic Portuguese man whose last name was Diniz. Vera looked for an exciting life and thought that this rich Portuguese will fulfill her wishes. She and the Portuguese did not hit it well. His father thought that a change in location would help and bought the couple an apartment in Shanghai. Vera and the Portuguese went to Shanghai sometime in the early 1930s. Other than the fact that Diniz was physically abusive, there is no other information about this part of Vera's life. "She left Diniz at some point and later she met my father Jason Joseph Isaac who by then had also left his first wife. My parents did not have a legal marriage because both were married to people who would not grant them a divorce. My birth certificate shows the last name as Diniz..."

Jason Joseph Isaac was born to a Jewish family outside of

Baghdad in 1908. After his father's death, he went with his mother to Hong Kong where her grandfather's brother, the Wise Sage Eliyahu Isaac, the cantor of Ohel Leah Synagogue, who later became the cantor of Ohel Rachel synagogue in Shanghai, lived. In his early twenties, Jason Joseph Isaac went with his mother to Shanghai. In 1930 he married another Baghdadi Jew named Mozelle Toeg. That marriage resulted in three daughters. The marriage broke up sometime in the early 1940s.

Isaac and Vera met in a nightclub where she worked in Shanghai. The Jewish Baghdadi and the Orthodox White Russian Vera from Harbin had three children out of wedlock. Rita was born in 1947, but her birth certificate registered her as a Diniz. They left Shanghai in December 1949 on a cargo boat named 'The Wooster Victory' that carried refugees. It was a lengthy voyage until it reached the Israeli port of Haifa. Neither part of the couple had any citizenship, legal marriage certificates, or other forms of documentation. They had arrived in Israel as Jewish

Fig. 37: Jason Joseph Isaac and Vera Dobrolovskii in Shanghai

refugees sometime in early 1950 and stayed there almost a decade until 1959. They became an Israeli Jewish family, and by now the legality of their marriage and the status of the children were taken for granted. The now Jewish family left Israel for Canada in 1959. Soon after that, the father changed his family name from Isaac to Davies out of fear of Canadian anti-Semitism.

Their Shanghai photographs reveal a style of life that was at odds with the hardship of the Japanese occupation of the city. Although in some of the photographs Isaac is seen wearing an armband indicating that he is a Jew, there was no mention of refugees nor of hardship. In the photos, their lives looked like an endless party and nightclub dances. "Their generation was secretive. I was not told much of their or my past," Rita Davies wrote.

A past has its twists. In this case, it starts with an Anti-Semite Russian Orthodox background in Harbin, and finds a Jewish connection in Shanghai that leads to a new identity in Israel, which changes again in Canada. It presents problems with glocalized memories, an imagined past, motives, identities and geographies, and the connection between them. The Jewish connection was coincidental but helped to form a new dimension to the identities of the players and especially to those of their descendants.

Movement from familiar geography to another, especially when the new differs drastically from the old, creates forces that may bring a change in the identity of the traveler, and lead to a creation or alteration of a past that either was not there or wishfully imagined. Harbin and Shanghai, two Chinese cities themselves with different pasts, harbored such changes. These railway and port stations existed for an exchange of goods and human cargo. They helped to form reconstructed or imagined geographies and assisted in changing or creating new identities. These, in turn, accelerated the invention of imagined histories.

Vera's past was one of these creations.

These mental histories exist everywhere because reality has its limits. What is real to one may not be factual or true to another. And because truth, is the state of being in congruence with fact or reality, it must wander on and on and never come to rest.

General Lin Hu

In considering an individual's past identity, the case of Chinese Air Force General Lin Hu, a decorated national hero, may demonstrate the complexity of historical investigation in determining a motif or reconstructing a past when facts are manipulated, imagined, or lacking. This case is especially difficult because the Chinese General has European features, and because his geographies, spaces, and time are confused and guarded in a locked box that the Chinese military authorities refuse to grant permission to open.[190]

Fig. 38: *Chinese PLA Air Force General Lin Hu*

Lin Hu said that he was born in Harbin in 1928. He told that his father was Chinese and that his mother was Jewish and of Russian origins. His father died of unknown causes a few months after his birth. The mother died in 1932 or 1933 and was buried in Harbin.

The boy and his older sister, whose name he does not remember, were put in an orphanage home located near the Harbin train station. At some point, the sister was taken by someone and her whereabouts are not known. The boy was taken by a foster family who lived near the station. After a year or so they sent him to Shandong province to be with another family where he was treated very badly. They gave him his name Lin Hu.

General Lin Hu has no recollections of his past. He does not remember the name of his mother, although he says that he went to visit her grave twice—first at the age of seven, and a second time in the early 1950s. He claims that his mother's tombstone had a Star of David engraved on it, but cannot say in which cemetery it was.[191]

This 'remembrance' has led his two daughters, now middle-aged oriental-looking women, and their offspring to believe that they are Jews.[192]

All attempts to interview the aging General were refused by the Chinese military authorities for fear he may reveal air force secrets. General Lin Hu could not provide any new details except remember Harbin as not a pleasant place to be in. I thought that a psychiatric analysis of a deep hypnosis he would undergo will reveal certain information about his mother and the cemetery she was buried in. But this idea was refused as well.

His description of the tombstone and the Star of David on it may give rise to speculation that his memory is serving a certain truth. After all, just but very few Chinese know what a Star of David is.

In any case, the old cemeteries in Harbin have been demolished in the late 1950s, and records of the Jews who were interned there are in the Jewish archives of Harbin, which have been closed in 1985.

A Caucasian-looking Chinese Jewish Air Force General. What an unusual story.

Boris Kushner

Ron Kushner has kept many of his father's letters hoping that one day he would be able to understand their content. Ron and his brother Irving grew up in America and never learned Russian, the language in which the letters were written. Their father Boris lived in Harbin.

The contents of Boris Kushner's letters were a surprise to us, wrote Ron. The first one appears to be addressed to my father from a spurned girlfriend (and refers to a second one). This is the first information we have about his love life and can't help you at all with regard to who the people mentioned in the letter are since this is the first we know about them.[193]

> *(Travel Permit Translation: Jilin Bin Jiang District Chief Executive & Office of Foreign Affairs of Harbin gives this permission because a Russian, named Boris (Berl) Kushner needs back and forth from Harbin to Shanghai. Please send the passport to make sure this permission work when being checked. According to the regulations please attached one Yuan revenue stamp. Boris (Berl) Kushner has to receive this permission in person. October 28th, 1922 – The person who gave this permission: xxxxxxxx – The validity of this permission is for 6 months.)*

The second letter addressed to Ricky is a complete mystery. We suspect it was addressed to someone other than our father but don't have a clue as to who he is and why our father has the letter. Our father lived in Irkutsk before he came to Harbin and passed through Chita on his way from Irkutsk to Harbin but, to our knowledge had never been to Kobe or London. And he never mentioned having a child before he came to America. Our thoughts fly in all kinds of directions trying to make sense of this letter, but everything is just speculation all the way from his having used an alias with some people to his carrying the letter because he expected to see Ricky someday and would deliver it to him.

Love is universal and so are physical needs:

…by leaving when you were supposed to stay. I'm kidding, don't be angry. I won't write you until I get a big letter. Ah, and you answer Mark, who from two… M. is a funny fellow, let him ask me, I'll tell him.[194]

I didn't send my regards to Ginzburg. This is unnecessary because he allowed himself to say something after you left, something he shouldn't have said. And furthermore, I know that he is a liar. Good luck! My best to you.

Warmest regards. M.V.

Hi, dear Boris!

It's a shame I didn't get your address and couldn't write to you the whole time. And you're worse than a little kid, too. Did you have no desire to drop a line to me personally, in other words, your Hello in a letter to M. I was not satisfied absolutely. After all, you could send them a letter for me, but if you didn't do this it is needless to say. Do you miss me or not? Do you love me? If so, do come back before it's too late. I miss you so much, if you want to know the truth. I come to M. only because I hope to meet you there or at least get a letter. I'm terribly sorry I didn't talk to you about so much, but it was because I was extremely nervous too. I didn't realize what was going on, but now I know that… I treat you very well and without you I would be very bad. I don't know if it's love or passion, but there's something. I am too righteous to say this or that without testing myself, but you are sweet, I care about your fate. You played on trick leaving me behind. You had to wait a little while longer, I'd get to know you and then…then we'd either be happy or we'd go our separate ways. If I wasn't older, a lot of things might have been different, but I was depressed about it, and I didn't do the right thing. Come back if you love me. I am waiting. Why didn't you hear my words to you last night: "Come back from Shanghai, I'm waiting"? Once more, listen to you or not, I say I miss you, I need you and I care about you. Come back! Going to America, will you forget me? It seemed to me that you were terribly nervous, parting with us, but stubbornness was stronger than me, and I did not show even the kind that I understand and see. Maybe you were nervous parting with M.S., but not me? Maybe your excitement and everything else was because of her?

But no, I'm not blind, I feel like I worried about you, so why did you leave? Write everything in detail; it is certainly in the extreme case, if you do not return. Somehow I don't believe I'll ever see you again. I have your photo on my table and I talk to you every day. You are better than alive there, your eyes are meaningful, you look eagerly in my soul and your mournful smile excites me to tears. There is nothing in my heart after your leaving, all first day I lay and didn't say a word to anyone, but life goes on, you have to break yourself and talk when you do not want and to laugh when willing to cry. Now I am writing from your room while being on a visit to M.S. I started tonight and I finish around 12. I'll go home, but you aren't here, there is no one to escort. I can't write anymore. The sisters came and, in general, ruined my mood. If you love me, write or come back, but sooner. The available addresses are: Third line, for me, or landing, be called for me, or to M.G., for me. Enough, I am finished, be happy and cheerful. Warmest regards, Ver... (sign)

... my darling!

Since we arrived to Chita and wrote each other on one letter, our communication broke again because I did not know that you left Kobe and I was sending my letters there, but I didn't get any answers, so I stopped writing to Kobe. Janson, the clerk of Tsentrosoyuz (Centrosoyuz) who worked with Buk in Vladivostok, said to me when we met that there was a request of Tsentrosoyuz (Centrosoyuz) from London about Buk, and we decided, that you are in London, but we couldn't understand why you don't inform us about yourselves. Indeed, it continued about a year and I think you have to, i.e. it would be possible to get word from the most distant countries of the World. But now I see in your letter, that you, my poor little soul, did write and cabled, but we got nothing except for this letter, which you didn't expect at all, which you sent in open form to Harbin Centre, and at long last unfamiliar comrades forwarded it to us here. You wrote it on March 2, 1922, and we got it on the 9-th of May. I am writing my letter now but I don't hope that you'll get it because in this almost three months you may be gone to Buk to London. And whether your friends from New York City will be so kind and accurate to send you these letters. And as I have no confidence that you'll get it, I have no desire to write a lot, but just in case I will write the most significant.

Our mishpocha (family) from Irkutsk — mother, Yakov, and his wife are alive and kicking, it seems, though that mom is carping about her heart, but she has quite a few years. Yakov is working in the firm "Truzhkop" as treasurer, he pays out wages in millions and billions because the Soviet money was so depreciated that a pound of rye flour in Irkutsk is 8,000,000 rubles. Mother asks us to take her here because her daughter-in-law offends her very much. I'm endlessly sorry for our mother, but you and I couldn't get along with her. Perhaps we will take her here for the winter, but to live will be extremely difficult because we are four here. Boris and Rose will finish a school year soon, and if we find the money, Boris and I will go to one of the local resorts. Rose will stay home as a hostess to care for Yanka, to cook him dinners.

But I think in terror that her dinners will transform my Yanka to real skeleton. We got a hundred yen you sent us from Kobe, and I'll report you in details how we spent them when you tell us your right address. Arrived to Chita, I sent a letter to Solomon, but there is no answer yet. In reality, those two brothers have completely disavowed us. I can tell nothing about Esther and Veniamin, most likely, they are not alive. As to Veniamin, maybe it is better for him, and Esther yourself has to be blamed for everything. When we regain contact, I'll tell you about our break with Esther, it was long ago and I didn't hear anything about her. Yanka and the guys extend warm greetings, and I send love and kisses to all three of you. Bless you.

Your Geka.

... I wish I could see all of you and your sweet son, I often take his postcard and look, and the more I look, the more I want to see him, to hold him. Please, for the sake of your boy, for the sake of all of us, pull yourself together and stop being so nervous, it's necessary that we still live and meet, I also promise you to "pull myself together." How much warm and heartfelt words I would like to say to you, but the unknown fate awaiting this letter deters me. As soon as we get your real address in London we'll have picture taken and send you our old funny faces.

I wanted to cable you, but when I knew at the Telegraph Office, that one word is worth 2 rubles 40 cop. coved by silver, so the most abbreviated telegram would cost me 5 or more rubles coved by gold because I don't know your telegraph address, I have to refuse with a mourn. All winter we borrowed the money, salary not enough, and that's why, having never in the hands of free money, can't wire you, to reassure you. And about my letter, if it reaches New York City and when it is sent to you, I'm afraid even to think how much time it will take. Write me, dear, a good letter; when I read this one, I cried so much that I thought my heart would burst. Once again I mentally embrace and kiss you all. I'm staying tuned.

Your G.

For many, time was not a fun party in Harbin. The two letters from Geka reveal not only an emotional weakness but difficulties in the daily life of the family as well. The aftermath of the 1917 revolution in Russia had a direct monetary effect on the economy of Harbin as the Ruble, one of the important means of life and commerce in the city has fallen to the bottom of the scale, and, as it lost its former value it became an untouchable mean of finance. And while the well-to-do lived in luxury, in large accommodations, others were crumbed in small apartments in which they had to share a small space with not just the nuclear family but with additions such as grandparents and sometimes even aunts and uncles.

Tova Zimin

Tova Zimin did not like to talk about her past. A journey to Harbin, her birth city, with her family in September 2012 rekindled her memories and when the family returned to her kibbutz Shamir in the Galilee, she sat down and wrote about her early childhood, her impressions of the city she grew up in, and about her meeting with Chinese students at Heilongjiang University in Harbin.

I was born in Harbin, northeastern China, in the Manchuria region. The city was founded in the days when the colonial powers tried to take a bite out of parts of China. It was actually a Russian city, under Russian rule until the Japanese War with Russia in 1904-5. Trumpeldor (the neighbor from Tel Chai) lost his hand in that environment and spent two years in Harbin in hospitals and in a POW camp.

During the revolution, tens of thousands of Russians fled to

Fig. 39: Moshe and Rosa Zimin

Harbin, and in the early 20th century, 20,000 Jews lived in Harbin with another 60,000 "white" Russians (and anti-Semites...). The Chinese lived in the shadow of the Russian and Jewish economies.

In 1931, Manchuria was occupied by the Japanese, and then Harbin in 1932, creating a rather frightening situation for the Jews. On the one hand, Jews were an economic force and the Japanese needed them, and also wanted to take advantage of the "Jewish influence" in the United States. On the other hand, the "white" Russian exiles were the Japanese natural allies, to the point of establishing a Russian battalion in the Japanese army that was intended to fight against the Soviets.

I was born into this reality in 1938 to a single mother, and we all lived in my grandparents' house. Grandpa, Moshe Zimin, was one of the leaders of the Jewish community and was an economically organized man. In 1940 he was called to run the Modern Hotel. It was few years after the kidnapping and murder of Semion Kaspe, the son of Joseph Kaspe, the owner of the hotel and a cousin of my grandfather. Joseph lost his sanity after seeing the body of his son and died heartbroken in France in 1938. The

Japanese who instigated the kidnapping wanted the hotel but never got it.

Hotel Moderne was the largest and most luxurious hotel in the city and was also a cultural, political, and social center. It contained a café and a theater hall, where artists and theater and ballet bands and singers performed, among others, the famous opera singer Chaliapin. We lived in one of the hotel suites. It was a luxurious childhood, and for the little granddaughter of the hotel manager, it was a world of its own. She was the little darling of the guests, she greeted customers who frequented the stores and restaurants, and the café. And she mingled with the people who were dressed in evening attire and smashing gowns.

All this was interrupted in 1945 when the Soviet Red Army occupied Manchuria. First of all, they arrested the leadership of the Jewish community, including my grandfather. One or two of them came back from the gulag years later, but my grandfather perished there.

We moved to the city itself, and thanks to my mother's golden hands, who opened a sewing salon for children's clothes, we suffered no shortage. Childhood became less generous, but I attended a Russian-Jewish school and had many friends for games and entertainment.

Where did the 60,000 white Russians go? Apparently one year of Red Army rule almost wiped out their presence in Harbin. Amazingly there were seeds of Chinese anti-Semitism, although most Chinese have never met a Jew in their days, in their opinion, Jews are smart, clever, rich, and have connections all over the world. They think that the Jews are almost a supernatural force.

In 1950, we sailed by sea to Hong Kong, and from there we arrived on a flight and landed at the Aliyah Gate in Israel, and from there they transferred us to a tent camp in Ramat Yishai. A tent for the family, an agency bed for the man, a fountain, and a dugout toilet.

*****

On October 14, 2021, I received a letter from 65-years-old Alexander Alkaev, aka Sasha Zimin, who lives in Samara in Russia. Samara, the sixth-largest city in Russia and capital of an eponymous region, lies on the Volga River in European Russia.

The subject of the letter was the "Zimin family. Harbin, 1921-1945".

What sparked my interest, wrote Alexander Alkaev, was that my ancestors emigrated from Samara to Harbin in 1921 and lived there until 1945. One of them, Moses G. Zimin, was one of the officials of the Jewish diaspora in Harbin.

Moshe Zimin is the cousin of my grandfather Mark Zimin (1901 – 1947), so Tova is supposed to be my 4th cousin. I am 65, my mother Natalia 87 years old, we live in Samara, Russia, one of the native towns of the Zimin family. Next is Orenburg.

The building of the factory, founded by Gedalya Zimin in 1909, is still situated in the old center of Samara.

I also discovered that Moshe's brother Joseph emigrated from China with his family and died in Sydney, Australia in 1994.

I've also found the Passenger list of Displaced Persons (departure April 24, 1950):

Moshe's wife, Roza Zimin, was born in 1891

Moshe's daughter, Esther Zimin, was born in 1914

Tauba Zimin, who was born in 1938, but her whereabouts are unknown. Nevertheless, it can be said in confidence that Tauba, and Tova are the same person.

It's a great event for all members of the Zimin family in Moscow, Samara, Ekaterinburg, Valencia (Spain) and Rugby, ND, USA, wrote Alexander Alkaev.

Tova Zimin never knew about her connection to a family in Samara, Russia.

I informed Tova of the new findings and introduced Alexander Alkaev to her.

On October 21, 2021, I received a letter confirming the establishment of communication between them.

"Sasha Zimin contacted us a week ago and there was a very exciting conversation," wrote Tova Zimin. Thank you so much for making contact. Another interesting detail is that what he did not write down but should be informed is that the son of the family who went to Australia, Robert Zimin, relocated to Israel and died several years ago. He left two children. Robert was the cousin of grandmother Ester. The brother in Australia, the young brother of Moshe Zimin, was a younger brother from another woman. Robert Zimin was a psychiatrist specializing in child development and autism.

Thus, the connection between Samara, Harbin, Moscow, Ekaterinburg, Valencia (Spain), Rugby, ND, USA, Australia, and Israel has been made. It is the unpredictable nature of human destiny that may change the worldview and identity of people when they move to new geographies. Tova Zimin, the darling of the luxurious Hotel Moderne in Harbin, turned into the socialist ideal when she arrived in Israel. Her Kibbutz, Shamir, belongs to the socialist movement "Hashomer Hatsayir" which beliefs in a classless existence.

*****

There is an oft-repeated legend in the American Jewish Community. The child asks the parent, "Why was this town started in this spot? The parent answers: That's where the peddler's horse died."[195]

"What the peddler achieved was more than making a living for himself." In his quest for survival, he was bringing new or recycled merchandise to the attention of the dwellers, and in doing so he created ever new wants and thus helped lay the foundation for a mass market. "In many ways, he was performing the functions now divided between advertising men, salesmen, mail-order catalogs, and radio announcers."[196]

Harbin's bazaars were not simply market areas in which goods of all kinds were traded. They were also urban living spaces with a specific life form; one could even say a distinct microcosm within the city topography. People with highly varied cultural backgrounds came together here on a daily basis, traders with their families as well as customers, who sold or bought goods, traded and haggled, organized themselves in interest groups and networks, exchanged opinions, knowledge, and cultural values as well as carried out conflicts among themselves. For many of the city's inhabitants, the bazaar was not only the center of their business activities but the center of their whole lives.[197]

"In a period when even newspapers were scarce, he served as a major agency of communication between city and countryside, between one county and another, one state and another. By keeping alive these vital channels of communication, he also served as an important link in cementing the unity"[198] of the space where people functioned.

"These fashion frills were only a tiny part of the early 'street' inventory that was supposed to supply the pioneers' needs 'from the cradle to the grave, from a baby blanket to hardware for coffins, from drill bits to black powder to demijohns of whiskey — in other words, the essentials and a few luxuries for every room, the front parlor, bedroom, kitchen, and, of course, the outhouse."[199]

The bazaar, and urban retail trade in general, is one of the spheres of life in a multicultural city in which primarily intercultural contacts, conflicts, and processes of negotiation determine daily life. This seems particularly evident in the case of Harbin, which, due to its favorable situation as a crossroads of Northern China, quickly developed into a center of regional and long-distance trade. Bazaars are a "contact zone"[200] by their nature. This is also the case for many streets and squares frequented by traders and customers, situated near a bazaar or adjacent to one, which often fulfilled a similar function with respect to trade, as well as to a host of vendors who used the streets as their trading zones.

The term "contact zone" describes "social spaces where disparate cultures meet, clash, and grapple with each other, often in highly asymmetrical relations of domination and subordination."[201]

Harbin's rapid economic upswing was closely connected with the dynamic development of neighboring Fujiadian, which many referred to as the Chinese Ghetto. Directly adjacent to Harbin separated only by the railway tracks, the Chinese settlement of Fujiadian quickly grew to the size of a town. The railway tracks from the bridge went onto a section of land called Mostovaya and continued on toward the station. Even though Mostovaya was small, it had a few warehouses and other buildings on it. It was not as narrow as just railway tracks.

A significant and constantly increasing number of Chinese who were employed in Harbin as workers or traders lived in cheaper Fujiadian, which lay within walking distance of the central areas of the city of Harbin, especially Pristan. Close to thirty thousand daily "border crossings" between Fujiadian and Harbin Pristan' in 1911 impressively document that for commuters in particular a high level of mobility between the two neighboring cities was part of everyday life.[202] While the border between Harbin and Fujiadian in the "normal" practice of day-to-day life was very porous, its significance became apparent in a very drastic way in crisis situations.

Until 1932, Fujiadian was under the Chinese administration and it only became part of the city of Harbin under Japanese rule as part of the newly founded state of Manchukuo. This situation of close proximity between two de facto districts with different administrations and differing legal systems enabled many inhabitants to circumvent Harbin's diverse trade and business regulations in neighboring Fujiadian without forgoing the advantage of location.

Although the small merchants, shopkeepers, and peddlers were not directly involved in international trade, in the long run, they would certainly have been able to profit from the changes it wrought for the city and its population. During the construction of the railway and of the Russian settlement, Harbin primarily attracted immigrants from a Russian cultural background, among them many Jews, who then became involved in trade and commerce. From the beginning of the twentieth century, however, more and more people from China and, in smaller numbers, from Japan, Korea, and other nations arrived.[203]

Although trade blossomed in all parts of Harbin, it seems to have differed in type and extent, depending on the quarter of the city. This assumingly was due to the very different ethnic or national composition of the quarters, as well as their specific infrastructure.

Not including the suburbs, the three most important quarters of Harbin were "Old Harbin" (Staryi Kharbin), then "New Town" (Novyi gorod), and finally and in particular Pristan' (Daoli), situated on the banks of the river Sungari.[204]

In the 1920s and afterward, Old Harbin was Russian-dominated. Probably because it offered poor transport facilities and was quite far from the central quarters of Pristan and New

Town, Old Harbin was the least urbanized quarter and lost its initial importance after only a few years.

New Town, the official and residential district of Harbin, was dominated by Europeans, mainly Russians, although in this quarter the percentage of Chinese and Japanese residents was higher than in Old Harbin. In around 1924, the population of the New Town was composed of 71.7% Europeans, 25.5% Chinese, and 2.8% Japanese.[205]

Pristan' was doubtlessly the most heterogeneous, multicultural part of Harbin. In addition to the Russians, many Chinese lived here[206], along with the Japanese and the majority of Harbin Jews. Pristan quickly developed into the center of trade and industries of all kinds. Around 1911 about 40% of Pristan's residents were tradesmen, storekeepers, or skilled workers.[207] Pristan' hosted one of the two major bazaars of the city, and large streets like the "Chinese Street" (Kitaiskaia Ulitsa) were lined with stalls and street vendors. The area around "Chinese Street" and the fourteen-row Pristan's bazaar was predominantly inhabited by Chinese and this part of Pristan' was often referred to as the Chinese quarter.

It was here, in the central area of Pristan where Jews lived, had their community social institutions, stores, and other properties such as hotels, apartment buildings, and trade yards.

In the small streets that crossed Central Street (Kitaiskaia Ulitsa), they had their specialty stores; butcheries, groceries, dairy products such as milk and cheese, bakeries, wineries, shoe, and watch repairs.

Reuvim Traub

June 4, 2011

I am sending you a poignant letter sent to my great-grandfather in 1923 from his son in Harbin. I am eager to find out what happened to the family and will be doing some more search to find out if they went to the US. If you can publicize the letter or give me any information about people in Sydney Australia I could speak to, that would be most useful.[208]

We didn't have an envelope; the letter was in the box where my grandmother kept her letters from her husband. This is the only information I have about Reuvim Traub. We didn't know he existed and my aunt told me that even though she knew her father had been married previously, her mother never spoke about it.

kind regards. Dr. Phyllis Sakinofsky. Sydney Australia.[209]

Harbin February 7, 1923

Dear Father. It's been many years since I have last received your letter. I admit that I have not corresponded much because I have not had your proper postal address.

During this time, I have been through much turmoil. Prior to the war, I enjoyed prosperity, I owned jewelry and watch stores on China Street, house No. 21. Residential crises hit the town of Harbin during the years of the war with flat and house prices skyrocketing. My trade did not stand those huge expenses and as a result I had to sell out all my stocks and close down the entire business.

I still was well off afterwards making good earnings on commissions and third party deals. However, the Russian Revolution brought about huge devaluation of Russian money. Unfortunately, I kept almost all of my assets in Russian Rubles that now have become worthless. So that I have got no possessions and my life-long work has turned out wasted.

I still do some go-between business, but the earnings are not as it used to be. Barely I can earn enough to feed us on daily basis. I keep wandering in the town from morning to night looking for any opportunity to earn even a penny. Rarely I am successful in these days because the town of Harbin has lost any communication with Russia. The entire population of Harbin suffers ever since business life has gone into stagnation.

Then I want to tell that I have got, thanks G-d, three daughters: the elder one — Yenta, 14 years of age; she studies in 4th grade of the Gymnasium. The second one is Etta, 8 years, we teach her at home. And the third daughter — Haya, is 2 years old.

I have to raise them all and give them proper education. Sadly, I cannot see ways to accomplish that, as I have got no income. I am devastated at this prospect. In addition to all my misfortune, my mother has passed away on the 5th of the month of Adar. She used to live with us in Harbin. Now I go to the synagogue three times a day to pray the Kaddish after her.

Few days ago I came to the synagogue to pray to G-d for my deceased Mother; I felt very anxious because my business wrong doings. Suddenly, I was presented with your letter posted to our Rabbi. Gladness left me speechless that my father I have not heard from for years was (thank G-d) alive and healthy. I would not need more to make me happy.

Dear Father, please write me frequently now as I have got any other relatives left apart from you — Dear Father. Please let me know about my dear sister and the whereabouts of uncle Azriel and his son Moissei. Please write me in as much details as possible. It will entertain us here, in Harbin as we feel very lonely and we have not got any relatives.

It would be good for us to leave Harbin at all as the business is going really bad. Also, we are worried for our daughters — they witness lots of wrongdoings and promiscuities in Harbin. It is impossible to enter Russia now and we have not got money to escape elsewhere either. I just do not know what to do.

We will take a photo of ours very soon and post it to you so that you will know the entire family. Please be well and forward my best wishes to my dear sisters, to your spouse, and to all other relatives. Please, write me letters in Yiddish.

Please, accept sincere best wishes from my wife and daughters. My wife and my eldest daughter will write you the next letter.

I am looking forward to your response.

Your son, Reuvim Traub

R.M. Traub. 30, Polevaya Street. Harbin, Manchuria. China

Lord Robert Skidelsky

Lord Robert Skidelsky is a British economic historian, prizewinning author, and Emeritus Professor of Political Economy at the University of Warwick. He is a Cross-bench Life Peer and has sat under this title in the House of Lords since 1991.

A founding member of the Social Democratic Party, he later became a Conservative and between 1997 and 1999 served as opposition spokesman in the Lords, first for Culture, then on the Treasury. He was Chair of the Social Market Foundation (1991 to 2001), and since 2016 has served as a director and trustee of the School of Civic Education.

Lord Skidelsky was born in Harbin, China, where his father worked for the family's firm, L. S. Skidelsky.

From Lord Skidelsky,

Saxon Lodge,

Saxon Lane. Seaford. East Sussex.

31 August 2010.

Dear Dr. Ben-Canaan. My friend Iain Sheriden suggested that I get in touch with you. I am at the start of a journey of exploration into my past. I know you are a great expert on Russians in the Far East, and I would like to establish touch, and keep in touch. I would be interested to discuss the question of anti-Semitism in

Harbin — I have read an essay by you on this — since it was never mentioned by my father.

Next year, I will probably come back to Harbin, as part of a longer visit to the Far East to take in Vladivostock, where my father's family established itself before the Revolution.

Yours sincerely, Robert Skidelsky.

*****

In 2005, Robert Skidelsky wrote a long essay about his family's experience in Harbin. He was invited to China for a lecture and took the time to visit his family's hometown.

A railway contract brought my Russian family to Manchuria 110 years ago, wrote Robert Skidelsky. Now that China's European past is unfreezing, I am welcomed back like a long-lost son to my birthplace, Harbin.[210]

I had been plotting my return to China for about a year, and now an invitation from Lanxin Xiang, author of a book on the Boxer rebellion, to lecture in Shanghai in September 2005 made it possible. I say "return," because the last time I had been on the mainland was in 1948, when I was nine years old. I was born in Harbin in Manchuria in 1939, came to England when I was three, and then went back to China with my parents in 1947, living for a little over a year in Tientsin (now Tianjin). We escaped to Hong Kong just before the communists took the city.

Why had we gone back to China in 1947? The brief answer is that the Skidelsky family-owned large properties in Harbin, and leased the largest private coal mine in Manchuria — the Mulin Mining Company. After the second world war, my father, a British subject since 1930, decided to reclaim the family business. In a spectacular piece of bad timing, we reached Tientsin at the moment when the communists were seizing control of Manchuria from the nationalists. We hung around in Tientsin waiting for the reversal of fortune which never happened. I remember thinking even then what a bad general Chiang Kai-Shek was to allow his best army to be cut off in Manchuria.

When you are building your own life, your family history is a matter of supreme indifference. But now I am fascinated by my family origins and wish I had listened more attentively to family stories told by my parents. They help me make sense of my own life.

The Skidelskys were one of the leading Jewish-Russian families in the far east. My great-grandfather Leon Skidelsky started his career in Skidel, now in Belarus. At some point in the 1880s, he moved with his family to Odessa on the Black Sea. In 1895 he won a contract to build the last stretch of the Trans-Siberian railway, which ran through northern Manchuria to Vladivostok. Leon made Vladivostok the family home. The Skidelskys were one of ten Jewish families allowed to live there. My father, Boris, was born in Vladivostok in 1907.

By the time Leon died in 1916, the family owned residential, industrial and mining properties in eastern Siberia, had 3,000 sq km of timber concessions in Russia and Manchuria, and was one of the region's largest employers. The Manchurian side of the business was managed from Harbin by one of Leon's sons, Solomon. The family firm supplied coal to the Chinese Eastern Railway and exported timber, plywood, and flour to London and New York.

In 1918 the Skidelskys left Russia, losing all their properties there, but with several million dollars in cash. My father's widowed mother moved to Paris, and sent her four sons to English public schools. Back in Harbin, great-uncle Solomon acquired a 30-year lease of the Mulin Mining Company in 1924. This became the mainstay of the reduced, but still substantial,

Skidelsky fortune. Harbin, already a big Russian city, swelled with White Russian exiles from eastern Siberia. The European sector was laid out with broad streets and avenues, fine houses, banks, shops, restaurants, cinemas, and an opera and ballet company. In the 1920s it was known as the "Paris of the east."

When my Paris grandmother lost her money in the stock market crash of 1929, she went to live in America and my father Boris went to Manchuria to work in the family business. He married my mother in 1936, and I was born three years later. My father fought for Britain during the war, but the Harbin Skidelskys, who were stateless, went on supplying coal to the railway, now taken over by the Japanese, who occupied Manchuria from 1932 to 1945. When the Soviets entered Manchuria in 1945, Solomon and his brother Simon were carted off to Russia, and perished in one of Stalin's gulags. The Chinese communists took over the Harbin properties and the coal mine. In 1984 I received a cheque from the British government for £24,000 in full settlement of a claim for compensation which amounted to £11m.

My maternal grandfather, Veniamin Vassilievich, turns up as mayor of Manchouli, in Russian Manchuria, in the early 1920s, before moving to Harbin. He was a literary agent, and I remember as a child receiving a letter from him in very old-fashioned Russian, full of lofty moral guidance. My grandmother's family probably came from Bessarabia. My mother Gali was born in Harbin in 1918.

My family history is a microcosm of the first wave of globalisation—based on the railway, steamship and telegraph—which opened up east Asia to the world market over a century ago. The Skidelskys' rise and fall mirrors the fate of this cosmopolitan world, which was mortally wounded in the first world war. It shows how easily politics can capsize economics. Wealth did not save my family, and others like them, from revolution, nor did economic interdependence save the world from fascism and communism.

Today there are no Skidelskys left in the far east. Following the communist victory in 1949, China was closed off to the rest of the world for 40 years. Harbin, together with ports like Shanghai and Tientsin, became a purely Chinese city, filled with the melancholy ruins of a dead European culture: the Bund in Shanghai, Victoria Park Avenue in Tientsin, the Bolshoi Prospekt in Harbin.

26th September, Beijing-Harbin.

A heavy fog hangs over Beijing. Lanxin says it is mainly pollution. We're on our way to the dowager empress's summer palace in the Garden of Clear Ripples, because there are photos of me there in 1948. The palace was looted by the British and French after the opium war of 1856-60, and the empress built a replacement using naval funds, which is why China was defeated by Japan in 1895. Or so legend has it. It was damaged again after the Boxer rebellion and rebuilt in 1902. It is a wonderful lakeside site full of fine buildings. The most amazing construction is a boat made entirely of marble.

In the afternoon, I give a talk at the China Institute of International Studies, a think tank said to be close to the foreign ministry. Ambassador Ma Zhengang, formerly in London, introduces me with a long explanation of current Chinese foreign policy. Then we hurry off to catch the plane to Harbin.

On September 26, 2005, we arrive at Hotel Modern at 8pm. This is the old hotel which, I'm told, my great-uncle Solomon used for assignations with a lady friend. I am in the suite in which Madame Sun Yat-Sen stayed in 1927 and Chaliapin in 1936. My mother told me about his visit and how they met and how he took her out. She was 18 and very beautiful. The suite is grand, but awkward. To turn off the bath tap one has to walk through the shower. There's an elegant desk but when I plug in my laptop the lights go off.

Harbin in the morning, I am at the Jewish cemetery on Imperial Hill[211] outside Harbin. There is a tombstone of my great-uncle Moses, who died — presumably in poverty, as his stone is modest — in 1951, aged 76. The original grave, in the city, saw a deep burial in 1963. My father used to tell me stories about Moses. He was noted for his good taste and extravagance, and possibly for that reason was eventually excluded from the family business. After the communists came, he was allowed to stay on in Harbin because he had not been active in the Manchurian business, but of course there was no more money coming in. The grave is well kept up. A bunch of flowers is thrust into my hands, which I lay on the grave. I am called on to make a speech. What can I say except that I am here to honor my father's family, Harbin and the Jews of Harbin. Graveyards are always melancholy, but even more so when the dead have no connection with the surrounding living.

In the old days of the "eastern Paris," Jews embedded in a community of 200,000 Russians and the same number of Chinese. The Jews were caught between the pro-Soviet and antisemitic Russians.

Solomon Skidelsky won the Mulin coalmine concession from a local warlord, Chang Tso-lin, because both loved poker, but Solomon was the better player. He let the warlord win for six months, and put him in such a good mood that he signed the contract for a 30-year lease without demur.

The Skidelsky Villa on the Bolshoi Prospekt in Harbin is bigger and grander than it appears in the photographs, but now a shadow of its former glory.

When the family built it on a hill above the old train station it was set in spacious lawns and looked out on to open fields, now the town has crept up on it and it is closed in by skyscrapers. The house was looted in 1945, and like so many similar properties, minimally maintained as an institution—in this case a People's Liberation Army leisure center.

The house is on two floors, with a central staircase made of wood curving down to the front hall. It had everything modern that those days could offer. Central heating with a furnace in the basement. Running water in copper faucets. Bathrooms and bathtubs were all equipped with the latest trends, spacious rooms, high ceilings, sunrooms, and tall windows.

The central staircase started at the entry space on the first floor and went in grandeur all the way up to the second.

Just imagine Solomon and his wife (or paramour) descending to greet their guests. There was something royal up in the villa on the hill overlooking the old grand train station and the view of Pristan that stretched all the way to the Sungari River.

Robert Skidelsky did not return to Harbin again. He framed the check of 24,000 British Pounds the Chinese government afforded him for the family properties, as a reminder to the better times his family had in the far eastern city. As usual, there is always a hope that one regime will be replaced by another and then all properties will be returned to their righteous owners. The framed cheque from the Chinese government for £24,000 will serve as a witness for the family's Harbin properties and fortune which amounted to £11 million 65 years ago.

Ella Levin

It takes a brave man to jump off a moving train for the sake of a sale, but the clothes hawkers had the easy courage of men who did this on the regular. They leaped off the front carriage as the train chugged into a station with no stop, bundles of cheap

Chinese pants and jackets on their arms, exchanged hurried words and cash with waiting Russians and jumped back on the last carriage as the Trans-Siberian trundled steadily toward Moscow.[212] This was the scene everywhere along the Chinese Eastern Railway that left the Trans-Siberian and pushed south toward Harbin. Railway was new to Manchuria and the peasants took advantage of the transport that collected many people into a one space. Bravery was not the issue. Survival and making ends meet were the agenda that dictated man' doings.[213]

Ella Levin remembered coming to China on November 20, 1917.[214]

In China, she said, there was no such thing like in the US, where you can buy an outfit ready to wear. In Harbin everything had to be made by a tailor, in all cases a man, or dressmakers, usually a woman, or shoemakers so it had to take longer to prepare the things that you all needed.

So, second-hand vendors were ready to serve with their goods anyone who did not have much cash or needed something in a hurry. These came very handy later after the family settled in Harbin.

Our first home was with my father's other brother Leiba. After we rested from the very hard and long trip that took 21 days, we started looking for an apartment. Every night at eleven o'clock we would go to the newspaper edition to look over the ads about "to let", but could not find anything that we wanted. Father heard that there was a landlord named Barack who had a big lot but had no money to build a house on it. So father and one more Jew who needed an apartment, they both gave Mr. Barack 10 thousand dollars, 5 for each one, and he started building a two family house, made of stone. The house cost him 35 thousand, and the 25 thousand he got in the bank.[215]

So, one worry we had was settled, but there was another and

Fig. 40: Grandfather Boris Levin and family in Harbin

worse worry, just to our luck, when we came to China all businesses there were not going on, there was not any import and export, and therefore there were no sales with cash money. People who came to Harbin from many different countries were talking in many languages and were handling all kinds of money.

In the center of Kitayskaya Street was a big beautiful house, owned by a Mr. Zaauna. This was a tea and coffee house. Inside of this house was a very large front room, filled with very many tables covered with snow-white table cloths, and around these men who were well dressed, like to fit such a beautiful place, and made all kinds of deals, with mostly big profits. For example, when a Chinese at storekeeper got a transport of some kind of things from the U.S. he had to pay for it with his own money, and got the money through the men at this coffee house. But because there was no import or export now the businessmen, including father and Leiba were going about with their noses down.

In a part of Harbin, there was the China town that was called Fundedian (Fujiadian). There lived mostly the rich Chinese people and they had a Birsha[216], like Wall Street, so every man of the Zazunovsky who had money, started going to the Fundedian Birsha.

The influx of White anti-Bolshevik refugees after the 1917 revolution gave new life to the Russian community in China.

The city of Harbin buzzed with exiled intellectuals, noblemen, and businessmen; the fallen Russian princess, now a high-class courtesan, became a Shanghai cliché. Harbin's department stores were packed with Russian goods, its streets lined with churches and tearooms; the exiles' daughters debuted at balls and picnicked on the river.[217]

It was a different picture than that painted by Traub, although that was a few years later.

The Jewish community, strongly represented among the refugees, exploded from 500 people in 1903 to over 20,000 people and two synagogues in the 1920s, as the city flooded with refugees from the Russian revolution. Russian hatreds reached all the way to Mongolia, where White general and lunatic mystic Roman Ungern-Sternberg conducted a brutal pogrom in 1921; Harbin's many White and Jewish papers buzzed with tales of his atrocities.

Harbin's Jews got on better with their Chinese neighbors, in general, than did the other Russians, who were often notoriously contemptuous of the Chinese they lived among. They thought Japan—that power great enough to beat even Imperial Russia— was the side to bet on; Harbin residents lined the streets to cheer Japan's invading Kwantung Army into the city in 1932, and young men trained in a specially established cadet school in Tianjin to be the administrators of a Russia they thought would be "liberated" by the Japanese. In 1946, though, they cheered for the arrival of Soviet troops—only to see their parents and grandparents who had fought against the Bolsheviks in the revolution shipped back to Moscow for execution.[218]

Susan Levin's father was born in 1911, on Yom Kippur, in Russia near Vitebsk, an industrial center some 500 km from Moscow, now Belarus.

Father, Joseph Boris Levin, said his first memory was the

smell of burnt horse flesh. My grandfather Boris had a coal refinery plant, it caught fire, and the fire reached the stable full of pure breeds.[219]

My grandfather Boris was born in 1880. He had very light blue eyes. His father's name was Shepsel. He was honest and authoritarian and loved horses. My grandmother, Ella Levin, was born the same year as Boris. Her father and grandfather were rabbis. She was from the intelligentsia and in love with a poet, but because her parents had died very young, she was obliged to marry Boris, a "crass businessman".

Boris and Ella had four children, Louis (1907), Doris (1909), Joseph (1911), and Lilian (1913). They lived in a large house with servants and fireplaces in every room. Boris was very strict with the education of the children, and private teachers came to the house to tutor them.

My father was 6 in 1917 when Nicolas II fell from power in February, and when he abdicated in October. At this moment the Levin family fled Vitebsk and Russia with money and government securities hidden in the lining of their clothes. Boris did not sell his estate, the coke plant, his carriage, and horses. But he left with the equivalent of 42,000 US dollars.

They crossed Siberia on the Trans-Siberian Railway. It took three weeks to reach Harbin, in Manchuria, about 8000 kilometers distant by train. The wagons were full of people fleeing the Bolsheviks but also the terror of the White Russians. At each stop, soldiers mounted on the train and shot anyone hiding or taking out money. The Levin family must have been well-dressed, but somehow survived the trip.

Boris' younger brother, Leiba, had arrived in Harbin in 1905, at the time of the Russian-Japanese War. With the First World War, Harbin became an international city, full of men of all countries, most looking for new opportunities and fortunes and some escaping conscription. There were 45 languages spoken in Harbin at that time.

Father's daily life in Harbin was probably too exciting for a young kid. Their Russian maid Olga seduced him — at 9! And at 10, he went to the synagogue every day for nine months to recite Kaddish for his father....

"In this city at the crossroads of waterways and rail lines, Jews without a homeland lived by exchanging goods and services such as maritime insurance, furs, or currencies. For example, in order to buy English tea, you had to pay in British pounds.

It was at Mr. Zazuna's elegant tearoom on Kitaskaya Street, close to the home of Boris and Ella, that these men without a country met to discuss and do business. The stock exchange (Birsha) was nearby, in adjacent Fujiadian. For 3 years Boris went six days a week to Mr. Zazuna's coffee house and to the Birsha to buy and sell whatever with the money he had brought with him from Vitebsk."

The denouement came in August 1921. Boris had invested all his money this time in furs, which were being transported on the Chinese Eastern Railway and then the Trans-Siberian railroad, but the goods were confiscated at the Chinese-Russian border "by the Bolsheviks," according to Levin lore. Boris went to the border to try to recover his investment. He disappeared, maybe died of a heart attack... or something else. He was 41. It seems foolish of Boris to have traveled to the Russian-Chinese border. He was intelligent, well-read. There were 20 newspapers in Harbin full of articles about the bloody civil war. Did he have a choice?

It took three weeks before Ella was notified of the death of her husband. Overnight, she and her four children had become penniless. Over the following weeks, Boris's friends repaid Ella money that Boris had lent them, enough in any case to be able to immigrate to the US, where Ella had a half-brother. The trip from

Harbin to Newport cost $3,000.

Ella wrote in a letter that during the nine months she had to wait for a visa Boris' "intelligent and cultivated" friends regularly came to take tea with her and that their discussions were often lively.

The family took passage on a Canadian ship that sailed on August 5, 1922, from Yokohama, Japan, to Vancouver, Canada. From there, 3 days and 3 nights on a train across the American continent to Newport, the upscale sailing port created by wealthy Bostonians.

Joseph (Joe) Boris Levin

Susan Levin's father Joseph (Joe) Boris, was 11 years old. He went to school but also soon began working. Before school, he made deliveries for the butcher where his older sister Doris worked, and after school, he worked in the grocery store that Ella ran. In the evenings he played drums in jazz clubs, and on weekends he played polo with the gilded youth of Newport. It is said that Joe proposed marriage to the woman who would be Susan's mother, an American from New York and Alabama, when they were out riding and her horse ran away with her.

On December 7, 1941, Joe Levin and Florence Edelbaum were to marry. That was the day of Pearl Harbor. Their marriage was postponed for a week and then Joe was called up into the Air Force, was based in Kunming, China, In 1944 he returned to Harbin, where the offspring of Boris' two brothers, Hirsha and Leiba, and sister Genia still lived. They emigrated to Israel after the war.

*****

Harbin has surely one of the most extraordinary and varied histories of any city. It owes its existence principally to the Russian workers of the China Eastern Railway, who built up the town at the turn of the 20th century.

The second wave of Russians came in the 1920s when the city was flooded with some 100,000 White Russian refugees fleeing the Revolution, making it the largest Russian enclave outside Russia.[220]

At Harbin, though still well inside China, the traveler finds himself back in Europe. He might easily believe he had crossed the line into Russia and was brought up in one of its most typical cities. Streets, architecture, customs, and inhabitants, are all on the Russian typical.

In 1931 Japan seized Manchuria and set up a puppet government. In the mid-1930s many Russians fled Harbin for the Soviet Union, where most were arrested, of course, for espionage or counterrevolutionary activity; some 30,000 were shot. Others moved to cities including Shanghai, Tientsin, Peking and Tsingtao.[221]

There are quite a few Germans and Norwegians, and altogether many foreigners, not counting the Russians. These are White Russians, refugees from the Revolution, and have a strange standing in China. They are people without a country, and their lot is a sad one. In 1945, when the Soviets occupied Manchuria, many of the remaining Russians were sent to labor camps. Manchuria was not completely in Chinese hands until 1952. By the mid-1960s, there were virtually no Harbin Russians left.[222]

Central Street resembled Moscow's Arbat Ulitsa[223], and there were Russian banks, shops, restaurants, and hotels. Twenty-two churches graced the skyline—including the onion-domed St. Nikolai Cathedral, an architectural gem built of wood without nails in the old Russian style. "It was like a little Moscow or Paris here, we had an opera here. There were so many magazines and newspapers and the cultural life was on a very high level. Unfortunately, all that was destroyed."[224]

Raisa (Rinia) Slavutin

Many of the Chinese men and women that worked in Jewish households form a lifelong bond with the families that employed them. It could be a serviceman that ran the house logistics, was in charge of maintenance, a woman who served the patrons of the house, and cleaned their clothes and their beds. It could be an amah, a Chinese women who nursed the babies and watched them grow with some Chinese genes they swallowed with her breasted milk, and it could be a cook who learned the Jewish costumes, cooked kosher dishes and went to the market each day for fresh produce.

Goldie Zyskind's mother Raisa, wrote about their Chinese cook named Sooza Jen, before she died in 1996. As part of this process, she wanted to pay tribute to a Chinese man who had been a special part of her family for many years.[225]

Mother was born Raisa (Rinia) in Harbin to Esther (Borodavkin) and Jacob Slavutin in 1925 where she lived for the first 10 years of her life. Her parents, and brothers Abraham and Nathan moved to Dairen where they had a guest house/hotel called El Dorado, and then later to Shanghai in 1941, where she worked there for cousins the Toochinsky family. Here she met my father, Chaim Gabriel Zyskind, a refugee from Warsaw, whom she married in 1945. The couple emigrated in 1946 to Australia where Goldie Zyskind and her sister were born.

Raisa Zyskind: "I am not good with dates. If this story is never published—don't worry. I am having a ball with it. It should have

been written many years ago —
like 50–60, but I never had the
guts …… I am tying up some
loose ends in my life now, and
this is a very long loose end to
complete."

My parents fled Russia
during the revolution and
settled in Harbin — Manchuria.
They were a middle-class
Russian Jewish couple who
started out life on a modest
scale. After their first child was
born, mother hired a young
Chinese boy — aged about 14
or 15 to help at home. He was

Fig. 41: Chaim Gabriel Zyskind and Raisa
Jacovna Slavutina — wedding photo

modest, quiet, and most willing to learn. In no time at all, he
learned perfect Russian, Jewish Russian cooking, and ran the
household like clockwork. He was slow but methodical and
nothing was ever not done on time. He was not a servant but a
friend and family. He ate with us at the table, the food we ate and
we would not have had it otherwise.

He was the backbone of my life. I don't think he spoilt me,
but I adored him. His name was Sooza Jen, but we called him
Soozachka — a diminutive for someone you love dearly. He had
a heart of melted butter but tried to keep a stern exterior to keep
up my mother's disciplinarian ideas. However, I could always
crack a little grin from him under most circumstances.

At the times when our grandmother lived with us, we became
kosher, and he knew all the tricks. No sooner would we use the
wrong knife or fork it would go with a vengeance into a huge
pot plant to make it kosher again. With the admonition of "not

having respect for grandma — how many times do I have to tell you, etc." We loved ham sandwiches — a most forbidden fruit, and when he would smell it on us we were made to strip in the outer room and scrub ourselves silly.

I can always see him squatting and polishing the silver with a cork and ashes from the Samovar- no Ajax or stuff like that then. I would sneak in behind him, put my arms around his neck — kiss him and make him fall. I bet he heard me coming and pretended not to. Always growled for interrupting his work — but I know he loved it.

At some stage he got married — his wife and family lived in the country. He went there once a year for Chinese New Year and then there would be another baby. He did not want to bring them over to the city and we never met his family. I think he wanted it that way.

We had a modest home and he lived in the little attic. It was spotless, tiny, tidy to perfection. My joy was to climb up those rickety steps and escape to my dreamland. Oh, those beautiful Chinese magazines that he kept in perfect formation on the floor. Oh, the paper cutouts on the walls in all shapes and sizes, and most beautiful of all his Chinese flute from which he produced the most beautiful, sorrowful tune at the end of each day — we knew his work was done and he was relaxing.

But one day — a very sad one for me — he told me I was not to go up there ever again. No explanations — no asking why — nobody told me, and it broke my heart. I was about 10 and he accepted the rules of the household. How he must have felt!

We had a lot of Chinese peddlers coming to the street. The little wagon with ice cream — what a taste, candied apples on a stick and other goodies — but my mother had this thing about them being dirty and getting a tummy ache, but I did not give up — my Soozuchka always found the penny I nagged him for, and he never had to answer for an upset tummy.

Then the Japanese came to Harbin and made life very difficult for white people. My parents decided to move to Dairen and mother told our friend we could not afford him anymore. He insisted to come—just for his food and board—they could pay him later when they had money. He would not take no for an answer. In Dairen we had a summer resort hotel, which was not a place he could get used to and we saw he was unhappy. So mother got him a job with two elderly, single brothers. But it was not family and he was again unhappy. Then an aunt of mine needed help and he went to work for her. He was with my family for 17 years—each of them I cherish. So he was happy again.

But all good things come to an end. The Japanese took over Dairen and life became impossible, especially for the Chinese people who worked for the foreigners. He had to report regularly to the police station to tell them what went on in the household. If he said nothing he was beaten, if he would invent a white lie which my aunt told him to do—he could not lie, so one day he gave up and took his own life to protect his beloved foreign family.

I can see him still—slim and tall, shiny black hair, Chines pants, and a jacket with always something in his hand wiping cleaning. My regret is that we never took a photo of him, but his influence on my life is enough"

Mum found out about his death when she was in Shanghai and "was devastated. I love the Chinese people—if they are your friends, it is for life. But are they?"

Solomon (Monia) Berman

Solomon (Monia) Berman wrote that from an early age, his two children, both born in Australia, questioned him about his life in

China. To my regret, he wrote, I never made any effort to pass on to them the experiences and memories that I and my family lived through in China. Maybe it was because I felt that life as a Jew in China during the Second World War was far easier than in Europe. Life in China, even under Japanese occupation, for most foreigners, in particular Russians, was unpleasant, that is until the war in the pacific began and Russia joined the allies in their fight against Germany and Japan. It was at this time that life in China became most difficult and which almost threatened our very existence.[226]

My father, together with his three older sisters, was brought to China by his parents in 1910. He was two years old. Born in Irkutsk, at that time Siberia's principal city, to a middle-class Russian-Jewish couple.

Unrest in Russia was slowly gathering momentum, as various groups wished to bring about political reforms.

It was about this time that my grandfather, at the early age of thirty-four years, died, which added grief to the already heavy burden and worry of an uncertain future for his young wife; my grandmother, and mother of four very young children.

It was not long before my grandmother remarried and a decision was made to migrate to China. The political situation in China at the beginning of the twentieth century was very unstable, but work opportunities for foreigners did exist in the larger urban centers and offered some degree of security.

The constant warfare between various warlords was being waged in the rural and mountainous regions of China. Frequent famine brought about by drought and floods seemed to occur with monstrous regularity, this, combined with the primitive agricultural practices, added to the burden of the long-suffering peasants trying to eke out a living for their families and inevitably resulted in men leaving their farms in droves and heading for the cities where they had a chance to find enough work to sustain themselves and their families left behind in the rural village.

The most sought-after forms of employment for the Chinese, was domestic service in private homes; gardeners, cooks, childminders, and chauffeurs.

On arrival in China, my father's family settled in Harbin.

Harbin was, for all intents and purposes, a Russian city on Chinese soil. Russian personnel took up residences in the suburbs, businesses were set up, and schools were established for the children of Russian nationals. Even most major streets were re-named in the Russian language.

This was the scenario into which my father's family settled and we children were sent to typical Russian schools, wore Russian-styled uniforms, and studied subjects that were in every Russian school curriculum.

The social structure was very well defined. Foreigners lived in enclaves, thus the Russian enclave became Mother Russia. Very few Chinese nationals could afford to live in these areas, thus creating unofficial segregation. The majority of the local Chinese lived in the poorer areas in the outer suburbs. The area in which the Chinese nationals lived became known in colloquial Russian as 'Kitaigorod', or Chinatown, or the Chinese ghetto.

In 1927, just before the Japanese occupation of Manchuria, and on reaching conscription age, my father traveled to Vladivostok to register for conscription in the Russian army. He was rejected due to his weak eyesight, but decided, before returning to China, to apply for Russian citizenship. By this time the civil war in Russia was well and truly over and the Bolsheviks, now known as Soviets, were victorious. My father returned to China as a Soviet Citizen. The attitude of the Japanese authorities to passport-holding Soviet Citizens, living under Japanese occupation, was less than positive, but was still tolerable. It was later when Russia declared war on Japan that living in China became more difficult.

On his return from Vladivostok, my father entered the fur trade by serving an apprenticeship with one of the largest fur companies in Harbin. The fur trade was flourishing in China, especially in Manchuria. It's forest and mountains were teaming with wildlife; foxes, beavers, mink, sables, and even tigers crossed the border from Siberia. A very lucrative trade existed between privately owned fur trading firms and countries like America, England, and Europe. No permits or licenses were required by the hunters and the trappers who were predominantly Chinese and no limits existed on the number of animals taken. Prices paid for pelts were very low, compared to the value of high-quality skins on the markets of the western world. The low prices paid for pelts coupled with the low wages paid to highly skilled Chinese craftsmen, employed by fur houses of Manchuria, meant that profits were very high and businesses flourished.

In 1933, while still working as an apprentice, my father met and fell in love with my mother. Her name was Ljuba, which in Russian means 'love'. She also was born in China to Russian Jewish parents. My mother's family history began in Khabarovsk, some six hundred kilometers northwest of Vladivostok. Her parents decided to travel to China for the same reasons as my parents did and as many Russian Jews did in those early years of unrest and occasional Pogroms which marred national stability for most Jews residing in Russia at that time.

My mother's family settled in Harbin in 1910. One of seven children, and second youngest, my mother always claimed she was the favorite. Never a high achiever academically, my mother made up for it with a bubbly and vibrant personality and classical beauty. She managed to combine a cheerful disposition with a serene almost aristocratic demeanor that attracted my father to her. Although very popular and with many suitors, my mother accepted my father's proposal seeing in him a hard-working and honest man and someone who could offer her security in a troubled world. In 1934, having completed his apprenticeship, my father took his now pregnant wife; my mother, to live in Dairen, a major seaport situated on the tip of the then Kwamtung peninsula. It was in the October of that year that I entered the world much to the joy of my parents, and of grandparents who were still living in Harbin. I only met my grandparents once when as a twelve-month-old baby I was taken to Harbin to be presented to all my relatives. My mother had every intention of taking me back to Harbin when I was older, but fate decided otherwise.

In 1940, at the age of six years, after a bout of measles, I contracted polio. No vaccine against the disease existed in those days and depending on the severity of the affliction, the prognosis was not very good. In my case, my chances of survival were minimal. I clearly recall a scene in my nursery when a Japanese doctor told my mother of his diagnosis. My mother burst into tears on hearing the news. My dear Aunt Esther, my mother's older sister, who was at the time living in Dairen with her family, spoke tersely to my mother. She perceived that I was very much aware of what was going on and was quite distressed. An ambulance took my mother and me to the hospital. The next six months of my life are but a faint memory.

I was totally paralyzed; I could not speak or move. It was three months before I showed any sign of improvement. I spent some four months in the hospital before being discharged. My rehabilitation was slow and painful. I could not walk, for the lower part of my body and my legs were paralyzed completely. Over the next two years, I had to learn to walk again. I survived.

My Aunt Esther and Uncle Jasha, were my favorite relatives. One of my favorite games was Bandits; uncle Jasha would put me on his back and let my cousins play at being bandits. I was often captured, and a demand for ransom was delivered to my uncle. A very vigorous barter ensued, which sometimes lasted until my aunt Esther would step in and resolve the issue by naming a price for my release. The whole concept of these games was based on real-life incidents. It was a common everyday occurrence to read in the newspapers, of gangs of bandits operating outside cities, who specialized in kidnapping wealthy citizens and demanding ransoms for their release. Mostly, victims were released unharmed if the ransom was paid. Occasionally there were horror stories of slayings, usually occurring if a ransom demand was refused. It was not uncommon for a family or relatives of a kidnapped victim to receive a finger or an ear, to induce the payment of ransom. Our game was eventually brought to an end when my cousin Nathan, managed to drop me on my head, much to the horror of my mother and aunt.

The school my parents enrolled me in was a Catholic convent school whose motherhouse was based in California. Maryknoll Academy was a prestigious missionary school, run by nuns, with branches located in several the larger cities of China. Although a Catholic school, it accepted children of diverse backgrounds, even those belonging to the Jewish faith, if they could afford to pay the high fees charged by the school.

The school itself was composed of campuses. Each campus was housed in an ordinary house purchased by the convent and modified to accommodate some fifty or so pupils. Each house was kept spotlessly clean, with highly polished floors, which were, for some reason, Father Ryan's foremost ambition to keep that way. One of the most inflexible rules, he set, was that we were to wear an old pair of socks over our shoes to protect those floors and to keep them clean. Putting socks over shoes worked well except when shoes were dirty or muddy after the rain.

However, great fun was to be had to throw mud-caked socks at each other on the way home from school, much to the distress of our poor mothers.

Relationships between foreigners and Chinese nationals were much more amicable. In many instances, where Chinese were employed as house servants, or home help, they were treated as members of the family. It was very common to have nannies, or 'Amahs', as they were known, to live in with the families employing them. Their main function was to look after young children, and that always meant virtually twenty-four hours a day. In many cases the sole care of children was entrusted to an 'Amah', enabling mothers to engage in a variety of social activities.

I clearly remember our Amah, who was in our household for many years. She was brought in to help my mother to look after me soon after I was born. Both my parents loved and trusted her implicitly. She completely dominated our family, so much so that until the age of three years, the only language I knew was Chinese. I was told, in later years, that even mum and dad had to converse with me in Chinese, but as I became older and started playing with children of our family friends, I soon learned to speak Russian. Oddly enough, after switching to Russian, my knowledge of the Chinese language diminished, and although I could still converse in that language, my fluency did not progress.

In 1940, my sister Mira was born. Our Amah, as expected, took over the nursing when my sister was six months old. I do not know her name or where she came from.

Our Amah was a portly woman of about thirty years of age when she came to live with us; she was not very tall and had very tiny feet. As a result of the binding of her feet. Being a rather large woman on tiny feet, she had considerable difficulty when required to walk in inclement weather, especially against strong winds. In winter, when the roads were icy, it was totally out of the question for her to keep her balance. To watch her trying to negotiate a slippery stretch of road and keep upright was like watching one of Charlie Chaplin's movies. We often took bets as to how many times she would slip and fall.

I remember, many occasions when I caused my Amah pain and anxiety by running away and hiding from her during our daily walks in the park nearby. She would be pushing a pram with my baby sister in it and me walking beside her. The distress caused her to cry when she had to search for me while also trying to keep an eye on my baby sister. Very soon, after my sister reached the age of two years, a governess was engaged by my parents to start my education, prior to my enrolment in the convent school. This event made Amah's task of looking after us somewhat easier.

Winters in Manchuria were very severe. The first indication of winter's approach took place in about late October when the first load of coal was delivered to the house. The central heating system in all the houses in our neighborhood was powered by steam; every house had a furnace which was located in the cellar.

The furnace was attached to a boiler which then distributed steam into elements known as 'batteries' which were in every room of the house. The furnaces were operated by Chinese stokers employed for this specific function. They were provided with living quarters usually located somewhere near the boiler, it provided warmth during the winter months. Furnace stokers were a rather nomadic lot, alone and without family ties, they would spend the winter months in keeping the boilers working. In exchange, they were provided with food and shelter, as well as nominal wages. At the end of the winter period, they would drift away, and reappear in late autumn to again take up their duties.

Another sign of approaching winter was when my mother gave instructions to have winter window frames inserted into the windows. Once double glazing was installed, the countdown to winter, as far as we kids were concerned, began. Usually, the very first snowfall of the season was heavy. Everything would be under a thick blanket of snow, sounds became muted, and even passing trucks, cars, and trams would sound quieter.

One day I was returning home with a few of my friends from a movie. Our route took us past a local vegetable market. In China, almost everything offered for sale was kept in wicker baskets of various shapes and sizes. Normally I would pay little attention to these baskets as they were part of every shop and marketplace, but something drew my attention to a row of such baskets just as I was passing that particular shop. At first glance, it appeared as though the higher baskets were placed on some kind of metal frame, except there was an unusual curvature at one end of the frame. My friends were already ahead of me when I decided to take a closer look. What I thought to be a frame was in actual fact a pair of runners, typical to racing sleds. I asked the shop owner to remove the baskets from the top of the sleds, which made him think that I was either mad or up to some mischief. Reluctantly, he obliged and I had a glimpse of what turned out to be a professional American racing toboggan, brand spanking new, but under a large layer of dust and dirt. I held my breath and very casually enquired if he would be prepared to sell it to me. After a short barter with the shop owner, we agreed on a price and I said I would return shortly with the money. But this was only half of what I had to achieve to gain possession. I had no money of my own and laid all my hopes on persuading my mother to let me have the sum of money I required, which though not very much, was a lot more than my weekly allowance, which I had already spent at the movies.

I managed to persuade my mother to advance me the required sum of money. I remember running all the way to the shop, and to my great relief and joy I took possession of the sleds. I spent the rest of the evening cleaning and polishing them until they were truly a sight to behold. Brand new, never used, brightly colored, and varnished, they represented a dream come true to a young boy. Overnight I became a celebrity at school and among all my friends.

My father was a very temperamental man and given to outbursts of violence, not to any excessive degree, but enough to lash out, on occasions, and slap my mother. I wanted to protect my mother, but at the same time was terrified of my father's outbursts. It is fair to say that these outbursts did not last long and always made my father feel guilty and motivated to make it up to my mother by giving her love and sometimes gifts. My mother, being a gentle and very loving person, always tried to convince me that my father was a good man and only reacted that way under stress. I came to agree with her in later years because I did love my father.

Or cook's name was Sooza. The name, I suspect, was an affectionate derivative from a proper Chinese given name, which none of us knew. He was originally employed as a cook by my aunt Esther, who, with her husband, owned and operated a resort hotel in the seaside town of Hashigoura. The hotel, under the name of El Dorado, was very popular amongst the social circles of foreigners. Quite small, and unpretentious, it was renowned for its style and good food, of which my aunt and uncle were very proud. The hotel was also renowned for its pickled cucumbers and tomatoes, grown in its own vegetable garden and pickled by my uncle Jasha.

I remember, at the end of our every stay at the hotel, Sooza would bring a large can of pickled cucumbers and pickled tomatoes and place them in a taxi.

By 1942, World War II was in full swing and the economy of the world was suffering, even in China. Trading with the outside world was increasingly difficult, and exports and imports of goods were largely restricted, as the Japanese gave priority to the movement of war materials. All this influenced the economy in general and the hospitality industry in particular.

My auntie and uncle saw the 'writing on the wall' and a decision was made to sell El Dorado. Soon afterward, they and their family moved to Shanghai. My father too wanted to relocate to Shanghai, but being of Soviet citizenship was not permitted to reside in Shanghai.

Sooza, being a Chinese national, would have had great difficulty to relocate to another region, and it was decided that he would come and work for our family as a cook, which he did for nearly two years. He lived with us in his own quarters with his young nephew, whom he brought from the village from which he himself came. The youngster helped with the house chores and regularly sent the money he earned to his parents. Among Sooza's duties, apart from cooking and baking, was to go to market and do the family shopping. It was on these occasions that the Japanese secret service began intercepting Sooza and whisking him to their headquarters, where he was interrogated, sometimes for hours. They believed that my father was involved in espionage. Suza was often tortured during these interrogations. They always released him in the end after threatening him with all kinds of reprisals if he told my parents about his treatment at their hands. Sooza trusted my parents so completely, that he always told them about his treatment at the hands of the Japanese secret service even showing them the bruises and wounds that were inflicted on him. It so distressed my mother that she insisted that he leave us and offered to arrange for him to work for some other family, who were not Soviet citizens. No doubt that removed from our household, the Japanese would have no reason to persecute him the way they did.

Sooza steadfastly refused to leave us, so great was his sense of loyalty to our family. The secret service persisted in their cruel quest, until, after a period of almost two years, he could take it no more. One Saturday afternoon, my father took me to a cinema.

During the movie, a caption appeared on the screen, asking my father to go to the manager's office where he was told to return home immediately. He collected me and we left for home. On arrival, we found our house full of police and secret service agents. Our governess took charge of me and both my sister and I were confined to our nursery. I was told that Sooza had been taken ill and had to go to a hospital for a long time. It was years later that I learned that Sooza had hanged himself in his room. He was found by his nephew, crying hysterically the boy ran to my mother. Not fully comprehending what the boy was screaming, she followed him to their quarters and was confronted by that dreadful scene; Sooza's death had a devastating effect on my mother. Long, drawn-out interrogations followed, one after another of both my parents. Devoid of any sensitivity and compassion, the Japanese authorities refused to accept that Sooza's suicide was brought about by nothing other than their own brutality towards him. Sooza's nephew returned to his village and we never saw him again.

Solomon (Monia) Berman's life in China came to an end in the 1950s. He and his family boarded a ship that took them to Hong Kong from where they flew to Israel only to stay there for a short period of time before ending their long journey in Melbourne Australia.

Bob Sitsky's Amah

Amah

As you know, there was a lot of racial prejudice among Harbin's European "colonials," and I saw it also in my childhood in Asia. It occurs to me that you might get some stories no one has told if you ask former residents of Harbin about inter-racial couples they knew. Racism is not usually part of idealized Harbin memories, though Bob Sitsky touched upon it in his memoir when talking about his Chinese nanny. There's a nanny story for you. She raised him and he never even knew her name, just "amah."[227]

I can see her now — she is dressed in faded, blue pants and jacket. Her feet are bound, misshapen, and triangular looking, much smaller than feet should be. She pads around the house on them and one cannot hear her steps. Her grey hair is tightly bound behind her head. I can still remember the smell when I sometimes saw her remove the binding from her feet and I observed her deformed feet. I remember that she had very few teeth left; the ones she had were thin and yellow-looking.[228]

I only knew her as Amah. She was just there for the family — there was no effort made to find out facts about her family. I did not even know if she had children of her own. To me she seemed 'old' but probably she would have been about 50 years old when we parted. She was with our family for a very long time and it must have been very

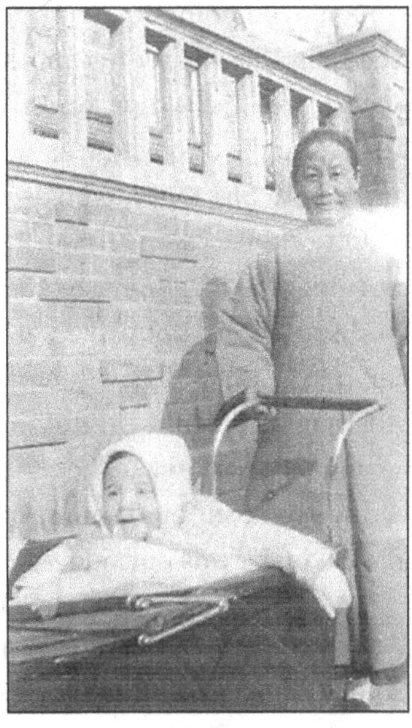

Fig. 42: Amah and Mara Sitsky 1932

hard for her after our departure.

When I was a toddler, my Amah had a unique way to settle me down when I became hyperactive—she put me on her breast. This was the Chinese way of handling toddlers. Mother did not approve of this type of behavior.

Once, when I woke up in the middle of the night, I was shocked to see her standing next to my small child's bed. I must have been very small at the time, maybe 5 years old, as there was a safety rail on the bed. I think she was pulling on my penis. When I asked why she was doing this she said she was trying to make it bigger—it was probably a Chinese custom.

She lived in our house. She had a bed in the alcove on the ground floor near the dining room. Once, when she was sick, we placed her in a small cottage located in the back courtyard and we asked the people living in the adjoining houses to look after her.

I enjoyed going to our large kitchen at the back of our house. It is there that I saw her mold her millet buns for cooking. She would give me a portion of the millet bun that I quickly ate up. I thought the taste was wonderful, but my mother was not impressed! She regarded it as peasant food.

On one occasion, Amah did not come to the house in the morning. We went over to check and found her in a deep sleep; loud speech did not wake her and neither our attempts to shake her into waking. The Chinese family living nearby came over but they also could do nothing. A local doctor was called and he managed to wake her. Apparently, she had overdone the bedding and suffered some type of oxygen deprivation. We were all shaken by this episode.

On our last day before leaving the city, my father gave Amah a substantial amount of cash to help her in her future and she said that she would return to her village. Her younger sister came to help her move. My parents gave Amah quite a lot of

Fig. 43: Amah holding little Alex
Nachumson

Fig. 44: Leon Nachumson -
Harbin 1929

goods from our house; we do
not know whether she sold them or took them with her to the
village.

As we were sitting down, in the Russian tradition, just before
our last rickshaw ride from our house, she came around to say
goodbye to all of us. She was crying.

Leo Vainstein

City directories are useful for placing people in a particular place
at a particular time. They typically tell where an ancestor lived
and worked and can help locate descendants in census years.

Generally, a city directory will contain an alphabetical
list of citizens, listing the names of the heads of households,
their addresses, and occupational information. Sometimes a
wife's name will be listed ben parentheses or italics following
the husband's. Other helpful information might include death
dates for individuals who had been listed in the previous year's

Fig. 45: Amah holding Ima. Harbin 1930

directory, names of partners in firms, and forwarding addresses or post offices for people who had moved to another town.

City directories are a map that records the space and time of a place as well as the people that were there in that particular year. In comparing directories of several years, one can find movement trends, changes in lifestyle, newly established streets, as well as the city's expansion and in which direction.

In addition to the alphabetical portion, a city directory may also contain a business directory, street directory, government directory, and listings of town officers, schools, societies, churches, post offices, and other miscellaneous matters of general and local interest.

In this, a city directory provides an accurate image of the place at a particular time with many of its functions.

A city directory functions as a 'code word' for a certain space in a particular time. It offers a large, cumulative, composite panorama of life, in our case in the capital of the Manchurian region of China. It is a history of a space in a particular point in time.

It can tell of the center of power, the economy, and the center of culture. It does not, however, relate to the macro of a region, but explicitly about almost everything that exists within the boundaries of the space — the city. It is the micro of the place.

Add to this all the spaces that usually one does not find in a directory, what

Karl Schlögel calls 'the non-places of those years'[229] — the movements of human cargo in stations, the black markets, the spaces of street vendors, the line in front of a movie theatre, the shacks and hostels, and prostitutes' dens...

Micah Winston was born 1994 in Toronto, Canada. His grandfather, Leo Vainstein ("Yeye" as he called him), was born in Harbin, in 1935, and moved to Japan around 1950 with his parents and brother, and eventually left Japan in 1953 by ship to immigrate to Canada. His parents and brother kept the surname name "Vainstein", but he changed his name from "Vainstein" to "Winston" in Montreal in 1962. Winston sounded much safer than the old Jewish name. Two years later, his father, Jonathan Winston, was born. He lived in Toronto, Canada before residing with his wife in Zurich, Switzerland. Micah Winston has heard all the stories as a child of his family growing up in China, but now have taken it upon himself to study the matter in more depth. His grandfather, Leo Winston, was still living in New York in 2021, but for medical reasons, sadly unable to provide any information to assist. His grandfather's brother, John Vainstein is living in Toronto but doesn't remember much about his youth in Harbin, China.

Micah Winston's grandfather, great-grandparents and great-great grandfather all lived in Harbin. It was possible that his great-great-grandfather is actually buried in the Harbin Jewish Cemetery. He saw his grandfather's name listed on the headstone

Fig. 46: David Leib Vainstein

transcriptions, but there was, unfortunately, no picture that he could compare with what records he had. Micah Winston was anxious to find anything about his forefathers.

He found his original surname Вайнштейн, in the Kharbin city directory 1926 on page 156. It seems, he said, to be translated as "Weinstein", "Vaynsteyn", or "Vainstein", depending on which Russian you ask. So it was translated as "Vaynsteyn", but it's all interchangeable, it seems. (Apparently the first character, "B" of Russian, is spelt as a "W", but pronounced like a "V" in the English language. It was all there on page 156 of the directory.

All Kharbin 1926

Vaynshteyn, Vladimir Solomonovich [son of Solomon] — (Yelena Leybovna [daughter of Leyba]), lawyer, 11 Pekarnaya [St.], tel.:3977

Vaynsteyn, Zandel' Izelev [son of Izel'] — (Golda Isidorovna [daughter of Isidor]), corner Diagonalnaya / 4 Konnaya St.

Vaynsteyn, Kel'man Leybov [son of Leyba] (Enya daughter of Shimon), 32 Kommercheskaya St.

Vaynsteyn, Leyba Vigdor — (Khaya daughter of Yakov), Malaya Shkolnaya 7, ap. 7

Vaynsteyn, Leyba Izelev [son of Izel'] — (Moisey son of Leyba), Kommercheskaya 32.

Vaynsteyn, Nekhava [son of Iosif] — (Khava Gal'neevna [daughter of Gal'ney?]), teacher, 46 Diagonalnaya, ap.2

The directory revealed a couple of interesting points:

He noticed that Kelman, Enya, Leyba, and Moisey all lived together at 32 Kommercheskaya Ulitsa (32 Commercial Street).

Kelman was his great-grandfather and Moisey was his brother. This told him that the "Leyba" and the "Enya" who are documented as buried in Harbin, are indeed his great-great-grandparents. They were his only direct ancestors actually buried in Harbin. The rest left Harbin in the late 1940s for Yokohama, and eventually Canada. He also found through the city directory that Leyba had a brother in Zandel, considering they both lived in Harbin, with the same surname, and same Patronymic name in "Izel".

Most people may be able to find some information about their relatives. However, the information is mostly like a milestone, or what I call "tombstone history".

What is lacking is the way they lived and how they interacted with their environment.

Below is the information Micah Winston was able to put together about his relatives:

David Leyb Vainstein (Лейба Изелевич Вайнштейн) — Great-great Grandfather. Born about 1870 in Anan'yiv, Ukraine. Lived in Harbin from around 1910until death in (possibly 1920s). Left Ananyev due to ongoing pogroms against Jews. Had two children — Kelman Vainstein and Michael "Moshe" Vainstein.

Kelman L. Vainstein (Кельман Вайнштейн) — Great Grandfather. Born April 10, 1896, in Anan'yiv, Ukraine. Lived in Harbin from 1910 until about 1950. Left Ananyev as a young child due to pogroms against Jews. One brother: Michael (Moshe) Vainstein, born March 22, 1899. Met and married wife "Raya Tunkel" in Harbin around 1930. Left Harbin for Yokohama,

Japan around 1950 with wife and two children

Yana Tunkel (Яна Тункель)—Great-great Grandfather. Born December 30, 1971, in Shirvint, Lithuania. Lived in Harbin from around 1905 until his death (date of death unknown). No knowledge of why they left Lithuania for China. Had 4 children: Raya, born in Harbin, Fania, Liza & Misha (born in Lithuania). Wife: Rebecca Tunkel (born January 7, 1876, in Podbrodze, Lithuania.

Raya Vainstein—née Tunkel (Рая Вайнштейн)—Great Grandmother. Born July 1, 1908, in Harbin, China. Father is Yana Tunkel. Lived in Harbin from 1908 (birth) until about 1950 when the family left for Japan by sea. Had 3 Siblings—Fania, Liza and Misha born in Lithuania.

Leo Vainstein (Лео Вайнштейн)—Grandfather. Born June 24, 1935, in Harbin, China. Parents: Kelman Vainstein and Raya Vainstein—née Tunkel. One brother: John (Yana) Vainstein (born September 8, 1941, in Harbin, China. Left Harbin with parents Kelman and Raya around 1950 for Yokohama, Japan by sea.

The city directory can provide a snapshot of the space, a past that is like a tombstone. It has the names, the dates, and on occasions some of the geographical movements made. All of the rest is within the memory of the next generation.

David Udovitch

History has shown that there are times when people who are either under stress or persuasive propaganda make irrational decisions that affect not only their well-being but their life.

Stalin's propaganda campaign that showed the Soviet Union as the ultimate heavenly space, lured thousands of exiles from the former Empire to return to that hostile land they escaped from. Some managed to survive but many others lost their life.

The David Udovitch life story[230] was told by a recording on tape in 2010. "The explanation to why Sonia Udovitch and her children decided to go back to the Soviet Union was that in 1932 the Japanese had occupied Manchuria. The Japanese established a puppet government in Manchuria, and their relations with Soviet Russia were bad after the Japanese entered Manchuria so the railway that was built by Russians at the start of the 20th century — belonged half to the Chinese and half to the Russians was taken away from them."

Under pressure from the Japanese, the Soviet Union had to sell to Japan half of what belonged to the railway. Japan considered that the Chinese Government of Manchuria as a puppet government. All the Russian employees who were working at the railway, and those living in Manchuria with Soviet passports, were offered to go back to Russia where, as they were told, life was better. Many decided that there was nothing else to do in China. In Manchuria after the railway would be sold there would not be any work or any kind of jobs to do, so a lot of them decided to go back to Russia. Sonia Udovitch also decided to go with 2 of her children.

The story of the Russian Jews living in Harbin is that after World War II ended in 1945 and the occupation of Manchuria by Soviet troops, there was no connection with the South like Shanghai. The south of China and Harbin was somehow cut off from communications. We found out about the establishment of the Jewish State of Israel in 1948 by radio.

In 1948 those people who were living in Shanghai had an opportunity to go to Israel straight away. But the Jewish people living in Harbin were not allowed to go to Israel until 1950: it was an exception to the rule because no Europeans were allowed to go anywhere from Manchuria at that time because the Chinese communists were in power in Manchuria after the Russian troops went back to the Soviet Union in 1947. The Chinese Communist Party was in power in Harbin and in Manchuria.

The other part of China was still occupied by a Chinese anti-communist government, so there was no connection with one part of China and with Manchuria.

That is how Stella's parents, her sister and her husband, and one child, and Stella's brother decided to go to Israel, and we, David and Stella, were left behind because we had a paint factory business at the time. We decided to stay for a while until the situation changed.

Last time I was telling the story of how I was crossing the border with my brother, Israel, to Harbin and China. This was illegal. I spoke about the first few days we were hiding in stacks of hay. During the nighttime, from 11:00 p.m. until 4 or 5 a.m. we were walking. This was in October 1931. It was nighttime otherwise you can't walk in the light, so the guides who were taking us to the border were always selecting the nights of the full moon otherwise there was no possibility of going across.

I told the story of how we met the border guards when 2 of them were sitting behind the fire and we had to cross in the path between 2 hills. They were sitting on one side, and we had to cross not far from them. The idea was that one of the guys was crawling first in the military manner as close to the ground as possible and not to get their attention as they were both armed. So one was keeping an eye at the border guards and one of our guides was watching the patrol and then my younger brother was crawling also across this hollow and then me, and then 2 women, one after the other, and the last one crossing was the guide. This was the most dangerous point that we made during the crossing of the border.

The next day we also were hiding. In the night time by approximately 3:00 on the 6th night, we saw the light of a Chinese city on the Chinese territory. There was full light in the city and we were on the top of the hill. The feeling was that we got what we wanted we crossed the border and we were mostly nearly on the Chinese territory. The feelings were of happiness that all this trip took 6 nights to come to the point of our destination. Of course, at the time I was 11 years old, and my brother was only 9.

We didn't think about our brother and sister that were left there, the guides refused to take them because my brother was 7 and my sister was 5 and they didn't want to take them because they were afraid that they weren't able to walk.

So, on the first attempt when we were crossing the border with the whole family we were caught and this time we left not only our brother and sister there but we left our mother that was in jail and at the time we did not know how long she would be in jail. So, on crossing the border we stopped for a while at one Chinese house that's called "Phanza" which is made of clay and straw and in the middle of the house there was a kind of brick bed warmed with cakes of coal underneath and in the 2nd part of October it was getting colder and we were happy to be in a Chinese house. In the morning we entered the City of Bogranisa (Pogranichny) — in Chinese it was called "Soi Hen Ho" (Suifenhe).

It's the last station on the western Chinese railway going from Harbin to Bogranisa, and then the next one was in Russian territory. We spent one day and night in this house of the guide's friends. This is their usual place where they take the people who they took over the border. We slept there all night. In the daytime, we went to see the town.

The funny thing is that I remember as a young boy that I was so afraid of anybody in uniform while walking in the Chinese town. As a matter of fact, a lot of Russians were living there. I was always afraid when a policeman was walking on the same side as I was, so I tried not to meet him, and I walked on the other side of the road.

Anyhow, the next day we took the train to Harbin. With us came the woman who was in our party, and one of the guides.

What happened on the way, that I will always remember, was that the guide was a bit drunk, and he was laying on the top layer of the train, and we were sitting down. When the military came to inspect the train, and the train was moving they noticed that our guide had a revolver in his belt, and so he was arrested and the lady who was in our party was also taken from the train.

So, the two of us were left on the train with nothing but only 2 tickets. I did not have my father's address, but I had the address of a place in Harbin where my father's friend had a business. It was a knitting factory, and the name of the family was Grovener. The name of the street was number 116. I remember the address because all the letters that were sent to my father in Harbin were to his address of living or business because father used to call there twice a week to collect the mail. This was just to avoid the military looking into the letters.

My father, from one point of view, was always cautious, and on the other side he wasn't because he was talking to my mother on the phone and was naive. He told her that nobody was listening to what he was saying. Actually, all the conversations between Russia and the foreign countries were all controlled and were all strictly monitored.

We were traveling to Harbin on the train, and it took the whole day. By the time we reached Harbin, the funny thing that happened was that I didn't know that before Harbin, the center, there was an old Harbin and we didn't know where to get out. So we got out at the Old Harbin and asked the name of the street that we had to go to. We were told that it was not here but at the next station so we quickly ran back to the train and continued to the City of Harbin.

When we got out at Central Harbin, we didn't know which way to go and nobody met us. For some unexplained reason, the guide didn't inform father when we were coming so we were going to Harbin just with the few notes in the pocket and the address of someone. When we got out of the train and into the street, we started moving in the direction just opposite the station moving in the direction of the Russian cathedral. We asked somebody where the street was and they told us we had to go in the opposite direction. So, we went in the opposite direction and when we reached the place we called it an arch. On this we noticed that some people were coming in our direction with waving flags and someone was firing, like firing from weapons or something.

Even at 11 years of age I already read a lot of books in Russia, and I read about the demonstrations against the government. So when I saw this demonstration we were a bit frightened and started running in the opposite direction. Then as I looked around and saw that nobody was running and that they continued going in the same direction where they wanted to go and no panics, I saw there was nothing. So we stopped and let the demonstration go through. We did not know what it was but later on, we were told that it was a Chinese funeral procession and they were firing crackers and carrying mostly white flags meaning that it was a funeral procession. So, this episode is still in my head and I will always remember and tell this story to my friends.

We went to find this place in Jagolina Street and found this knitting factory and my father was called by phone and came to pick us up. As a matter of fact, this was Mrs. Warner's father and mother, they were crossing the border also before us and they came from some part of Siberia and before going to cross the border they lived in our place for a few days to add to this I have to say that few other people also departed from there for the border crossing trek, and also Michael Pilichinsky who is living here, he and his sister, at the time she was 16 and he was 14. They also came from city of Legastock and lived in our place for a while and were then taken by guides across the border. Their father was a friend of our father from the city of Legastock, and their father also was living already in the City of Harbin and they were friends with my father and they met occasionally and that's why my father was recommended to stay there on the way from Negia and then across the border.

My father took us to the place of his living. At that time he was a partner in a business that was selling fodder. Fodder is used for oil cakes and wheat bran and for corn and flour. But most of the selling was hay and wheat bran which was used to feed the dairy cattle. In Harbin at the time, a lot of Russian refugees lived in the area where my father had his business and house. In that area were living a lot Russian refugees and they were heading to this dairy farm. It was all in the backyard and you would have between 2 to 5 cows that were giving between 20 to 25 liters of milk per day and somehow even milk was cheap at the time at 5 cents a bottle, and a liter is only a bottle and a half.

People somehow managed to live on these earnings, and milk was also delivered to the shop and to the other houses. There were few dairy farms that had about 12 cows and up to 20 and a few of them were Jewish families that worked in this and my father was selling this for all the dairy farms. Later on, I was like an incasta, which is the one who goes and collects the debts. Most of the trade was not with cash and I had to go see a few customers and collect every second day because it was my job after school. Before the shops were closed, I was helping with the deliveries, with the men who delivered the goods. I was going with them and looking around and it was kind of a pleasure for me to go on a horse, on a small horse delivering approximately 5 bags of bran or 10-15 pieces of hay and I was always trying to get on the delivery done. This life in October 1939 until the next year we were living in a place where father had a room behind the business. One room only, and there were 3 of us living in the room. We would have breakfast together and at dinner time my brother and I used to go across the road to a kind of restaurant which was conducted by the Russian refugee committee and we had our dinner there.

The funny thing of course that I have to tell is that my father was kosher. He was always kosher in Russia, and so in Harbin. By this time somehow he couldn't afford to have kosher food for his 2 sons, and he was having the kosher food delivered to his place when he was working and the meals they prepared for him and for his partners. His partners were a well-known family by the name of Vidocha. Three brothers working in the business and one of them was partners with my father in this fodder shop selling corn and flour and the other 2 brothers were engaged in the delicatessen and the small cafe they had next door. The food was delivered to these 3 brothers and my father was having his share delivered as well for exactly the same amount he was paying to them. We were going to this small restaurant or its called eating place or Stalova, a cheap cafeteria in Russian and having dinner there. But usually, we were buying one dinner for two.

There was not much money that my father gave us for that and he was always trying not to show to the people that we were going to that restaurant and that nobody would see that we go there because he was ashamed that his sons were going to a restaurant that was treife, not kosher.

By the end of summer in Harbin there was a flood and all the city and this part of the city that we were living in and having business was also flooded and we had to leave the place and go to some part of the city that was higher and wasn't in danger of floods, so we moved to the new city called Novegora (Noviy Gorod). The name of the street was Sunzinka, Sunzin (Tianjin) the name of the city in Manchuria[231] and we were living in that street where we rented a room and we were living there again with my father.

That time was Autumn 1932. There was a cholera epidemic, and there were a lot of refugees from the flooded areas who were living just on the streets in tents and some without tents and because of shortage of clean water, the epidemic of cholera was spread. I was sent to prepare myself to enter the school. Before this, when I first arrived I was going to a Russian school but somehow it had a Chinese name. Most of the people of course were Russians and the subjects were in Russian. I was going there because the son of a friend of my father was going to that school. So on his advice I was going to the same school.

Later on when my father found out that most of the Jewish kids first were going to Talmud Torah, a Jewish school that was on the corner street. However, we could not afford to be send to commercial school and I had to have the entry exams. I was sent to a teacher in Komner Street and he was living there during the flood because his house was flooded. He was on the first floor and I was going there 3 times a week. He was giving me lessons for the exam that I would have. So I entered school in 2nd class. Second class at the time was 3 pre-school classes and then 1st class, 2nd class and up to 7th class. 7th class was graduation so it means that actually 10 years people were going to school. When I was 7, I entered this school I was 12 years of age and I was in the 2nd class. Most of the boys and girls that were in my class were a bit younger than me. Because they started at 5 or 6 years of age and by the time they came to the 2nd class they were only 11 of them around. I know that some of them that graduated from school were only 14½, 15 years of age.

I graduated from school when I was 17. We were living in the place that wasn't flooded in the new Harbin called New City and at that time we were told by father that our mother was coming to us from Nicolva. I remember that when we left the city of Nicolva my mother was still in jail. But father was trying to get her out to bring her into China.

At the time in 1932, we had the Japanese entered Manchuria and occupied the region. Because the Russian border was very closely guarded and the border patrols were increased it was very difficult for my mother to cross the border. As usual, father also sent her guides to take her from Nikolva to Harbin.

When we left she was still in the prison. But then she was sent to 3 years' exile into one of the cities that were given to her. It meant that you could go and live in the city in any place inside the 7 main cities in Russia. And you had to work once a week or once a fortnight with the local military to show that you were there. And mother was given 5 places in Russia where she could go into exile and live there and report to the military. My mother selected the city of Tushcan.

At that time my father arranged with the guides to take her across the border. As she was in jail for 11 years, and she was not a healthy woman and the conditions in the jail were bad, not only from the poor food but the conditions: they were mostly sleeping on the floor, and all in one room.

There were about 7, 10, 11, or 12 women in one room, and my mother she got TB. She was so sick that in crossing the border she wasn't able to walk and the guides had to hire some workers to carry her on to the station across the border, and then in the Chinese territory also because some of the way between the border and Harbin was flooded and the radio line was disconnected.

She was carried by men on the carriage for many, many kilometers to reach the rail line, and then she arrived in Harbin. We met her after school at home, and of course, it was a very pleasant surprise even though we were told that she was coming and mother was living with us for a while until a lot of floodwaters receded and we went back to the part of the city we used to live before. The room that we were having was not big enough for us, and then my mother came, and we had to take another room somewhere. Father rented a flat in a poor part of Harbin. We were below the middle level of living because father at that time worked in the business already and my impression was he was always in need of money and he wasn't able to have much. Later on, he established his business as he was bringing hay by railway, by carriage, railway carriages up to 20-30 tons at a time and was selling it at the station where they arrived.

For a few days the people were coming and buying hay there and they knew him from his previous business and that's how he was earning a living. But life of course was very difficult for the whole family because the flat where we were living was in a very bad place. The house was dirty, not only because it was cheap. It was very far from the center of the city, and I was going to school and my brother was going to Talmud Torah. But after my mother arrived we ate kosher food. She knew how to conduct a kosher house, but it was also very hard for us because it was much more expensive.

Anyhow, we were living in the place and my mother was sick. Later on, I found out that she had TB. At that time there was no medicine, and she was using old methods of medicine to treat it but there was no cure and the basic medical help was not very good. I especially remember that she was going to the slaughterhouse and drinking fresh blood from the killed cow there because somebody told her that it will help her. Life wasn't easy for all of us. It was going on for a few years, until we moved to another place and it was also far away from the center and there were no buses at that time or transport so we went to school walking in the summer and winter and we weren't really well dressed because father was always short of money to buy warm clothing.

My father wasn't able to buy leather shoes or leather boots. In the wintertime, we were wearing what was called Kotonskin but you can't go to school wearing this so we had to have some kind of shoes. My father wasn't able to buy a pair of shoes for $5.00, so he was buying us tennis shoes that came from Japan and it was possible to buy them for $1,50, $1.75, $2.00 or gym boots in the wintertime. This is what I was wearing to school instead of leather shoes.

It was all wet because most of the people in my class came from more or less wealthy families and I was the only one that was wearing cotton trousers not woolen ones in the summer because woolen trousers cost $6.00—$7.00 and father couldn't afford it, so he was buying copy ones that cost $2.00—$2.50 and he was buying it twice a year because they were not that strong and because others cost $6.00. We were wearing these trousers for 2 years at least until we were grown. The same thing was with the shirts.

Most of the boys were wearing woolen shirts and in the summer light cotton ones with the school buttons and I was wearing also one which we bought in the market and they had ordinary buttons and, on my photo, taken at school all the boys are in the shirts with shiny buttons and my buttons were ordinary black buttons and I looked different from the other boys. On top of all this because I was not wearing the proper leather shoes I got sick in my legs. I was perspiring at the time very badly and my feet were perspiring and they smelt and it was a problem for me in the class. It was a problem for me for many years.

At that time when we were living in that flat, in the autumn we used to buy small ducks, they were growing fast and by the time it was cold and there was no place for them to live during the winter, we killed just before the New Year holiday, Rosh Hashana. Father was a kosher, and a religious man, he used to bring the shochet to our place and he was killing these ducks just before wintertime.

In the area where we used to live, there lived also Russians. One of them was a butcher. They had a son and daughter. Their son was Nikolai, and their daughter later moved to Shanghai but she married in Harbin. She got married when she was 16, and then went to Shanghai and then from Shanghai to Australia.

Her brother, who is dead now used to live in Kraznadar in the same city where my sister, Vera, lives now, and we were always enquiring about each other. Her brother was a strong good looking man but he was not allowed by the Japanese into the Russian military patrols. These Japanese were training Russians for sabotage war in case they will fight Russians they were anticipating that Hitler will beat Russia and the Japanese will enter the war and occupy the Far East. They trained these Russians, mostly white Russians for the future, When the Soviets entered the war in 1945 and occupied Manchuria, all these Russians that were serving in this military attachment, they were all arrested and sent to the works in Siberia on forestry, and many of them died there but Nikolai survived. I met him at Krasnadar when I visited our sister for the first time.

That life we used to live wasn't very good because the building itself had very big windows. In the wintertime, it was cold there and mother suffered from all this because we used it as a bedroom and we all tried to be in the one room where the stove was. Mother started to get worse and worse. Life wasn't very easy for my mother so she was just getting on only because she was still young. At that time she was only 33 or 34.

After she had 33 days of not eating anything, only drinking, she felt somehow better. But after that and in a few weeks' time, she had a stroke and was taken to the Jewish Hospital and she died there on May 4, 1935. I was at that time 14½ years and my brother, Israel, was 2 years younger. My brother was going to Talmud Torah school and I was going to a commercial school. My brother couldn't join this school because the fees were very high. I was there only because I had a scholarship from the Jewish community as a person who had good results at school.

In each class in the Jewish community had one or two Jewish boys or girls that were not able to pay for the school fees, and the Harbin Jewish community was paying to the school some amount of money. The fees at the school were at the time for instance in the 3rd or 4th year were $130 to $140.00 a year. In the 7th class, it was $170.00 to $180.00 a year. It was paid quarterly or monthly. So just to say what was the amount of my compared with the wages, the wages at the time for water at the factory just without any profession was between $25.00 – $30.00. The people that were working in the shops or the big shops were getting between $30.00 to $60.00.

When my mother died in the Jewish Hospital, we were allowed to see her face: it was a custom in Harbin to see her face only for a few seconds before the funeral. Funerals then usually weren't like that the body was taken to a synagogue and then from one synagogue to another one, and in our case, it was from what is called the new synagogue where father and I were going, and from the new synagogue, it was taken by a carriage to the cemetery. The cemetery was between the Chinese town and the Russian town at the edges of the city. It was a very big cemetery. Whoever looked after they had a sort of tradition and there was another prayer said: a prayer said at the first synagogue, and then at the second synagogue, and prayer also said there.

We had a problem with burying my mother. On her passport, she was Ana Pantilimono but not Sara Brama or Sara Abram as she was named after conversion.

Somehow when the passport was made in China when she arrived in the passport it was written that she was a Jewish but the name was Ana Pantilimono. It's a real Russian name. Ana of course is like Hannah and Pantilimono is not Jewish at all. So father had a one or two days of negotiations and it all finished well after father found somebody that was a witness in the city where mother was converted by the Rabbi Ashkanasiv. Rabbi Ashkanasiv was later on a chief Rabbi in Shanghai and he was a friend of my father.

By that time I already had my bar mitzvah which was conducted in the new synagogue and everybody knew that I was attending the Jewish lessons in the school and that my brother was studying in the Talmud Torah school so it was a dilemma not to allow my mother to be buried in the Jewish cemetery when both sons were Jewish. We were left without a mother living in that flat. We were living there for a while and in the meantime, the financial situation with father was really bad and we tried to let one of the rooms, we had two rooms with a kitchen at the time and we were trying to let one of the rooms so that paying of rent would be much easier. The rent as I said was about $40.00 and father just couldn't earn money at that time he was trying to do some commission work and was saving or buying things for us.

After my mother died we understood that the financial situation was very bad so we were getting dinner from the Jewish refugee dining room. It was delivered to our place, and we were having our meal at home after school. In the summer it was all right, but in the winter the fellow who delivered it would bring it all cold and, by the time we would come home it was waiting for us on the stove. If the stove was not hot we would have to start it. This flat didn't have any blinds or window coverings. In the summer it was all right, but in the winter it was very difficult because everything was open. If we wanted to go to the toilet, we had to go fully dressed with our coat on.

The toilet was working in a very particular way. It was a big hole and it was for the whole building. You go out and you sit above a hole and you do whatever you want to do. In the summer it was a bit cold. But in the winter it would freeze and the Chinese men who came to dig it and then carried in the baskets.

But at the same time there were some areas in Harbin where, for instance, Stella's parents used to live, a place where more wealthy people were living and they had a heating system in their flats and they had inner plumbing and good sewerage and for a toilet they had hot water. But that place where Stella used to live the price for a flat was not less than $60, $70 or $100.00. They had 4 bedrooms, 5 bedrooms actually they used to pay $100.00. $100.00 a month was a big amount of money and the people back there in business, all the wealthy people could afford to pay that much. So our idea at one stage to get a room somewhere in this area was just impossible. Then father decided that there was nothing he could do in Harbin because there was no work at all.

So in 1936 father decided that he has to go and do something somewhere else. First, he went to Tianjin. He went there because in Tianjin there used to live the family of Hwatkin. The family of Hwatkin were relatives of father from Siberia. Father decided to go there himself.

This is how he left my brother, the two of us by ourselves. I was 16 and he was 14. By that time we were living in another flat, a smaller one. At one stage we had a tenant. It was a friend of mine, he was Chinese and she was Russian. Later on, we found out that she was working in a brothel.

Father of course was helping us by sending some money every month so that it would be easy for us to pay for the flat. The food we were eating from the Jewish free diners. For breakfast, we ate just milk and bread. We did not always have money to buy sugar.

We both, Israel and I, were treated badly by surrounding boys, and it was always a problem when we were going home from school. I was in my uniform and Israel was in a special uniform for — but they all knew that we were Jews. Of course a few times we were beaten on the way home. So we had to go in such a way home that we did not pass the places where these boys were. It was always a problem to get home without any insults.

As father started himself a base in Shanghai, we decided that Israel would go to Shanghai and live there because he was not successful at school and father told him that he would be with him there and he will find work in Shanghai. Israel was not successful in the courses in Shanghai so father found him some work on a ship with his friends and he was working there. At that time I was in Harbin and I moved as didn't need any kitchen so I moved to a room. I was living with a Russian family renting one room. I was still going to school and after graduating from school I was trying to get into a Japanese institute that was established in the city of Changchun. The idea was to teach some Russians the Japanese language and Japanese culture and that we had to live there and talk only Japanese and learn the culture, as the future leaders of the Russian immigration, the Russian society in Manchuria. I filled an application and attended some exams but was not accepted because the Japanese commission decided not to have a Jew in that institute.

All I have to say is that by that time I graduated from school with honors and my name was put on what's called the "Golden Box" that was hanging in the main hall.

When I graduated I was 17 years and a few months. After the application to the Japanese institute was not accepted I and a friend of mine, Mr. Kemik who is living now in Israel, we decided that we would apply to the Russian Railway Institute. It was not a big school, but later it was very good because the teachers were mostly from the university that was conducted by the railway. After the sale of the railway to the Japanese, the institute was closed and all the teachers that did not go to Russia stayed behind were available. They were the institute's backbones. They had chemical and electrical and mechanical classes. Mr. Kemik, and I entered the institute. The situation was not very good for us because the institute was conducted by a Russian immigration committee, and antisemitism was there. Not all amongst the lecturers but amongst the students. Mr. Kemik Snr, was a tailor, and he was making some suits for a Japanese fellow by the name Makmamura, who was one of the chiefs at the Japanese security police and was having a hand in that institute as one of the advisers, helped us.

So we entered the institute. It was not in our part of the city, it was in the part of the city called Navagora, New Town, near the railway management offices and classes were mostly in the evening.

While we were attending classes the Japanese decided that they start a proper institute not only technical but an institute of commercial science and they called it North Manchuria University. There were two faculties, one commercial and one industrial technical. They moved it first to Pristan, the area was very close to us, it was a Jewish area and as a matter of fact it was on the same street as our commercial school for the first few months, and then they got a big place in New Town in the place called the Ukrainian Club. They had a three-floor house and the institute was established there.

I enrolled there. For me it was not easy because I had to travel there. I had to travel by bus and train. I was going there for 4 years and it was not that easy for me because I had to give lessons to make some money and to survive because father was hardly sending anything.

At that time people were trying to leave Harbin and go to the South of China and from there to other foreign destinations. It was 1937-39 when the war started in Europe in 1940.

After the occupation of Manchuria, the free movement of money was forbidden and whoever wanted to transfer money at across was not easy. So, somehow with the connection that father had in Shanghai with his friends there, we started transferring money and I was making money. I did this by taking money in Harbin from people that found out about me or if I found them. They gave me their money and I was going to the Japanese Bank and transferred this money to Japan. I was doing all this before the start of the war on the Pacific, I was contemplating going after graduation to the United States because I was in contact all the time with my later mother's sister who was living in California.

After I graduated from the university, I was not well graduated because I was not able to get a diploma, I was getting only a certificate of graduation.

In conclusion about my life in Harbin when I was going to school and in my first few years of university, I was always helped by the Jewish community by paying my school fees, and I was getting free meals. I feel obliged to the community that during these hard years I was helped so much.

David Udovitch left Harbin for Shanghai and from there, as a married man, to Australia. His English never improved yet his detailed memories of his daily life and struggles in Harbin contribute to the understanding of the course of human events, activities, and the path of the existence of an individual and a family, through the actions and events that occurred to them in Harbin.

Yehudit Karlik-Bein

Yehudit Karlik[232], now Bein, was born in 1940 in Harbin to Sophia Wertzman-Vigdorchik and Michael Karlik. The extensive Vigdorchik family came to Harbin from Herson in Ukraine between 1907 and 1910. Her mother with her parents and two brothers reached Harbin in 1910 after an 18 days' journey by the Trans-Siberian Railway across Russia, and then from Manzouli to Harbin on the Chinese Eastern Railway. Her mother was then a two-year-old child. She later graduated from the Generozova middle school in 1923. Yehudit's father was born in Balata, in the Odessa district in 1917. His parents moved to Vladivostok and he came to Harbin in 1930. He opened a textile-furs business and was doing fairly well.

Not like most others, she remembered the years of World War II as comfortable and safe. "During the war, when the whole of Europe was aflame, we enjoyed a comfortable life. Perhaps our parents wanted to hide from us the surrounding realities, but we enjoyed a wonderful childhood and adolescence, and the echo of the war reached us as a muffled thunder."

She remembers her home at number 22 Konnaya Ulitsa. It was called "Dom Antipasa", the Old and the New synagogues, her school "Talmud Torah", the great Churin store, and, especially, the tall tree on Artilleriiskaya Street, with hundreds of colorful strips of paper hanging from its branches.

"The "Antipas House", where we lived, was one of the tallest in town, equipped with an elevator, a rare luxury at the time. At the entrance lived a Russian couple. The man was what we called "schweitzar", a door-keeper. He checked the people who entered and asked them who they come to visit. I do not know till today if he was for or against us."

The majority of the tenants at the Antipas House were Jews, amongst them Mrs. Olga Arkus, who led a tragic life. "Olga was a wealthy Jewish woman who served as the president of the WIZO organization in Harbin. She owned a pharmacy and also produced perfumes. Her only daughter lived in Tsingtao."[233]

In the building lived also the Kuhl family. Mr. Kuhl was the headmaster of the Harbin German School. Shortly after the occupation of Harbin by the Soviet Red Army in 1945, Mr. Kuhl was arrested and evicted from his apartment with his family.

A Soviet army colonel moved into Kuhl's apartment which was next to Mrs. Arkus's flat.

Olga Arkus established good relations with her new neighbors and often invited the colonel, his deputy, and Sashka, his orderly, to her apartment.

One morning the colonel advised Olga to stay at her apartment and not to go out. In a matter of minutes, several soldiers came, emptied her flat of all her possessions, put her belongings on a truck, and arrested her. She was transferred by train to the Grodekovo prison where she was put in a cell together with 40 male Chinese. She was the only woman there.[234]

When high officers visited the prison she seized the opportunity and shouted that she, a Russian woman, was put there for no wrongdoings. She was interrogated and released and was given travel papers. Making her way back she reached Harbin at night. She spent the night at the house of the Zuckerman family, Zuckerman was the owner of a chocolate factory, and then she moved in with the Karlik family. All of them lived in the Antipas House.

While in prison, the Soviet authorities in Harbin seized her apartment and confiscated her pharmacy. They appointed a Mr. Schuster, a well-known Jewish Soviet, as the receiver of her property. Her complaints to the Soviet authorities brought to her second arrest in April 1946 and she was put on a military train heading to the Soviet Union. Shortly after, it was reported that a body of a woman was found near the tracks. The body was that of Olga Arkus. "They slashed her throat and threw her out of the train."[235]

On the top floor, there was only one small apartment with a lot of aquariums with colorful fish swimming in them. There were also many windows, from which the whole of Harbin could be seen like on a palm of your hand.

Yehudit Karlik, like many children of her age, was attended by a nanny, "niania" in Russian, whom she "inherited" from the Dr. Chaplick family. Her nanny was kind and noble, and it was only natural that she loved her very much. The nanny was a tall, good-looking woman, well-educated and intelligent. She was a widow of a Polish officer. When Yehudit was five, her father decided that she was sufficiently mature and can do without a "niania". She left the Karlik home, but came to visit on occasions for years. She died just before the family left Harbin. Yehudit and her mother attended her funeral at a Catholic church in Novy Gorod (The New City). With her nanny gone, she started attending the "Talmud Torah" kindergarten.

"Each summer, during the hot months of July and August our family used to move to "za-Sungari" on the other side of the Sungari rive). In the spring of 1945 I "caught" a severe case of measles and instead of going to "za-Sungari" we went to live with our friends in their farm way out of the city. There they gave me plenty of goat milk, which was supposed to have been a potent remedy against the illness. This was also my luck to have missed the entrance of the Red Army into the city.

There was, however, an episode, which I cannot forget till today: one day in 1946 my mother and I were walking along the "Naberejnaya", the Sungari embankment, when we saw a band of strange men, armed with rifles, coming in our direction. They were tired, some barefoot, dressed in tattered khaki. But the most striking thing about them was that they walked in total silence. Passersby, silent too, looked at them in bewilderment. Much later, mother told me that they were the "Ba-lu din", soldiers of the Communist Eighth Army, who marched to the municipal prison on Kommercheskaya Street to liberate their comrades, who were imprisoned there."[236]

Synagogues played an important part in the children experience. During the High Holidays all the Jews of Harbin attended services at the synagogue. Father, who was an active member of our community, attended the "New" Synagogue, but his mother continued, as ever, to go to the Old Synagogue. Yehudit believe that the younger people mostly attended the New Synagogue. The children, however, changed from one to another. She remember well Rabbi Kiselev, who sat to the right of the Ark, once in the "Old" Synagogue, another time—in the "New".

"My father's seat was in the fourth or the fifth row on the right-hand side of the aisle. Next to him sat Mr. Oumansky, father of Garik Oumansky. Facing my father, on the women's balcony sat my mother. She chose her seat purposely: Not being able to read Hebrew and despite her prayer book having a Russian translation, she watched father praying below, and, to keep face, when he turned a page, she followed him.

Before the prayer for the dead, the "Yizkor", the Gabbai, the manager of the synagogue,) used to thunder at us: "Children, out!", and we used to pour into the yard. There we played marbles or "kartinki" ("pictures"), a pack of portraits of film stars, placed on the ground with a square frame around it. The contending players had to knock the pictures out of the square by hurling a "bitok", a piece of flat iron or an old shoe heel."[237]

The area of the children's activities was rather limited. It was just a narrow rectangle from Novogorodnaya to Kazachyia Ulitsa, and from Diagonalnaya to the Sungari embankment.

When Yehudit was about seven, her uncle, a great football fan as she described him, used to take his son and her to the football games. We walked on foot from Pristan to the football field, across the old water carrier. She and her nephew were fans of the opposing teams, "and one of us cried bitterly at the end of each game". One team, however, was an exception, it was called "The Red Star", because the star of the team, Borya Zvibel, was Jewish. "We were also very proud of our sports yacht, "Kedma", whose crew were members of the "Maccabi" club. She remembers well, Dima Kaufman, Teddy's brother, and Shmushkovich, who set out on it along the Sungari River.

For Yehudit, the Jewish school "Talmud Torah" was a world all its own, completely separated from reality. Black benches screwed onto black desks with a cavity for an inkstand. The desks were covered with names and drawings, carved by the pupils' pocket knives. The school belonged to the chain of schools of the religious party "Agudat Israel", but in her time it was a "modern school" where Hebrew was spoken in "Ashkenazi" dialect. Later, with the occupation of Manchuria by the Soviet Army, the students had to wear a Red Star badge.

When the Soviets prohibited the study of Hebrew, the Hebrew teacher, Mr. Nadel who lived in a small house in the schoolyard, used to take the students to his apartment and gave them "private" lessons of the language and the Old Testament.

The school was situated close to the Karlik home, and the young girl was allowed to go there without being accompanied her mother, which was the custom. Mothers used to bring their children to school and pick them up after classes. In winter they used to bring with them warm blankets to protect the children from cold, which sometimes dropped as low as minus 30 degrees Celsius!

On Hanukkah[238] and at the end of each academic year they had parties, prepared by the Parents' Committee. There were a lot of tasty refreshments, dancing, and, first and foremost, a performance produced by the parents and acted by the pupils. Once they even had a professional producer!

Nothing was taken more seriously than birthdays. All the girls arrived at a birthday party in thoroughly starched dresses, with ribbons in their curls. Boys in formal suits and ties. They sat at the long tables covered by spotlesswell-starched table cloth and loaded with tarts and sweets. Behind stood the mothers and made sure that the children "behaved properly as befits children brought up in good homes."

When the meal was over, each one had to exhibit his or her talents, for there was hardly a Jewish child who would not be given musical education, even in families of meager means. Yehudit's specialty was not piano or violin. She sang—Russian war-time songs and romances.

Then came 1949, the beginning of the great aliya to Israel. Those were intoxicating days of expectation and hope to begin a new life in the old-new country of their own. She remembers how thrilled they were when a short news documentary has shown Golda Meir, the first ambassador of Israel to the USSR presenting her credentials in the Kremlin.

At the beginning of 1950 the class at school was all but empty. Every day another pupil came to say goodbye: "We are leaving for Israel!" One day she came home from school and asked her mother, "When are we going to go to Israel?".

Soon after, when she was ten, her mother asked "Do you really want to go to Israel?" The answer was in the affirmative. She opened the door of the drawing room and said: "Look carefully at what you see, and remember that you will never have it there." She answered: "Mother, I promise you that never will I ask for anything. Nor will I ever complain".

Then came the preparations for the journey. Lists were made of what to sell, what to buy, what to take with them, and what to leave there. The reports from Israel were vague. Some advised the immigrants to take any object they can lay their hands on, even a broom or clothes-pegs, and to buy dark colored bedding, because in Israel there is not enough water for laundering.

The Karliks sold their beautiful furniture, which hurt her mother a lot, while the children, were delighted in sliding over the parquet floors in the empty apartment.

On April 20, 1950 they left for Tientsin, and, from there, by boat, to Israel.

Yehudit Karlik-Bein lived in Harbin ten years, but had just few opportunities to play with Chinese children. They did have Chinese friends on Diagonalnaya Street. They had two sons her age, and they played occasionally in their yard. "We had a good friend by the name of Liu, whom we called Liulka.

When in Israel Yehudit was very proud when she was called "Chinese", and proud of having a passport where she is registered as born in China.

Max Star

Max Star traveled to Harbin in 1914.[239]

When we stopped at Pogranichnaya at the border of Russia and China, he recalls, we were taken into a customs house on the Chinese side and searched thoroughly to determine if any of us were smuggling opium. Dealers in the narcotic paid thousands of dollars to people who would smuggle opium into China, and all of us had been warned by the train conductors that customs was very strict and penalties high for smugglers. Men and women alike were thoroughly searched.

Afterward, we were allowed to go into the town which, although owned by the Chinese, was under Russian control. I located a small Jewish community of ten families, a doctor, dentist, druggist and a few merchants. No further Jews were allowed to settle there by order of the Russian Government.

It was a warm and comfortable sunny day, and since it was close to our High Holidays, Rosh Hashana and the Day of Atonement, I decided to stay over for a few days.

Walking up the main business street, I noticed that most of the people were primitive types of mixed nationalities—Chinese, Bashkirs, and Buriats—all of whom spoke a little Russian. I saw some merchants that seemed to have Jewish names and went into their shops to visit with them. After pleasant moments spent with them, they directed me to the synagogue. At prayer time, some ten people were gathered there. The deacon was a Chinaman who knew the entire ritual prayers and could take care of the Synagogue as well.

I finally took my leave of this place and entrained for Harbin, noting that the trains were built of heavy armored steel, and the conductors were Army men carrying pistols. I learned these precautions were necessary in Chinese territory since Manchuria was not too well developed, the people still wild, and often formed into bands to attack the trains and rob them. To protect themselves against attack, they would shoot steam from the sides of the train, the passengers would lie on the floor, and the conductors and guards would shoot it out with the bandit gangs.

In Harbin at the Jewish Community Center, a place was found for me and some other new arrivals. We were fed, and those without money were given

Fig. 47: Max Star

a few cents. We were housed in the classrooms of the Hebrew school. Everyone was always alert to protect the women from the many Chinese who were always trying to kidnap or lure white women. Most of the Chinese men there were single, as few Chinese women would leave their native China for the Russian-dominated territory.

Harbin was a large city, but badly out-moded and old-fashioned. Most of the city was slums, where the Chinese lived. In the European quarters lived the business people, government workers, teachers, white-collar workers, a few Chinese merchants, and the two regiments of soldiers who protected the city and the railroads.

Shortly after arriving, I was invited to take charge of the Jewish Center. They wanted me to work with them, especially in warning the women not to go out walking at night, as there were bands of Chinese who would attack any white woman and often throw them into the Sungaree River. The city was Internationalized, and the police force was unable to cope with its problems. Each church or religious body had the responsibility of warning and watching its people.

In the business section of Harbin, I noticed that all labor was Chinese because they would work so cheaply. Many of the businesses themselves were owned by the Chinese, since few could compete with their low expenses, few of them hiring salespeople, but doing everything themselves. From three to six people would open a business, living in the back of the store and taking turns waiting on the trade, cooking, and cleaning.

Europeans in business there were mostly importers or owners of factories or large stores.

I saw a meat block placed right in the middle of the street, where a butcher was doing business, selling the black, poor meat there in the open amidst thousands of swarming flies. The Chinese do not eat much meat, but at holiday time they chop a little in with their vegetables.

Further down the street, something was boiling in a large kettle. I thought at first they were heating something with which to tar the street, but found to my surprise that they were cooking barley soup. Many came running toward me, pleading: "Captain, give me something to eat." The soup was selling at three cents a plate, so I bought some for them, being repaid by the color that returned to their pale cheeks as they drank it.

Back at the Center, one of my jobs was to help set up accommodations for everyone, as they arrived. I went to the lumber yard and picked up some lumber, then tried to get a truck to deliver it. I found two Chinamen with a horse and wagon who wanted two dollars to deliver the lumber. I was about to give them the job when I saw a mob of Chinese running toward me, begging me to let them carry the lumber on their shoulders for a small sum. I gave them the job, thinking it was better to give twenty people a job than to help feed two men and a horse. We had to take the lumber over a mile, and it was accomplished with much changing of the wood from shoulder to shoulder, and many rest stops. I had to keep a close watch to see that none of them wandered away with the lumber.

The Chinese in Harbin were treated very poorly under the Russians, but when I walked over the tracks to a town called Fujiadian, which was under the Chinese regime, I found conditions even worse. Stores had stocks worth perhaps twenty-five dollars, and six or eight children helped run them. People ate very little, there was no furniture in their homes, their clothes were in rags and if they had an income of fifty cents a day, it was considered a lot. The Chinese police were very rough, in addition.

I tried to find a job for the two or three months I expected to be there, although I knew it would be difficult, what with the abundance of cheap Chinese labor.

I spoke to a lumberman, who told me he paid little or nothing for his lumber as, during the winter, he took a number of Chinese with him to the woods across the river, and for six or seven months they cut lumber and put it on the frozen river, and when the river thawed, they followed the logs down the river to Harbin. He obviously needed no extra help.

The Jewish Center decided to build a larger place for their classrooms and shelter. I was put in charge, as an assistant to the architect. The Chinese laborers we hired tried to work very fast, and we had to keep a steady watch on them to be sure they mixed the mortar well and built the place properly. It kept me busy going up and down the scaffolding to make sure the work was being done properly.

My pay was very small, and I had to buy a pair of shoes that cost me twenty dollars. My pay hardly covered my expense of eating, plus the shoes, which in peacetime would have cost five dollars. The job was finished in two months, and I was sure that my money from America would have come by then.

I decided to go to Vladivostok because I could not stay in Harbin any longer, since the Russians controlled Harbin and mistreated the Chinese. The Chinese had been weak about complaining to the Tzar about their treatment.

The trip to Vladivostok took three days. The city when I arrived was old-fashioned, and the streets had wooden sidewalks. Chinese and Japanese held most of the jobs. The Jewish Community gave me a place to sleep and bread to eat. It was a small community and they were unable to do much for those who came their way.

Max Star's stay in Harbin was very short. His memoirs did not reflect his impressions of the Jewish community. He was interested in the Chinese and their life under Russian domination. Nevertheless, his notes paint Harbin in a way others did not. After all, it was a city in China and the majority of its inhabitants were Chinese. The Russians were there as colonizers, part of a Russian scheme to annex the region of Manchuria into its imperial holdings. As it happened, the Russian saga in Manchuria was historically very short, almost as relatively long as Max Star's stay in Harbin.

Nick (Nikolai) Cherniavsky

Nick (Nikolai) Cherniavsky met Irina Spalwing in the White city of Vladivostok on the Siberian warm water east coast. They were in love, and it was a love like a classic novel: her parents bitterly disapproved of the match. The two youngsters eloped and were married in Harbin.[240]

At the ceremony, they exchanged wedding rings of pale Siberian gold. Each was inscribed around the inner rim with delicate Cyrillic characters: the ring he gave her read "Nikolai," and the ring she gave him read "Irina." Both rings bore the date: 14 IX 1922.

They were stunned by what they found in Harbin. The builders of Harbin hadn't created a Manchurian city, but a Russian one. It had wide radiating boulevards and big stucco buildings painted in bright pastels; the skyline was tangled by Victorian terracotta ornamentation and dotted everywhere by ornate onion-ball church domes.

They treated the place as a kind of substitute Russia without the Bolsheviks. By the early 1920's, Harbin had downtown department stores crammed with Russian and imported goods. Its cafes and corner newsstands sold newspapers representing the furiously contending monarchist, fascist, liberal, and radical factions. Its boulevards were lined with ornate tearooms and restaurants. There were theaters where great actors staged the Russian classics, and movie houses showing the latest films of Chaplin and Valentino. There was even a yacht club, which filled the Sunghuajiang River (a name soon Russified to Sungary) with bright European-style sails in the long summer afternoons.

When Nikolai and Irina arrived, the talk in Harbin was of the imminent fall of Lenin's government. Nikolai himself, during his first year or two in Harbin, attended lots of urgent meetings about the plans for post-Bolshevik Russia.

In the meantime, he had to support himself; Irina was already expecting a child. So he fell into one of the century's newest and most essential trades: auto mechanic. The streets and the countryside surrounding Harbin were crowded with luxury automobiles, and they all needed a reliable garage.

Irina gave birth to their only child, a son, in April 1924. They named him Nikolai, Nick. His family and Russian friends always called him Kolya.

After Nick's birth Nikolai begin to wonder what sort of future his family could have in Harbin. The great re-conquest of Russia was on indefinite hold, and in the meantime, Harbin's own situation was growing daily more perilous. Those were years of revolutionary chaos in China; Manchuria was a shadowy and shifty domain of contending warlords. The people of Harbin often saw interminable, dusty armies of one or another faction marching across the grasslands, and silent gunfire in the distant hills on summer nights. Sometimes the armies swept through the villages along the river collecting conscripts; now and then their officers entered the city to hire mercenaries.

Then, too, the city itself was changing. After the Reds solidified their hold on Russia, the stream of refugees across the border dried up; but with war and revolution tearing Manchuria apart, people from the surrounding countryside were flooding into Harbin for sanctuary just as the Russians had done a decade earlier. At the start of the 1920's, the population of the city was around a hundred thousand, and by the late 1920's, the population had doubled, and almost all the new arrivals were Manchurians and Chinese.

Nobody talked about Harbin becoming a melting pot; the Russians kept to their sections of the city and they expected their new neighbors to do the same. But a kind of infiltration of the local culture began even so.

During the long and bitterly cold winters, the Chinese started a tradition of carving ornate ice sculptures in the public parks. There were huge dragons and dreamy cloud spirits and bristlingly-armored ghost warriors silently bellowing and calling and leering among the massed snowdrifts and the thickets of bare trees; sometimes the artisans would hollow out unobtrusive gaps in the sculptures where candles or even incandescent bulbs could be hidden, so that at night the milky ice would glow from within, in wavering and mysterious pastels, like trapped spirits. The Festival of the Ice Lanterns, they called it. Irina and Nikolai and the other Russians found it beautiful but somehow disturbing. It was as though a florid Asian dreamworld was seeping up into Harbin's strict European proprieties.

Nikolai decided it was time to go. To leave Harbin and replace it with another destination. Maybe it was the rumor that the Japanese were going to invade and take the whole of Manchuria for themselves. One day in the fall of 1926 he told Irina that they were leaving.

They packed up their few possessions and set off by train south to the Chinese coastal city of Darian. There they booked passage on one of the tramp steamers that bobbed from port to port all along the shores of Asia. For most of the voyage, there was nothing to look at but the blank ocean and a featureless line of land off to starboard. Then one morning they came out on deck and found something new: the blue water for miles around them was stained by a turbulent tawny-yellow murk. This was the sign that they'd reached their goal, the point where the currents of the great Yangtse River emptied into the China Sea. The steamer turned towards the west and made its way up the wide river delta, to the mouth of one of the Yangtse's tributaries, the Huangpu. The river was a gorgeous swarming riot of freighters, junks, steamers, yachts, sampans, and warships. Upstream, around a slow glittering bend, there came into view the vast sprawl of Shanghai.

Nikolai's years in Harbin were over. These years were spent through the reasoning that politics, especially those of old Russia, were the gravity of his life there. He spent his days working on automobiles and at night he sharpened his oratory skills in endless political debates.

Olga Keks

It is all but human nature to tell those who are in the distance that the place you are living in is a paradise. People made long journeys moving from one place to another and looking for ways to construct their life in a new space. These new lives were shielded by their owners so that their relatives or friends that were in faraway lands would think that Harbin was heaven on earth. Most concealed their true conditions while describing life as a continuous celebration. This, as I have argued earlier, is the case with "imagined history" in many of the memoirs written many years later. They tend to romanticize former life and fall upon nostalgic sentiments to beautify the state or mode of living and existence as it was not.

Olga Keks questioned the notion brought forward in the many articles and memoirs that Harbin was heaven where people spent their time in the luxury that life could offer.[241]

My early childhood in Harbin, she wrote, was clouded by my family responses to the tragedies that befell them. My uncle, Michael, a young engineer of putei soobshchenia returned to the USSR in 1936 and disappeared without a trace. Only recently, did I discover that he was arrested and later was executed. My grandfather's brother was similarly executed in Ulianovsk. His other brother was arrested by the Japanese in Harbin and his horribly mutilated body was returned to his wife for burial. Finally, my mother, a dentist, was informed-snitched by an informer White Russian émigré, arrested, and water tortured for some two weeks. Do you think we look back on life in Harbin with any kind of nostalgia?

Olga's whole family was dispersed among the treacherous ruins of dictators' and imperialists' conquests. Most did not survive the ordeals. Other families shared this kind of fate as well. And, for most the trauma was so great that they were left with these dominating memories that shadowed all other experiences.

Olga Keks was trying to explain the reasons why the former Harbintsy consider Harbin as the Garden of Eden. There must be a way to discover the backgrounds and names of the Harbintsy who were slaughtered on Stalin's orders, and how many families it affected. This is my powerful rebuttal of Harbin as a metaphor for human bliss, she wrote.

Epilogue

"In much of the rest of the world, the shape and character of big cities were determined by Indian rajahs, Persian emperors, European kings,"[242] and the creativity of the settlers. They wrote their histories and we read them at their will.

A typical family story is repeated in virtually every town—always told as though it were unique to that family. The founder grandfather (or father) walking on a street on the weekend sees some kind of activity in progress. 'What is all this commotion and mish-mash?' demands the Patriarch.

'It is an argument about who was first here', explains the New Generation.

'What's it for? Who needs it? All these people waste their weekend for nothing', they all know where they came from, and they do not change anything!'

'But is it necessary?' the New Generation asks patiently.

'We must do this regularly or we can't know what our life is all about,' answers the Patriarch.

Thus, the Patriarch takes the New Generation by the sleeve and guides him to his home office, where he unlocks a desk drawer that the New Generation has never seen before. From the drawer, the Patriarch takes out an old, worn, dirty canvas pack, and from the pack, he removes and spreads on the desk a few dozen old photographs, dozens of worn-out papers, and other assorted documents.

'This,' says the Patriarch, pointing to the pack's pitiful contents, 'is the inventory of our life in the old country. Everything else—

that's the future, or whatever we can make of it here.'[243]

In a strange way, Harbin became a temporary destination for the Jewish quest to find a free and safe space. This was manifested with the arrival of several Jewish migrating groups.

The first was that of the wealthy and well-to-do industrialists who were ready to seize opportunities when the Tsarist regime allowed them to settle in Manchuria and transport her goods to the motherland and beyond. It followed Russia's Finance Minister Count Witte's declaration that the Tsar should permit "the best of the best" referring to Jews to settle in the new imperial acquisition and move Manchuria's resources by the newly constructed Chinese Eastern Railway.

The second group of Jewish migrants was composed of white-collar professionals who wanted to exercise their expertise in a free and welcoming place where they can fulfill their aspirations. Among these were medical doctors, journalists and writers, accountants, musicians, real estate opportunists, and others.

The third group of Jewish migrants was that of the unfortunate refugees, those who fled the pogroms in the Russian pale of settlements, the families that tried to escape the after-mass of the Russian Revolution of 1917 as well as the destruction of World War One, and later those who looked for possible routes of escape to new destinations before and during World War Two.

Another group of Jewish migrants that should be included are the Jewish soldiers that fought with the Russian army during the Russo-Japanese War of 1904-1905. At the end of the war, some elected to stay in Harbin where they later brought their families to.

Common to all these groups was the Jewish tradition and culture which served as a historical bond and made it possible to set up a vital Jewish community in the new city.

Unfortunately, life in Harbin was not heaven or paradise,

and the new place did not bring about safety to the members of the Jewish community. Antisemitism was part of the scene. They found out that the age-old prejudice against them was very much alive in Harbin, and that this could accompany them wherever they went.

And, contrary to attempts by several writers, especially those who are biased toward the extreme-right revisionist movement, to paint Harbin as a Zionist fertile soil, it was not so. It is true that a thin part of the community's leadership had Zionist aspirations and that two of the youth movements were founded on the Zionist ideal, most of the community preferred destinations other than Palestine or Israel.

Dr. Abraham Kaufman for example, advertised his Zionist beliefs and affiliations everywhere he was. Yet, the President of the Jewish community in Harbin for almost 40 years never left the city of his own will, nor did his sons. One went to the USA very early, and the other was forced to leave China after the October Revolution.

The Jewish case of Harbin presents an interesting diasporic phenomenon in which a group of strangers can construct a community that functions well and that offers its members exchange of ideas and ideals, lively discussions on matters that concern them, and the building of social and economic institutions that cater for their needs.

As we have seen in the stories of families and individuals, history is made of the "little" pieces of life that not only matter to them but that may influence the social, economic, and political makeup of the community.

History is not just a macro tale of the past. What I am interested with is the micro-history of the space and the people that functioned there. And, as we have seen, the stories present a variety of personal lives — some with good memories and comfortable existence, and others with suffering and hardship. Reading each of the stories gives sense to the place and the function of the tellers. And considering them all together brings a deeper understanding of the space, the time, the circumstances, and the consequences of life. Together the stories turn the little pieces of life into a large event.

Stories of individuals have transformed the pasts of Harbin into fanciful geographies, mostly imagined. These pasts have been packed into suitcases that moved from one space and time to another, changing, creating new stories, or hiding portions, while neglecting to note what was real.

More than 40 foreign nationalities gathered in Harbin to make the city an international cosmos. Among them, Jews from different geographical locations. They brought their former spaces with them, created a new local existence, and maintained global connections. Their experience became glocal.

Upon leaving Harbin years later, they added another past to the suitcase, and this they brought to yet a new place. Over time, these pasts lost their boundaries and became almost one.

The case of Harbin is fascinating because it presents a blend of local memories, sometimes made of imaginary components, staffed in a box. As Thomas Lahusen writes: "The memory of previous times was preserved, re-, and deconstructed elsewhere around the globe."[244]

Studying the stories that serve now as evidence of that era is very difficult as these reflect traumas, nostalgic emotions, impaired remembrance, and too many generalities. It is not only the geography that concerns me but the background and character of individuals and their daily life.

Among the hundreds of stories and memoirs I have collected, almost all can be classified as 'Marker Histories', where the texts do not constitute full accounts but fragmented dates and names.

Each name and date represent a mark—a headline in the past of an individual, a family, or a community.

Other stories I have classified as 'Tombstone History' because tombstones carry names, dates, and on occasion a short line such as "In memory of our beloved son…"

Both categories are lacking what is in between the dates and the names. The life of the living, the daily concerns, and actions, the environment that dictated the routine and the unusual, the reasons why actions were taken, and how all of these influenced the daily existence.

In working on this subject, I found also an interesting trend that shows that most memoirs written in later years present only "marker histories". While others present an added value and thus are "tombstone histories". The markers are incomplete, very narrow in their scope, and remain a mystery as are the lives of their authors. Tombstone histories, on the other hand, provide more.

Diaries, however, may present a larger view of the particular past, yet may not bring it as it actually was, because the author may have had considerations and motives to present the past in a certain way—traumatic experience, political, social, or economic pressure, and, personal motives.

Letters, on the other hand, come closer to a real presentation of the past, for they were written in the actual time of the events and were much more direct and clearer in their representations. But this should not be taken as a rule because, as was argued in Olga Keks's story, even letters can hide the historical reality.

I was fortunate to receive a trove of letters written by a person named Shimon Fix, an accountant by profession who lived with his wife and 3 children in Harbin and had a unique talent for writing. His and his wife's letters are among the very few that brought the past as it was for the family into light. I felt it would be only right to insert his letters, in groups, between the other stories and memoirs so that it may give a true feeling to what actually was.

Manchuria, under the Russian sphere with the establishment of the CER, siphoned Jews from the whole of Eastern Europe and some from the west. Here they were able to develop their social and economic life to an extent that most never had before. They were able to practice freely their religion and beliefs, develop commerce, establish and attend their own schools, cultural centers, and social services, and form an almost free, modern, and enlightened society.

Yet, it is important to note, that not all shared the wealth Manchuria and Harbin could offer. Many families arrived with only their clothes on and found it difficult to find proper jobs, let alone kosher meals.

Reading the stories one should wonder whether the idea of all humans being born naked, meaning equal, is correct. Here you have the city of Harbin, born in the wilderness of Manchuria with nothing in it. Yet, as it grew, the city became a stage for social and economic classes. The minority was very rich, while the majority struggled to meet a level of measured survival. In between were the members of the middle class, rocking between the top and the bottom according to political, and socio-economic conditions brought about by shifting winds.

Although the structure of the communities resembled the traditional diasporic social and organizational makeup, it took a new turn that abandoned the shtetl mentality for the excitement of new possibilities—in fashion, studies, commerce, cultural experiments, and in politics. One could no longer see many bearded orthodox Jews with their long coats, white sox, and fury hats roaming the streets. Night clubs flourished, cinemas lit silver screens, music and drama production thrived, and prostitutes—including Jewish ones—had addresses. Gambling was part of the establishment, including within the rooms of the Harbin Jewish Culture Association and library. The Skidelsky Talmud Torah School did not restrict itself to teaching religion only but had an advanced curriculum that included sciences and literature. The newly rich built houses and villas, they opened hotels and practiced law, accounting, and real estate.

The Jews had left one geography that belonged to other times and came to a new one where they could change and develop new identities and manipulate memories of a past or pasts. They hoped that anti-Semitism would not follow and that they will be free of stereotypes and prejudice. They learned, the hard way, that these are like parasitic blood-sucking ticks, and cannot be got rid of easily; not even for the price of changing one's name.

An imagined past cannot bring concrete answers to an experience people did not have. It can bring questions that are based not on factual information but on assumptions. These can provide an exciting exercise in projections, probabilities, and in predictions made by extrapolating from past observations.

The changing political winds, the annexation of sovereign states to others, the weakness of economies, the swell of anti-Semitism, and the rise in nationalism across Europe served as catalysts for a large Jewish migration to faraway lands. Here they formed new dreams and established new homes, most temporary ones.

Different groups brought with them the cultures of the countries they left. But what united them all was not their European experience, but their common heritage, tradition, and the aged long Jewish culture.

In his book, Der Judenstaat, Theodor Herzl writes that the Jewish question persists wherever Jews live in appreciable numbers. He goes on to declare that wherever it does not exist, it is brought in together with Jewish immigrants.[245]

Thus, antisemitism should be considered as another form of bond that united the Jews in Harbin.

Some of the stories people told apply tangible perspectives to the study of identity and its relation to geography and time, especially to ways identity, geography, and memory may intersect and change.[246] These tales are based on oral and written memories, diaries, letters, and other publications. Some are centered on motives, nostalgic remembrance, selective memory, psychological blocks and forgetting, as well as political manipulations. These I call 'imagined history'. Others come as close as possible to historical reality.

People who came to Harbin brought their former geographies with them; creating a new local existence, maintaining global connections, and influencing global events, hence forming glocalized[247] communities. And, by dwelling in the diasporic past, the global village created its spiritual and intellectual theme park. They all formed not just a 'global village', but a 'glocalized space' with special spatial dimensions. When leaving Harbin years later, they added another past to their suitcase, and this they brought to a new place. For many, over time, these pasts lost their boundaries and became almost one.

This was the case with Rosa Clurman whose mother bought a small porcelain Buddha in a Harbin street second-hand bazaar in the 1920s and took it with her to San Francisco in the 1940s. She put the porcelain Buddha in her living–room and created a new glocalized space, almost a Chinese shrine where she and her former Harbinski friends would play mahjong every Thursday under the watchful eyes of her Buddha.

Harbin, born as a foreign city with a Russian flavor on Chinese soil, is a good example of a geographical transformation. A colonial experience that brings one geography into another and siphons many other geographies into it.

The case of Harbin presents a blend of local memories, sometimes made of imaginary components, sometimes nostalgic, and sometimes deceiving, staff in a 'glocalized suitcase'. These suitcase memories, when are opened, may bring a hollow tale of a rich past. Some, however, are detailed and full of information and thus excavate history to its full dimensions.

In many cases, a present perception of a past is influenced, among other things, by the experience of risks and threats, both personal and environmental. In these cases, former geography becomes a void, a black hole, nothing is left but a name. The new geography takes over and assumes the colors of its space and condition.

Altered memories are not necessarily nostalgia, but they do become so when one longs sentimentally for a certain past, tries to create or tries to hide it.[248]

There are also other considerations. Among them personal motives and official state political manipulation of events and the 'memories' that are attached to them. These influence collective communal memory and thus add another weight to imagined history. The opposite, then, is historical reality.

These mental histories exist everywhere because reality has its limits. What is real to one may not be factual or true to another. And because truth, is the state of being in congruence with fact or reality, it must wander on and on and never come to rest.

I wrote this record as a love letter to my Harbin, into which I came many years earlier from afar. As I made the city my domicile, I came to understand her character, know her personality, and most of all discover her Jewishness.

Acknowledgments

THIS IS A JOURNEY into a past that some glorified but others unveiled its true nature. It is a quest to uncover the stories behind personal testimonies, oral or written. Searching for the life of the people in the space called Harbin, I scoured historical materials, listened to and examined recorded interviews with individuals, memoirs, thousands of photographs, letters, and personal notes.

All of these provided an opportunity to open a wide window to the daily life of Jewish individuals and families in Harbin.

This is a unique, and maybe a first-of-its-kind journey into personal homes, private spaces to be exact, that grew dust on old and rusty shelves in the attics among many other family relics.

I owe my gratitude to many families who had their roots in Harbin. Their stories, their curiosity, their wish to uncover their life and those of their Harbińskie relatives, and the painstaking roads they took in order to understand what was there, in the faraway land of China, that affected their own lives.

Over the years I was privileged to be given letters, memoirs, photographs, and relics of hundreds of Harbińskie families who wanted to share their experiences with me and others, and to store their pasts in the archives of the Sino-Israel Research and Study Center under the Harbin Jewish Culture Association. These materials have served many research ventures over the past 22 years.

The collections in this undertaking are but just a few of the materials I have in my archives. However, the many stories, or what I call "histories" that are presented here, give a quality of accuracy to the past of members of the Jewish community in Harbin. Not all of them are full of details, but together they bring the essence of factual life and the memories of it, the flavor of daily life; the concerns, the worries, the celebrations, and the basic needs of individuals and families.

I owe my special thanks to several individuals that have shared their full family histories with me. Standing out are Jean Ispa of Columbia Missouri in the center of America, Anne Atkinson of Perth Australia, Irene Clurman of Colorado in the USA, Roman Ravve of Ukraine, Paul Kerson of New York, and Mara Moustafine of Sydney in Australia, among many others. Among all these stands my wife and partner Liang Yisha who has been my inspiration and strict editor. I have no words that can express my gratitude and appreciation to all of them.

Dan Ben-Canaan
Harbin, P.R. China
Winter 2022—2023

REFERENCES AND BIBLIOGRAPHY

Adams, Brus F. The re-emigration of Russians from China (1921-1960), University of Louisville, Kentucky, USA.

Lorraine Attreed. Making History: Interpreting the Past and Explaining Ourselves. 1998.

John D. Block. Escape: From Siberia to California. Chapter 8: Life and Work.

Boris Bresler. Harbin Jewish Community 1898-1958: Politics, Prosperity, Adversity. John K. Fairbank Center for East Asian Research Harvard University, Cambridge Massachusetts August 1992.

Andre Brink, 'Stories of History: Reimagining the Past in Post-Apartheid Narrative,' Negotiating the Past: The Making of Memory in South Africa, eds. Sarah Nuttall and Carli Coetzee, Cape Town: Oxford University Press, 2002.

Pearl S. Buck. My several worlds. January 1, 1960.

Bernard Darel, A Home for Jews In China', Los Angeles Times, 21 September 2004.

Field, Douglas R. Making Memories Stick. Scientific American, 2005.

Harry Franck. Wandering in Northern China.

Francis Fukuyama. The End of History and the Last Man. Simon & Schuster, 2006.

Ginzburg, Carlo. The Cheese and the Worms — A Cosmos of a Sixteenth-Century Miller. The John Hopkins University Press, Baltimore, USA, 1980. Translated by John and Anne C. Tedeschi.

Frank Grüner, In the Streets and Bazaars of Harbin: Marketers, Small Traders, and Peddlers in a Changing Multicultural City. Itinerario. Volume 35. Special Issue 03. December 2011.

Gould Hunter Thomas. An American in China: 1936-39 A Memoir.

Guang, Pan, The Jews In China Chinese-English Edition, China Intercontinental Press Beijing 2001 1st Edition.

Han Tianyan, Cheng Hongze, Xiao Hong. Family Stories of Harbin Jews.

Theodor Herzl, Der Judenstaat, cited by C.D. Smith, A Concise History of the Israel and the Arab-Israeli Conflict, Routledge 4th ed, 2001.

Cecelia Hurwich. Hunger in Harbin. A memoir. April 15, 2009.

Linda Hutcheon, Irony, Nostalgia, and the Postmodern. University of Toronto. January 19, 1998.

Kaufman, Theodore. The Jews of Harbin Live on in My Heart. The Association of Former Jewish Residents of China in Israel—Profil Publishing House Israel. 2004.

Kertzer, David I. Amalia's Tale—A Poor Peasant, An Ambitious Attorney, and a Fight for Justice. Houghton Mifflin Company. Boston—New York USA 2008.

Keyser, R. de & Vandepitte, P. Eds. 1998. Historical Formation. Design of Vision. VLG. Kuhn, D. 1991.

Krouk, Nora, Skin for Comfort, IPeNEWS, Vol 6, No. 1.

Thomas Lahusen (ed.), Special Issue: Harbin and Manchuria: Place, Space, and Identity, South Atlantic Quarterly 99,1, 2000.

Sandlin Lee, Saving His Life Sherwin Beach Press. February 22, 2008.

Yaacov Liberman MY CHINA: Jewish Life in the Orient 1900-1950. Gefen Publishing House, 1998. Israel.

Su Ling, An investigation of the Heilongjiang Academy of Social Sciences. Southern Metropolis Magazine, Guangzhou, 2007.

Moshe Lichomanov, Childhood Memories from Harbin. Bulletin, Igud Yotsei Sin Israel 2006.

Moustafine, Mara, Secrets and Spies: The Harbin Files. Vintage 2002.

Valerie J. Nelson. June 11, 2010 Los Angeles Times.

Mordechai-Modka Olmert (1908-1998) In his "Darchai b'Derech Rabim" An autobiography 1981.

James Palmer. China Borderlands, ChinaFile's project to document life on China's borders, in partnership with the VII Photo Agency. January 18, 2016.

Kaikki Oikeudet Pidatetaan, Modernisation and Conservative Backlash. Helsinki: The University of Helsinki, 2007, Helsingin yliopisto.

Hartley, Leslie Poles, The Go-Between NYRB Classics, New York, March 31, 2002 edition (first published in 1953).

Qu, Wei and Li Shuxiao editors, The Jews in Harbin, Heilongjiang Academy of Social Sciences, Harbin 2004. First edition 2004 and, second edition 2006.

George Radbil, Murder by the Church Gates. Biuletten' Igud Iotsei Sin, no. 356, 1998.

Phyllis Sakinofsky. Imprints of Memories, Shadows and Silences. Journal of Transnational Literature. Volume 2 No 1 November 2009.

J.D. Smele,"White Gold: The Imperial Russian Gold Reserve in the Anti-Bolshevik East, Europe-Asia Studies, Vol. 46, No. 8, Soviet and East European History (1994).

Snow, Edgar; Red Star Over China. Grove Press New York. 1968. (1938, 1944 Random House), 1961.

Robert Skidelsky, A Chinese Homecoming. Prospect Magazine. Sunday, January 01, 2006.

Max Star. The Lion's Den. Florida Grower Press of Tampa, Florida, 1964.

Henry Strage. The Dinaburg Family. Chapter 6 — The Manchurian Diaspora. December 2014.

Hayden White, 'The Value of Narrativity in the Representation of Reality,' On Narrative, ed. W.J.T. Mitchell, Chicago: The University of Chicago Press, 1980.

Jing Wang, Asian Newsletter May 6, 2006.

Wolff, David, To the Harbin Station: The Liberal Alternative in Russian Manchuria, 1898-1914, Stanford, California, Stanford University Press, 1999.

Notes

1   Boym, Boym S. The Future of Nostalgia. New York: Basic Books. 2001: XIII; see also Davis F. Yearning for Yesterday: A Sociology of Nostalgia. NewYork: Free Press. 1979. In Xu Jing Nostalgia, Identity, Ideology, and Place Making: The Case of St. Nicholas Cathedral in Harbin. 2022.

2   Kimberly Smith, 2000: Smith Kimberly. Mere nostalgia: Notes on a progressive paratheory. Rhetoric and Public Affairs 3(4): 505-527. p. 509.

3   Berliner David. Multiple nostalgias: the fabric of heritage in Luang Prabang. The Journal of the Royal Anthropological Institute 18(4): 769-786.

4   Bonnett A and Alexander C. Mobile nostalgias: connecting visions of the urban past, present and future amongst ex-residents. Transactions of the Institute of British Geographers. 2013. 38(3): 391-402. See also Blunt Alison. Collective memory and productive nostalgia: Anglo-Indian homemaking at McCluskieganj. Environment and Planning D: Society and Space 23: 717-38.

5   Wilson JL. Here and now, there and then: nostalgia as a time and space phenomenon. Symbolic Interaction. 2015. 38(4): 478-492.

6   Gvion L. Organized leisure as promoting nostalgia: Israeli senior citizens singing in Yiddish. Leisure Studies. 2009. 28(1):51–65, particularly in page 53.

7   Hutcheon L and Valdés MJ. Irony, nostalgia, and the

postmodern: a dialogue. 1998. Poligrafías 3: 18-41. See also Ben-Canaan Dan. Nostalgia vs. historical reality. In: The International Forum on the History and Culture of Harbin Jews, Harbin, China, 17 June 2006.

8   Su Ling, An investigation of the Heilongjiang Academy of Social Sciences. Southern Metropolis Magazine, Guangzhou, China April 2007.

9   Qu, Wei and Li Shuxiao editors, The Jews in Harbin, Heilongjiang Academy of Social Sciences, Harbin 2004. First edition 2004 and, second edition 2006 – English version by Dan Ben-Canaan.

10 Guang, Pan, The Jews In China Chinese-English Edition, China Intercontinental Press Beijing 2001 1st Edition.

11 See Dan Ben-Canaan, The Business of Stereotyping Business. Heilongjiang University School of Western Studies 2007. Economy and business have been two key concepts in China's policy-making in the past twenty years. It is well understood here that in order to be an active player within the global community, China should be using both economics and business concepts to its advantage. According to a statement in the Harbin Jewish Research Center brochure its goals are "to study the successful experiences of Jewish people in economy, science and technology, culture and education." The center's literature expresses China's friendship with the Jewish people and says that the Chinese "look forward to their return." But in fact their established goals contradict their statements. Their intention has been from the start to display their ability to fulfill a mandate given several years earlier, to recruit "Jewish money" from around the world.

12 Ehud Olmert, Prime Minister of Israel words of congratulation in the new 2006 album edition.

13 See Teddy Kaufman's preface to the new 2006 album edition.

14 Kaufman, Theodore (Teddy); The Jews of Harbin Live on in My Heart. The Association of Former Jewish Residents of China in Israel – Profil Publishing House Israel. 2004.

15 Letter of Theodore V. Orosz of Valley Stream New York, dated April 2006, after his visit to Harbin in April 2006.

16 Letter of Theodore V. Orosz of Valley Stream New York, dated May 27, 2006, after his visit to Harbin in April 2006.

17 Mordechai-Modka Olmert (1908-1998) In his "סיבר דרדב יכרד - Darchai b'Derech Rabim" An autobiography 1981. He was Ehud Olmert's father,

18 Wayne Mellon, e-mail letter to the author, dated October 14, 2006.

19 Sarah K G Jensen, Vincent Sezibera, Shauna M Murray, Robert T Brennan, Theresa S Betancourt. Intergenerational impacts of trauma and hardship through parenting. J Child Psychol Psychiatry. 2021 Aug;62(8):989-999. doi: 10.1111/jcpp.13359. Epub 2020 Dec 7. National Library of Medicine.

20 Prof. Jing Wang, Head, Foreign Languages & Literatures MIT. Chair, MIT Critical Policy Studies of China – Asian Newsletter May 6, 2006.

21 Linda Hutcheon, Irony, Nostalgia, and the Postmodern. The University of Toronto. January 19, 1998.

22 Hartley, Leslie Poles, The Go-Between NYRB Classics, New York, March 31, 2002 edition (first published in 1953), is a novel (set shortly before Queen Victoria died in January 1901), rich in thematic interest. In the prologue to his book, L.P. Hartley says: 'The past is a foreign country: they do things differently there'. The novel paints a detailed picture of rural England at the beginning of the 20th century, when Hartley himself was only five years old. The leisurely life of the land-owning upper classes, with their bathing parties, cricket matches and dances, and their sometimes cruel

manners and values, was to change radically as the century progressed.

23 Prof. Lorraine Attreed / Department of History, College of the Holy Cross / Making History: Interpreting the Past and Explaining Ourselves. 1998.

24 Fromm Martin T. Borderland Memories: Searching for Historical Identity in Post-Mao China. Cambridge University Press. 2019.

25 Ibid. p. 2.

26 Dr. Marilyn H. Stauffer, University of South Florida / Class Outline, June 23, 1997.

27 Keyser, R. de & Vandepitte, P. Eds. 1998. Historical Formation. Design of Vision. VLG. Kuhn, D. 1991.

28 See Prof. Francis Fukuyama article that forms the afterward to the second paperback edition of his The End of History and the Last Man (Simon & Schuster, 2006). It is a phrase that comes from GWF Hegel and, more popularly, from Karl Marx.

29 Qu, Wei and Li Shuxiao editors, The Jews in Harbin, Heilongjiang Academy of Social Sciences, Harbin 2004.

30 Adams, Brus F. The re-emigration of Russians from China (1921-1960), University of Louisville, Kentucky, USA.

31 Kaikki Oikeudet Pidatetaan, Modernisation and Conservative Backlash (Helsinki: The University of Helsinki, 2007, Helsingin yliopisto). Chapter One. p. 8.

32 Ibid, Chapter One. p. 8 (cf. title word "Antisemitismus" in Zentner/Bederftig 1985, 29).

33 Krouk, Nora, Skin for Comfort, IPeNEWS, Vol 6, No. 1.

34 Mara Moustafine, My family and its city: fifty years in Harbin, paper presented at the International Seminar on the History and Culture of Harbin Jews, 30 August – 2 September 2004, Harbin.

35 Moustafine, Mara, Secrets and Spies: The Harbin Files. Vintage 2002.

36 Wolff, David, To the Harbin Station: The Liberal Alternative in Russian Manchuria, 1898-1914, Stanford, California, Stanford University Press, 1999.

37 Elizabeth McGuire, book review To the Harbin Station: The Liberal Alternative in Russian Manchuria, 1898-1914..

38 Cipko Serge. Ukrainians in Manchuria, China: A Concise Historical Survey. Past Impeifect, Vol. 1, 1992. pp. 155 – 73.

39 Although, the placards on the walkway along the river, near Stalin Park, speak of the contributions of emigres from Russia. The Russian language descriptions did not hide the early Russian influences on the city. This, however, bears political and economic aims.

40 Snow, Edgar; Red Star Over China. Grove Press New York. 1968. (1938, 1944 Random House), 1961 (John K. Fairbank)

41 Kalman M. Shlifer response to questions asked by his niece Galia Perdo, in his home in an old-age facility in Zichron Yaacov in Israel on December 2, 2014. He was 87 then. He passed away shortly before I went to Israel to interview him in 2017.

42 The MicroWorlds Lab - A Humanities Unbounded Collaborative Project in History at Duke University.

43 Boris Bresler. Harbin Jewish Community 1898-1958: Politics, Prosperity, Adversity. A presentation at the Symposium on Jewish Diasporas in China: Comparative and Historical Perspectives, John K. Fairbank Center for East Asian Research Harvard University, Cambridge Massachusetts August 16-18 1992.

44 Ibid.

45 James Carter

46 The quorum required for Jewish communal worship that

consists of ten male adults in Orthodox Judaism.

47 The large community synagogue was opened in 1909.

48 Talmud Torah, a Hebrew term, literarily means a place where one studies the Torah, the law of God as revealed to Moses and recorded in the first five books of the Hebrew scriptures (the Pentateuch).

49 Chizuko Takao – Professor, Department of History, Rikkyo University, Tokyo (Japan). Fields of academic interest: Russian and Soviet Jewish history, Russian Jewish presence in the Far East. Author of *The Soviet System and American Jewry* (2006, in Japanese).

50 Chizuko Takao's footnote in *The Birobidzhan Project from the Japanese Perspective*. Mizrech, Vol. 1, November 2008. p. 38: As for Japanese understanding of Jews see Masanori, Miyazawa, *Nihon-jin no Yudaya-isuraeru ninshiki* (Japanese perception on Jews and Israel) (Kyoto: Showado, 1989); *Zoho yudayajin ronko* (On the Japanese discussion on the Jews) (Tokyo: Shinsen-sha, 1982); Miyazawa and David Goodman, *Jews in the Japanese Mind* (New York: The Free Press, 1995).

51 Takao, Chizuko, *The Birobidzhan Project from the Japanese Perspective*. Mizrech 東方 חרזמ, Vol. 1, November 2008. p. 38

52 Ibid. p 39

53 Diplomatic Record Office, MOFA, Files related to the Jewish Questions, vol. 1. As stated by Chizuko Takao.

54 Building at 83 Yamskaya Street [Today Daan Street] - From information provided by Charlie Clurman to his daughter Irene Clurman in 1997.

55 Ethel Clurman was born Feb. 20, 1900 in Odessa, Russia. Died April 4, 1994, in Reno, Nevada. She was the wife of Isak Grigori Clurman (referred to on the tape as "Grandfather," because he was Irene's Grandfather). She was the mother of

Charles (Ruvim) Clurman, (referred to on the tape as "Papa" because he was Irene's father); Sylvia (Tziva) Clurman and Israel (Izra, Izrick). She was the grandmother of Irene Clurman, Gregory Clurman, Nurit Epstein Eshtien, Rose Clurman Calander and Helen Clurman Pyne.

56 Martin Buber, Tales of the Hasidim.

57 Comprised of "Global" and "Local" to mean the entanglement of both in relation to the world.

58 T. Lahusen, Remembering China, Imagining Israel: The Memory of Difference, South Atlantic Quarterly 99,1, 2000, 253–268.

59 M. Featherstone, 'Global and local cultures', in J. Bird, B. Curtis, T. Putnam et al. (eds), Mapping the Futures: Local Cultures, Global Change, London: Routledge, 1993, pp. 169–87 here p.177, cited in J. Beckett, 'Against nostalgia: place and memory in Myles Lalor's "Oral History"', Oceania 66, 4, 1996, pp. 312–22.

60 Die Welt, (August 29, 1903) from The Pedagogic Center, The Department for Jewish Zionist Education, The Jewish Agency for Israel, (c) 1992-2004, Director: Dr. Motti Friedman, Webmaster: Esther Carciente.

61 Ibid.

62 Pavel Sudoplatov and Anatolii Sudoplatov, with Jerrold L. Schecter and Leona P. Schecter, Special Tasks: The Memoirs of an Unwanted Witness — A Soviet Spymaster, Boston, MA: Little, Brown & Co., 1994, p. 289.

63 Asya Pereltsvaig (October 9, 2014). "Birobidzhan: Frustrated Dreams of a Jewish Homeland".

64 Sun's father had in 1920 declared his support for the Jews and a homeland in Palestine. Sun Ke embraced his father's opinion; in the spring of 1928, he visited the small, vibrant

Jewish community in Palestine. The visit only strengthened his support for Zionism.

65   The Die Gelbe Post, a newspaper in German published in Shanghai from 1939 to 1941 by Adolph Josef Storfer (1888 —1944), a German Jew, reported the proposal and resolutions, carried a number of specific introductory articles about Yunnan where the settlement was supposed to be established, and discussions of job opportunities there by Jewish refugees in Shanghai.

66   Xu Xin, Nanjing University, Responses from Afar. Paper for Allied Powers' Response to the Holocaust Conference March 2015, The Hebrew University of Jerusalem, Israel.

67   Wang Jian, Escape and rescue, the Jewish people in the second war. Shanghai Jiaotong University Press. Shanghai, Pages 221-223 (逃亡與拯救，二戰中的猶太難民與上海, 王健著，上海交通大學出版社。)

68   Ibid.

69   Ibid. Note 4.1. Pages 221-233.

70   Paul Kerson. Our Ancestor Sol Kerson (1894-1984) – An Appreciation. A letter to all Fellow Descendants of Sol, (there are 20 of us so far). 4th of July weekend 2018. New York. The letter is in the Paul Kerson file at the archives of the Sino-Israel Research and Study Center in Harbin, China. "This 4th of July weekend 2018, I thought I would share with you the meaning of the story of our common ancestor Sol Kerson, admitted to the United States with less than nothing at age 22 by a friendly U.S. Immigration Officer 102 years ago, in 1916. He told me his story in detail over a three-day visit at his apartment in North Miami Beach, Florida in 1973."

71   Ibid.

72   Ibid.

73 Paul E. Kerson, a fundraising letter on behalf of "The American Friends of the Sino-Israel Research and Study Center. August 2, 2007.

74 Jack Steinberg, the father, was the son of Russian Jews who had escaped from Russia during the revolution to China.

75 Cecelia Hurwich. Hunger in Harbin. A memoir. April 15, 2009.

76 Ibid.

77 Giuseppe Garibaldi (Italian: [dʒuˈzɛppe gariˈbaldi]; July 4, 1807 – June 2, 1882) was an Italian general and politician. He is considered, with Camillo Cavour, Victor Emmanuel II and Giuseppe Mazzini, as one of Italy's "fathers of the fatherland". Garibaldi was a central figure in the Italian Risorgimento, since he personally commanded and fought in many military campaigns that led eventually to the formation of a unified Italy. He was appointed general by the provisional government of Milan in 1848, General of the Roman Republic in 1849 by the Minister of War, and led the Expedition of the Thousand on behalf and with the consent of Victor Emmanuel II.

78 Ibid.

79 Ibid.

80 The following text was transcribed from a recorded interview made on October 28, 1982, in Reno, Nevada. The interview, transcription, and editing were done by Irene Clurman, Ethel's granddaughter. Ethel was a native speaker of Russian and her grammatical errors in English were left unedited.

81 Pearl S Buck "My several worlds". January 1, 1960. This autobiography covers Pearl S Buck's childhood, adolescence, and young womanhood growing up in China as well as her eventual return to America.

82 Yiddish for synagogue.

83 General D.I. Khorvat was appointed as Director General of the Chinese Eastern Railway when it started operations in 1903.

84 She refers to the "Free Soup Kitchen".

85 Harbin Memories – Charles (Ruvim) Isaac Clurman. The following narrative is excerpted from an audiotape made by Charles Clurman on October 29, 1982, in Reno, Nevada. The interview, transcription, and editing were done by Charles' daughter Irene Clurman. A native Russian speaker, Charles did the interview in English, and his grammar was left uncorrected.

86 The Russian name for the Heilong River.

87 Now Zhongyang Dajie - Central Street.

88 Professor (Emerita) Jean Ispa. The University of Missouri. Department of Human Development and Family Science. Columbia, Missouri, USA. Prof. Ispa inherited all her grandfather's letters; written in the Russian language and were translated into English. Many of the letters she shared with the author. All entries herein of the letters by Shimon Fix, his wife, or any other related person, are the property of Prof. Jean Ispa and are presented in this writing with her permission.

89 Shimon Fix letter to his son Alexander. February 19, 1922.

90 Shimon Fix letter to his son Alexander. March 5, 1922.

91 Evgenia Fix letter to her son Alexander. March 15, 1922.

92 Shimon Fix letter to his son Alexander June 4, 1922.

93 Shimon Fix letter to his son Alexander June 25, 1922.

94 Shimon Fix letter to his son Alexander November 26, 1922.

95 Rostran was the Soviet transport company Shimon Fix worked for.

96 Shimon Fix letter to his son Alexander October 23, 1922.

97 From Yaacov Liberman MY CHINA: Jewish Life in the Orient 1900-1950 by Yaacov Liberman. PDF version. Gefen Publishing House, 1998. Israel. Permission was granted by the publisher on April 10, 2007.

98 Yaacov Liberman, My China. PDF version. P. 1.

99 Ibid. p. 2.

100 Ibid. p. 2.

101 Ibid. p. 2.

102 A ceremony celebrating a Jewish boy's 13th birthday, in which, according to Jewish tradition he becomes an adult. For women it is a Bat Mitzvah celebrated when a girl reaches the age of 12.

103 Yaacov Liberman, My China. PDF version. P. 3.

104 Ibid. p. 3.

105 Ibid. p. 3.

106 Ibid. pp 4-5.

107 Ibid. p. 5.

108 Ibid. p. 5.

109 Ibid. p. 6.

110 Ibid. pp. 6-7.

111 Ibid. p. 8.

112 Ibid. p. 8.

113 Ibid. p. 9.

114 Ibid. p. 9.

115 Ibid. p. 10.

116 The present Dongfeng Street in Daoli District.

117 An interview with Moses Grossman, MD. Interviewed by Jean D. Lockhart, MD. August 1, 1996.San Francisco, California. American Academy of Pediatrics. Oral History Project.

118 Lida was Sasha's friend – they had a sort of dating relationship in the summer of 1924. Now, in 1925, she is 19 years old.

119 Letter to Alexander from his parents in Harbin. June 30, 1925.

120 Han Tianyan, Cheng Hongze, Xiao Hong. Family Stories of Harbin Jews. Chapter 11. Translation from Chinese by Jutta Maurer.

121 Ibid.

122 Karen Glikman's letter to her cousin Sherry Smilo, with a copy to the author, "Trying to figure out what went wrong with our family." Dated April 3, 2013. Karen Glikman is the daughter of Joseph Israel Glikman.

123 Joseph Glikman's interview with his mother Chana.

124 Karen Glikman. Felger-Glikman Timeline. April 2011.

125 Galya Katz (Volobrinsky). HARBIN 1945 – 1952). February 17, 2005.

126 Prof. Hayim Tadmor. From Talmud Torah in Harbin to the Israel Academy of Sciences in Jerusalem: Personal Reminiscences. Paper presented at the International Seminar on the History and Culture of Harbin Jews organized by the Heilongjiang Academy of Social Sciences. 22.12.2007.

127 A September 1932 letter from Shimon Fix to his son Alexander Fix who is in the USA. Shimon Fix's letters are in the position of Prof. Jean Ispa, Shimon Fix's granddaughter who is in the process of translating them into English from the original Russian. Courtesy of Jean Ispa, February 2022.

128 Shimon Fix letter to his son Alexander and his wife Tanya. November 20, 1932.

129 Lindemann (Zydower), Anna Elsie. Émigré. On way from Fürstenwalde (Germany), to Shanghai. Interview: March 21, 2012. Length of Interview: 1 hour 10 minutes. Interview & Synopsis by: Zieva Konvisser. Videographer: Fred Safran.

130 Mara Moustafine. My family and its city: fifty years in Harbin. Paper presented at the International Seminar on

the History and Culture of Harbin Jews. 30 August – 2 September 2004. Harbin

131 Ibid.

132 Ungern Von Sternberg, The Bloody White Baron. Roman Fedorovich Nikolai Maximilian von Ungern-Sternberg was born in Austria on December 29th, 1885. His father, Theodor Freiherr von Ungern-Sternberg, was a Baron and Roman was his eldest son. He was an anti-Bolshevik Lieutenant General in the Russian Civil War and then an independent warlord whose Asiatic Cavalry Division wrested control of Outer Mongolia from occupying Chinese forces in 1921. Ungern-Sternberg's attraction to esoteric Buddhism and his eccentric, often violent treatment of enemies as well as his deep antisemitic convictions led him to the massacre of hundreds of innocent people including many Jews.

133 Mara Moustafine. My family and its city: fifty years in Harbin. Paper presented at the International Seminar on the History and Culture of Harbin Jews. 30 August – 2 September 2004. Harbin.

134 Ibid.

135 Ibid.

136 Harbin Photos and Documents from the Albin-Bialik-Krajmalnik Family. From the Albin Family Collection. Veronica (Vero) Albin July 2019

137 A letter from Veronica (Vero) Albin dated May 15, 2019.

138 In a letter from Shari Buxbaum dated Thursday, March 18, 2010. She is the sister-in-law of Sherman Jack Keller.

139 Valerie J. Nelson. June 11, 2010 Los Angeles Times.

140 George Radbil', "Murder by the Church Gates," Biuletten' Igud Iotsei Sin, no. 356, 1998, pp. 66-67.

141 Shimon Fix letter to his daughter Mira (Mirusya). June 10, 1939.

142 Shimon Fix letter to his children Alexander and Mira who are in in America. June 14, 1939.

143 Shimon Fix letter to his daughter. March 26, 1939.

144 Shimon Fix letter to Alexander and Mira. July 25, 1939.

145 The Alexander I. Pogrebetsky Family Archives of Rare Chinese and Asian Banknotes, Part 1, Archives International Auctions, Hong Kong, 2015.

146 Ibid.

147 "White Gold: The Imperial Russian Gold Reserve in the Anti-Bolshevik East, 1918-? (An Unconcluded Chapter in the History of the Russian Civil War)" by J.D. Smele, Europe-Asia Studies, Vol. 46, No. 8, Soviet and East European History (1994), pp. 1317-1347.

148 The Alexander I. Pogrebetsky Family Archives of Rare Chinese and Asian Banknotes, Part 1, Archives International Auctions, Hong Kong, 2015.

149 Over 500 lots of rare Chinese and Asian banknotes and scripophily will be sold at auction May 24th in Hong Kong, China. ArtfixDaily, 7 May 2015. Retrieved 13 October 2015. Results From Archives International Auctions' Sale Held On May 24. Antiques & Auction News, 2015. Retrieved 14 October 2015. Archived here. You can bank on it: Highlights from Archives International Auctions December sale. Barnebys. Retrieved 30 December 2015.

150 Shimon Fix to his son Sasha - p. 3 exert from letter 1930.

151 Memories of Rinia Zyskind nee Slavutin. Received on September 28, 2013, from her daughter Goldie Zyskind: "You reminded me that my Mother had in fact written about her life in China. She did this when she was being treated for her ovarian cancer and so sometimes she is not as articulate or punctuation sensitive as normally. However, I have left it as she wrote because it is her voice. I have only included

descriptions that give an idea of the times so I hope it is interesting and relevant.

152 She refers to Sun Island which was a holiday resort to the residents of Harbin.

153 Phyllis Sakinofsky. Imprints of Memories, Shadows and Silences. Journal of Transnational Literature. Volume 2 No 1 November 2009.

154 Hayden White, 'The Value of Narrativity in the Representation of Reality,' On Narrative, ed. W.J.T. Mitchell, Chicago: The University of Chicago Press, 1980.

155 Andre Brink, 'Stories of History: Reimagining the Past in Post-Apartheid Narrative,' Negotiating the Past: The Making of Memory in South Africa, eds. Sarah Nuttall and Carli Coetzee, Cape Town: Oxford University Press, 2002. 32.

156 Zvia Bowman. The Shichman History. September 18, 2018.

157 Myra Waddel - Extract from family history. February 11, 2017.

158 Myra Waddel Note: Dina, who gave me such a lot of information about the family's life in China, lost touch with Bluma many years ago.

159 Myra Waddel Note: Not knowing any of their husbands' surnames, I haven't yet been able to discover anything more.

160 Myra Waddel Note: Dina's story is in a separate document.

161 These were Dina's uncle, her father and her brother-in-law.

162 John D. Block. Escape: From Siberia to California. Chapter 8: Life and Work in Harbin. https://siberiaheritage.com

163 She is now a registered nurse and the wife Dr. Allen Nickel, an ENT specialist in San Jose, California. The Nickels have three adult children, one of them, Bob Nickel, worked with the Josh McDowell Ministry for many years and has now gone to Russia many times to spread the Gospel. He recently

became the business manager for "Leadership Ministry World Wide."

164 Shimon Fix letter to his son Alexander. April 23, 1940.

165 The Paul Soskin Biography. A pdf document provided by Anthony McKay on December 22, 2015.

166 My grandmother Lea memoir. Received from Rafael Medoff on Monday, June 8, 2020.

167 Simone Monnier Clay is a Professor Emerita in the French department at the University of California Davis. Among her research interests is the 1911 Harbin Plague.

168 Provided as a document by Liora Dankner, May 2012, Israel.

169 My mother and I visited Valentina L. Gesgorina in 1979 at Carnegie Hall in New York. We still have at our house my mother's black J. Beker piano she brought from Harbin.

170 Anne Atkinson is a Professor Emerita of history. She resides in Perth Australia. The information comes from a paper she sent me titled The History of the Burak Vickers Family. August 12, 2014.

171 In Wikipaedia for example.

172 Anne Atkinson notes that this was in the period of the Napoleonic wars, when part of Poland was annexed by Russia.

173 Other reports state that 430 died.

174 Published by the Liberty Hose Company No. 2, Pennsylvania USA on a website designed to report on incidents of fire and their causes for instructional purposes.

175 The family were Jewish and Bernard Darel, who was born in 1929, now lives in Tel Aviv. ` A Home for Jews In China', Los Angeles Times, 21 September 2004. There is no evidence that the Darel's bought the factory off the Buraks, or if, indeed, it was the same factory.

176 Soon the new transportation company is going to open

in Harbin, with the head of the former Sovtorglot freight forwarder, Mr. Fentsreido (Joe Fideraido) and British Citizen Mr. Irving, who have owned the transportation company which has operated in the Pacific Ocean region. This company will include the Sovtorgflot and Gosstrah dealerships (the first dealership for attracting cargoes and the second one for its insurance). The opening of this ` Transportation company ' will attract attention because the two of its directors being counter intelligence officers; the first from the USSR, and the second one works on the foreigners. GAHK Fond 830 Opis 3 File 49 - p14-15.

GAHK Fond 830 Opis 3 File 49 - Folio 1 - de-FIGAREIDO Yosif Michail Genrihovich, the Portuguese citizen 52 years, entrepreneur, the Trade mission employee. Closely connected to the Soviet Intelligence. Works in foreign circle. Lives: Vodoprovodnaya 35 apt. 1.

177 Moshe Lichomanov, Childhood Memories from Harbin. Bulletin, Igud Yotsei Sin Israel (2006).

178 Should be Lao maozi - A nickname for a paleface with a red beard.

179 Dina Vincow (Lichomanova), My "Talmud Torah" - Jewish School in Harbin Days. Text was written by Gershon Vincow on August 17, 2007.

180 Letter from Shimon Fix to his daughter Mirusia. March 19, 1940.

181 The little window in the door, according to the language of In-Fapchina.

182 Harbin Documents and Photographs from the Galat (Galatzky) Family February 11, 2009. Biography courtesy of Bonnie and Suzanne Galat, daughters of Alexander Galat. With the permission of Bonnie Galat, his daughter.

183 A Russian unit of length equal to 28 inches or 71 centimeters.

184 His friend Ronya Tsirulskaya wrote to him of her life in Harbin and her longing to travel. Her letter, originally written in Russian, was routed through the USSR to reach Paris. Ronya must have had a crush on my father…her letter is so beautifully flirty! With permission of Bonnie Galat, his daughter.

185 Henry Strage. The Dinaburg Family. Chapter 6 - The Manchurian Diaspora. December 2014

186 Olivier Thomas. My ancestors from Harbin. In a letter dated October 27, 2012.

187 Jean Ispa noted that literally, it means Honorable Bourgeois – which in pre-1917 times allowed Jews to live outside the Pale. The term by itself did not mean "Jewish." It was conferred on Jews with higher education or wealth or who had contributed in some way to the country.

188 Peter Berton (Alexander Menquez - pseudonym). Contribution of Jews to the Musical and Cultural Life in Harbin in the 1930s and Early 1940s. From an article that was presented at the Conference on Jewish Culture in Harbin – Harbin, June 2004.

189 He described all this in his autobiography "On Four Strings".

190 During the Korean War General Lin was a fighter plane pilot. He was shot down and imprisoned by the North Koreans who mistaken him to be an American pilot.

191 There are many difficulties in determining the truth. Partially because Lin Hu does not know either his birth name, or the names of his parents. Further suggested investigation, including advanced psychological hypnosis, which the daughters agreed to, was refused by the PLA on the grounds of 'secrecy'.

192 In a letter dated Monday, 4 April 2011, Lily Lin asks: "Do you think DNA test can prove if my dad's mother was a

Jewish or not?"

193 A letter from Ron Kushner dated Friday, October 19, 2018. My brother Irving recently came upon a trove of several dozen additional letters written in Russian. We have a way of translating them. After they are translated, if any of them appear to be relevant to your scholarly interests, I can arrange to send you copies of the letters and their translations.

194 The Boris Kushner Letters. Translation from the Russian handwritten letters by Gregory Shpektorov, Moscow. August 2018.

195 Paul E. Kerson, THE HAGGADAH – BOOK II - Where the Horse Died: American Jewish Peddlers and the Refounding of the State of Israel. New York 2008.

196 Leo Schwarz (edt.). Great Ages and Ideas of the Jewish People. Random House, New York, 1956. In Paul E. Kerson, THE HAGGADAH – BOOK II - Where the Horse Died: American Jewish Peddlers and the Refounding of the State of Israel. New York 2008.

197 Frank Grüner, In the Streets and Bazaars of Harbin: Marketers, Small Traders, and Peddlers in a Changing Multicultural City. Itinerario. Volume 35. Special Issue 03. December 2011, pp 37 72

198 Ibid.

199 Paul E. Kerson, THE HAGGADAH – BOOK II - Where the Horse Died: American Jewish Peddlers and the Refounding of the State of Israel. New York 2008.

200 Mary Louise Pratt, in Imperial Eyes, 4.

201 Frank Grüner, In the Streets and Bazaars of Harbin: Marketers, Small Traders, and Peddlers in a Changing Multicultural City. p. 42.

202 David Wolff, "Russia Finds Its Limits," 46.

203 Frank Grüner, In the Streets and Bazaars of Harbin:

Marketers, Small Traders, and Peddlers in a Changing Multicultural City. p. 43.

204 On the districts and suburbs of Harbin, see Kharbin-Futsziadian', 29-30; Bakich, "A Russian City in China," 134-35; Kradin, Kharbin - Russkaia Atlantida, 23-64.

205 Frank Grüner, In the Streets and Bazaars of Harbin: Marketers, Small Traders, and Peddlers in a Changing Multicultural City. p. 45.

206 Their proportion of the population increased steadily over the years, to more than 40% in 1924.

207 David Wolff, To the Harbin Station, p. 93.

208 A letter from Dr. dated June 4, 2011, from Phyllis Sakinofsky. Sydney Australia.

209 Phyllis Sakinofsky translated the letter from Russian into English. She made a note: "Interesting point about the translation. Yes it would definitely have been Yiddish not Hebrew because they were all Yiddish speakers and while I know the family was Zionist, I am sure they didn't speak Hebrew. So I really don't know he specified Yiddish, not Russian. Perhaps his father wasn't fluent in Russian and perhaps he wrote in Russian because he had access to a Russian typewriter. Fascinating. It is all swirling around in my head."

210 Robert Skidelsky, A Chinese Homecoming. Prospect Magazine. Sunday, January 01, 2006.

211 Huangshan cemetery at the outskirts of the city some 20 kilometers from downtown Harbin.

212 James Palmer. This essay is part of China Borderlands, ChinaFile's new project to document life on China's borders, in partnership with the VII Photo Agency. January 18, 2016.

213 James Palmer. A People's Friendship. ChinaFile, January 18, 2016.

214 A Few Words from Ella to her Loving Children. Written by Ella herself and printed by LL, word for word, as written. February 1951. First typing by Lou Levin, son of the author, 1951. Second typing by Joshua Ostroff, great-grandson of the author, July 1974. Courtesy of Susan K. Levin.

215 Ibid.

216 Stock exchange in Russian.

217 James Palmer. China Borderlands, ChinaFile's project to document life on China's borders, in partnership with the VII Photo Agency. January 18, 2016.

218 James Palmer. A People's Friendship. ChinaFile, January 18, 2016.

219 Susan Katherine Levin. My father's Family. Document written in October 2015, and was given to me.

220 Gould Hunter Thomas. An American in China: 1936-39 A Memoir.

221 Harry Franck. Wandering in Northern China.

222 Gould Hunter Thomas. An American in China: 1936-39 A Memoir. Written in pre-Communist, war-torn China by a young Yale graduate working for Texaco in Tsingtao, Chungking and Canton.

223 Arbat Street, or Ulitsa Arbat, is also known as the Old Arbat (to differentiate it from New Arbat Street). Arbat Street once served as a main Moscow artery and is one of the oldest original streets in the Russian capital. The Arbat District, through which Arbat Street runs, was once a location where craftsmen set up shop, and the Arbat's side streets show evidence of their past with names that describe various trades or products, like Carpenters, Bread, or Silver. Arbat Street is within walking distance of the Kremlin, so it's possible to visit this free Moscow attraction when you visit the heart of ancient Moscow.

224 An interview with Harbin Russian. The St. Petersburg Times 2001.

225 Cook Sooza Gen. My Mother's story of their cook Sooza Jen. I also read your article "Nostalgia" and found it very interesting. I always felt that my Mum had a very idealised memory of her youth OR perhaps she was young and protected OR perhaps kept her experiences to herself of Harbin and the Japanese Or all of the aforementioned. Received from Goldie Zyskind September 23, 2013.

226 Solomon (Monia) Berman. China on My Mind. March 23, 1996.

227 Irene Clurman in an email letter to Dan Ben-Canaan, October 29, 2016.

228 Bob Sitsky, Growing Up in Tientsin. Sydney, Australia, 2015. Chapter 18. Chinese Servants and Tradesmen. My Chinese Amah.

229 Karl Schlögel. Moscow 1937. Cambridge, Polity Press, 2012. p. 9.

230 David Udovitch dictated his life story to tape, prior to his death 6 January 2010. Elijah Udovitch, his son, provided the typed transcripts on June 23, 2014.

231 Actually, Tianjin is a northern port city not far from Beijing. It is not in what was Manchuria.

232 Yehudit Bein. Harbin Childhood, and all the "Children of Harbin". June 6, 2006.

233 Theodor (Teddy) Kaufman. The Jews of Harbin Live on in My Heart. The Association of Former Jewish Residents of China in Israel. Tel Aviv Israel 2006.

234 Ibid. p. 153.

235 Ibid. p. 154.

236 Yehudit Bein. Harbin Childhood, and all the "Children of Harbin". June 6, 2006.

237 Ibid.

238 Hanukkah - Is a Jewish festival (the festival of lights), lasting eight days from the 25th day of Kislev (in December) and commemorating the rededication of the Temple in 165 bc by the Maccabees after its desecration by the Syrians. It is marked by the successive kindling of eight lights. From Hebrew ḥǎnukkāh 'consecration'.

239 HARBIN MEMORIES FROM MAX STAR - Presented here are pages 144-150 from In The Lion's Den by Max Star, published by Florida Grower Press of Tampa, Florida, in 1964. This material was provided by Saul Marks, great-great-grandson of Max Star's aunt, Sara Rywka Staroletna. Permission to print the book excerpts was granted by Max's daughter, Dorothy Skop, on August 10, 2007.

240 Sandlin Lee, Saving His Life Sherwin Beach Press. February 22, 2008. Lee Sandlin memoir of Nick Cherniavsky - Harbin, Manchuria 1924 - Chicago 2007. The story of Sandlin's father-in-law, who emigrated to the United States in the 1950s. Originally published in the Chicago Reader, July 17 and 24, 1998.

241 Olga Keks letter to the author dated January 28, 2014.

242 Leon Harris. Merchant Princes – An Intimate History of Jewish Families Who Built Great Department Stores, Harper & Row, Publishers, 1979.

243 Ibid. An interpretation of Leon Harris's tale. In Paul E. Kerson, THE HAGGADAH – BOOK II - Where the Horse Died: American Jewish Peddlers and the Refounding of the State of Israel. New York 2008.

244 T. Lahusen (ed.), Special Issue: Harbin and Manchuria: Place, Space, and Identity, South Atlantic Quarterly 99,1, 2000. In Lahusen's introduction to the special Issue, p.2.

245 Theodor Herzl, Der Judenstaat, cited in C.D. Smith, A

Concise History of the Israel and the Arab-Israeli Conflict, Routledge 4th ed, 2001. p. 53.

246 According to Alexander B. Murphy, geographical thinking is vital for addressing some of the critical geopolitical, environmental, and socio-economic challenges. Yet the insights geography can offer on the changes are often overlooked because of the tendency to view geography in static, descriptive terms. It is important to understand how geography's concerned with spatial patterns and assumptions, mapping, and integrative place-based modes of analysis.

247 Glocal - Reflecting or characterized by both local and global considerations. Describing the seamless integration between the local and global; the comprehensive connectedness produced by travel, business, and communications; willingness and ability to think globally and act locally.

248 Field, Douglas R. Making Memories Stick. Scientific American, 2005.

Name Index

About The Author

Dan Ben-Canaan has been living in China for over two decades, and has known the country and its people intimately since the late 1980s. He is a Professor Emeritus of Research and Writing Methodologies at the School of Postgraduate Studies, Northeast Forestry University, and Heilongjiang University, School of Western Studies in Harbin. He also serves as Visiting Professor for Advanced Studies with the Postgraduate Studies at Heilongjiang Provincial CCP Party School. He is the founder of the Sino-Israel Research and Study Center (2002) attached to the Harbin Jewish Culture Association which he founded in 2014. His research focuses on the history of Northeast China, known in the past as Manchuria, Harbin as an international and transcultural city, the history of the Jews in Harbin and China, and the Chinese perception of the Jewish people. Among his books are *Echoes of Harbin: Reflections on Space and Time of a Vanished Community in Manchuria,* and *The Kaspe File: A Case Study of Harbin as an Intersection of Cultural and Ethnic Communities in Conflict 1932-1945.*

www.ingramcontent.com/pod-product-compliance
Lightning Source LLC
Chambersburg PA
CBHW012013110726
47993CB00009B/3050